FATAL RIVALRY

FATAL RIVALRY

Flodden 1513

HENRY VIII, JAMES IV AND THE BATTLE
FOR RENAISSANCE BRITAIN

George Goodwin

W. W. Norton & Company

NEW YORK   LONDON

First American Edition 2013

First published in Great Britain in 2013 by Weidenfeld & Nicolson,
a division of The Orion Publishing Group Ltd, London

For information about permission to reproduce selections from this book,
write to Permissions, W. W. Norton & Company, Inc.,
500 Fifth Avenue, New York, NY 10110

For information about special discounts for bulk purchases, please contact
W. W. Norton Special Sales at specialsales@wwnorton.com or 800-233-4830

Manufacturing by Courier Westford

Library of Congress Cataloging-in-Publication Data

Goodwin, George, 1956–
Fatal rivalry : Flodden 1513 : Henry VIII, James IV and the battle for
Renaissance Britain / George Goodwin. — First American edition.
pages cm
"First published in Great Britain in 2013 by Weidenfeld & Nicolson,
a division of The Orion Publishing Group Ltd, London"—T.p. verso.
Includes bibliographical references and index.
ISBN 978-0-393-07368-3 (hardcover)
1. Flodden, Battle of, England, 1513. 2. Great Britain—History—Henry VIII,
1509–1547. 3. Scotland—History—James IV, 1488–1513. I. Title.
DA784.6.G66 2013
942.05′2—dc23
2013021161

W. W. Norton & Company, Inc.
500 Fifth Avenue, New York, N.Y. 10110
www.wwnorton.com

W. W. Norton & Company Ltd.
Castle House, 75/76 Wells Street, London W1T 3QT

1 2 3 4 5 6 7 8 9 0

For Arthur, Cecily and Frances

CONTENTS

LIST OF ILLUSTRATIONS

Prologue

Late in the evening of Saturday, 26 March 1603, a dirty, bloody and dishevelled horseman of mature years arrived at Holyrood Palace in Edinburgh. That this was a gentleman of distinction was shown by the quality of the material, if not the condition, of his clothes. He demanded to be taken immediately to see James VI, King of Scots, and although the King was already in bed, James was wakened to receive him.

The gentleman rider was Sir Robert Carey, Warden of the English Middle March. He was also Captain of the Border castle of Norham in the East March a fortress reduced to ruins in 1513 by the invading army of King James's great-grandfather, James IV. Sir Robert was well known to James VI; as a young man, during an English diplomatic mission, he had got on famously with the King. So well in fact that James had written to Elizabeth I to ask whether Carey could 'attend on him at his court' more permanently.[1] Elizabeth had considered the matter with her usual deliberation and then refused the request. But James's relationship with Sir Robert and his family continued; and it was to Sir Robert's sister Philadelphia, Lady Scrope, that he sent a sapphire ring, to be returned urgently when the elderly English Queen had breathed her last.

Elizabeth had refused to nominate her successor throughout her near forty-five-year reign. Yet, at her magnificent Renaissance palace of Richmond in the small hours of the morning of Thursday, 24 March, she made a sign. To those crowded around the death bed, including Sir Robert and his sister, this was taken to favour her nearest in blood, King James. Though it was almost certain that the Privy Council would send formal notification to James, the Careys did not risk a delay. While the Council met, Lady Scrope waited at a window until she saw that her brother was outside the palace gates and could not be stopped. Then, furtively and unseen, she threw the blue ring to him. By ten o'clock that same Thursday morning, Carey was riding north at a furious pace. As early as noon on the Saturday he had reached Norham on the Tweed. He crossed the border and would have travelled the remaining forty-five or so miles[2] rather more quickly, had his horse not stumbled, thrown and kicked him. Weak with loss of blood from a head wound, he was forced to ride more slowly, making his arrival much later than planned.

The existence of the sixteenth-century Palace of Holyrood and Carey's mission in 1603 were both consequences of one event: the palace had been created to celebrate the wedding, a century before, of James IV of Scotland and Margaret Tudor, the eldest daughter of Henry VII of England. It was because of James VI's descent from Margaret, his great-grandmother, that Sir Robert Carey knelt before him now and saluted him by his title of King of England, Scotland, France and Ireland.[3]

The formal offer of the Crown from the Privy Council duly followed; and just a few days afterwards, on Tuesday, 5 April, James left Edinburgh. Late the following afternoon, the King approached Berwick with an ever-increasing host of Scottish and English dignitaries. He then crossed into his new kingdom;[4] the swift progress of the new monarch being in stark contrast to the slow sombre passage of the late Queen's torchlit funeral barge, as it made its final night-time journey between the royal palaces of Richmond and Whitehall.[5]

✥ ✝ ✥

The likelihood and consequences of a Scottish succession had been discussed by Henry VII and his Privy Council more than a century earlier. This was in 1501, a full two years before James's marriage to Margaret. As reported by their contemporary, the historian Polydore Vergil, there was a tense debate among the King's councillors:

Some were afraid that at a future date it might come about that the inheritance of the kingdom might fall to Margaret, and therefore they judged it wise not to give her in marriage to a foreign prince. But the King's answer to this was, 'What then? If this happens, which God forbid, I foresee that our realm will suffer no harm, since it will not be the addition of England to Scotland, but rather of Scotland to England as the most renowned part of the whole island, since it is always the less which is joined for glory and honour to that which is greater, just as in days gone by Normandy came under the rule of our English ancestors.' The wisdom of the King was praised, and by a unanimous voice they plighted the maid Margaret to King James.[6]

Henry VII was not quite right: though the crowns were united in 1603, the countries did not come together in an Act of Union, as Great Britain, until 1707. And even then they did so with different legal and educational systems and a degree of cultural separation. Scotland was not subsumed by England and much of the credit for that belongs to James IV. By 1513, his twenty-five-year reign had brought full royal control for the first time over what we know as the geographical entirety of Scotland. He was the owner of the largest warship in Europe and his country a naval power. And he had created the reality of an independent position for Scotland, rather than one of aspiration buttressed by myth. With these achievements, James IV can be properly described as King of Scotland as well as King of Scots. Had the schemes of King Louis XII of France borne fruit in 1513, James could have become the effective King of England as well.

Introduction

On 22 August 1513, 42,000 Scottish troops crossed the Tweed under the command of King James IV. It was the largest Scottish army ever to invade England.

This was James's third attack on his southern neighbour. In 1496, in at least notional support of the Yorkist pretender Perkin Warbeck, he had pillaged northern Northumberland and destroyed its fortified towers. In 1497 he focused his attention on just one target: the castle of Norham, fortress of the Bishops of Durham, which defended the Tweed crossing on behalf of England's monarchs. An attack on Norham was significant for strategic reasons, but also for symbolic ones: it was at Norham that Edward I had humiliated the Scots by meeting there to choose their king. James had bombarded the castle, but he had not taken it.

In 1513 it fell in only six days. Wark Castle just over the border from Coldstream was also taken easily. Both were captured before the relieving English army under the Earl of Surrey was anywhere near. James then moved against the castles of Etal and Ford. By 1 September,[1] all the fortresses of the English East March were either in James's hands or had been destroyed.

It had been an extraordinarily swift and successful campaign. James had assembled a vast army for two reasons. One was entirely practical: it was likely that, as at Bannockburn and in the ongoing wars in Italy, there would be a battle between the besieging and the relieving army. The other, like the attack on Norham itself, was highly symbolic. James had brought with him troops assembled by nobles from all over the geographical entity of what we now know as Scotland: he had united and unified his country to an extent that none of his predecessors, not even Robert the Bruce, had achieved.

The successes of late August and the first days of September were at one with a man of great intelligence who sought to make the most of modern technical innovation to display both power and panache. He now had time in hand with his mustered army to plan the victory in battle that would complete a historic campaign. James even had the advantage of knowing the enemy commander, the seventy-year-old Earl of Surrey, not merely as a former adversary but, if only for a short time, as a courtier companion. All seemed set fair for James for what would become known as the Battle of Flodden, fought close to the village of Branxton on Friday, 9 September 1513.

⁂

In late Medieval and early modern Europe there were many sources of competition. At the bottom of the social pile, the poorest struggled to gain sufficient sustenance for survival. Much higher up the scale, whether in cities, towns or countryside, the battle was for wealth, status, influence and power. At the very top of the social pile was the sovereign's court with its ruler, be that a duke, king, emperor or pope. The court provided the platform and the theatre for its master to demonstrate his fitness to rule, both to his own political nation and to the ambassadors of his royal rivals.

Medieval monarchs were elevated by God's sanction through anointing with holy oil and by the 1330s, the kings of France, England and Scotland had all incorporated anointing into their coronations. But by 1500 they and their Renaissance counterparts were set high above their subjects on a more everyday basis. They were no different to their predecessors in their aims, but they were in their presentation. By harnessing the greater prosperity, technological innovation and cultural dynamism of the times, they created and radiated an overwhelming magnificence.

Kings competed among themselves in the splendour of their courts and their tournaments. For James IV and Henry VII, that most unusual of kings, display became a substitute for war; but for James IV and Henry VIII it increasingly became a preparation for it.

More viscerally, kings competed to produce male heirs of their bloodline who would, they hoped, ensure that their success would be remembered in this world and their soul protected in the next by the appropriate number of masses for the dead. These two elements would best come together should a king be buried by his heirs in a place that combined both temporal and religious importance – as granted to Henry VII in Westminster Abbey and denied to the last two kings killed in battle on English soil.[2] Such a contrast in fate could mean the difference between temporal fame combined with everlasting life or, at best, oblivion.

It was because of such matters that the question of the royal succession was so important. In 1513 it gave added weight to the growing quarrel between Henry VIII and James IV. James with his Queen, Henry's elder sister Margaret, had a living child who was a potential heir to the English throne, whereas Henry and Queen Katherine of Aragon did not: and the exchange of taunts about the future added increasing bitterness to the rift between the brothers-in-law.

Ultimately, underlining all other forms of kingly display were those related to the activity and weaponry of war. For, should their 'peaceful and generous relations with other princes' fail,[3] they were expected to excel in the 'vigorous conduct of magnificent princely warfare'.[4] Henry VIII and James IV each had a supreme model to follow and possibly eclipse: for Henry VIII it was Henry V; for James IV, Robert the Bruce. It was on the battlefield where kings, directly or by proxy, would ultimately expect to decide their rivalries – with God and fortune pronouncing their judgment.

1

Uncertain Inheritors

It is one of the great myths of English and then British history that there has been no successful foreign invasion since the Norman Conquest. It was one Winston Churchill usefully perpetuated in 1940 and stylishly restated with the phrase: 'it was nearly a thousand years since Britain had seen the fires of a foreign camp on English soil'.[1]

In truth, there have been foreign camps aplenty since 1066, not least those of Prince Louis of France (1215–17) and William of Orange (1688).[2] There have also been a number of foreign-backed invasions under English or Anglo-Welsh leadership.

The threat posed by would-be usurpers to an incumbent monarch was not lost on Henry VII: having fled the country as a fourteen-year-old in 1471, Henry had returned fourteen years later to stake a claim against Richard III, landing on 7 August[3] at Mill Bay, Pembrokeshire, with a force of 2,000 French soldiers paid for and equipped by Charles VIII of France.

Just two years before, Henry Tudor's chances of gaining the throne had seemed slight indeed. Even on 22 August 1485, as dawn broke over the troops gathering at Bosworth, the odds against him had appeared overwhelming. Though he had gained adherents en route from the Welsh coast, Henry's forces were vastly outnumbered – that is until the non-intervention of the Earl of Northumberland and Lord Stanley, and the very late but decisive participation of the latter's brother, Sir William. Victory at Bosworth, and the death of Richard III on the battlefield, ensured that the crown was Henry's, but his reign seemed set to be a short one. His supporters may have been united in being anti-Richard, but most certainly they were not reliably pro-Henry.[4]

☙ ✠ ❧

Three years after Bosworth, on 11 June 1488, James III, King of Scots, faced the forces of his strongest nobles at Sauchieburn. The fate of the country was to be decided in a landscape where, just over a century and a half before, Scotland's greatest victories against the English had been won. Nearby were William Wallace's Stirling Bridge and Robert the Bruce's Bannockburn, the latter so close, that King James's battle was at one time given the same name.[5]

James III had inherited the throne at the age of eight and thus by 1488 had reigned for more than a quarter of a century. His adult rule had been one of continual uncertainty. It had seen dramatic changes of minister and of policy, driven by a King with a wilful and reckless propensity to antagonize his nobility and most senior churchmen.[6] Most calamitously, James had shown an ability to alienate the closest members of his own family. Relations with his younger brother Alexander, Duke of Albany, deteriorated to the point that the latter, with the backing of Edward IV of England and the army of Edward's brother Richard, Duke of Gloucester, invaded Scotland in 1482 and declared himself Regent.

Albany, however, arrived too late to capture the King, who had already been imprisoned by their half-uncles in Edinburgh Castle. He also lacked authority, being even more unpopular than his brother. His coup came to an end when English support evaporated in April 1483 with the sudden death of King Edward.

Richard of Gloucester, having seized the English throne as Richard III, was too intent on securing his own position to worry about Scottish affairs. This brought liberation for James and restoration to power. Albany sought exile in France, where he was accidently killed in a tournament by the future King Louis XII.

James's fortunes continued to improve. After the death of King Richard at Bosworth in 1485, the English crown passed to a new king of a new dynasty: Henry Tudor. Potential marriages were discussed: firstly of James's second son with Princess Katherine, sister of Henry's consort, Queen Elizabeth; then, in November 1487, following the death of James's estranged wife – allegedly poisoned at her husband's instigation – it was proposed that the widower James should himself marry Queen Elizabeth's mother, Elizabeth Woodville.[7] Strangely, the possible marriage of James's eldest son and heir, fourteen-year-old James, Duke of Rothesay, to another unspecified daughter of Edward IV, took a distant third place. Stranger still, the second son, so obviously more favoured than his elder brother and made Duke of Ross in January 1488, was also called James.

At the same time as the marriage plans, James III sought to place himself in a commanding position to achieve what must always have been, among all the twists and turns of policy, his main objective: to subordinate the nobility of Scotland to the power of its King. In so doing he was following the aims of his father and grandfather.

But King James utterly and unnecessarily overplayed his hand at almost every turn. His draconian approach for settling a long-running disagreement with Lord Hume over the distribution of church revenues was to accuse Hume of treason. Hume, a powerful noble in the turbulent eastern region bordering England, came to the conclusion that James was bent on the destruction of his entire family. This united other well-born nobles in fear of a similar fate. In response, James called successive Parliaments to give institutional form to the humiliation of his aristocracy.

There was also a deepening estrangement with the most important member of his own family. The King's son and heir, James, Duke of Rothesay, was kept secure more than thirty miles away from his father. Ostensibly, this was for the Prince's own safekeeping. However, on 2 February 1488, Prince James, supposing he was to be supplanted by his younger brother and thus fearing for his life, escaped and disappeared. To James III's impetuous moves for domination, so reminiscent of those of his distant cousin Richard II of England a century before, carelessness had been added.

The Prince became a rallying point for the King's enemies as they gathered an army. When the two sides met in their final battle at Sauchieburn, the King took the field equipped with Robert the Bruce's sword. But this was to be no Scottish Excalibur. The battle, for James III, was a disaster. His army was defeated, and the King who had sought to exert his will so extensively over his chief subjects found himself unable to control his own horse, which careered at speed off the battlefield. Separated from his troops, James was forced to take shelter at Bannockburn mill.[8] There, offering comfort for the King, a priest was admitted – or rather an assassin in priest's clothing – who produced a knife and stabbed the King to death.

As for the actions that day of the young Duke of Rothesay, the prince who now became James IV, one cannot find conclusive documentary proof. That is hardly surprising. The Prince had benefitted from the murder of a crowned and anointed king who was also his father. That alone led James IV to do penance for the rest of his life. But what if he had been more closely involved? Patricide was considered the most heinous of crimes; but for a king to kill his father would invoke an even higher level of damnation, both in this world and the next. No surprise then at the gap in the documentary record, for Prince James was almost certainly with the rebels at Sauchieburn. His presence there gave him another immediate difficulty: in siding with rebel subjects against the arbitrary power of the old king, he risked strengthening their power at the expense of the new. Personally and politically, James IV seemed to have begun his reign in a very dark place indeed.

2

New Kings

Henry Tudor, from the time of his challenge to Richard III and throughout both his reign and those of his Tudor successors, was depicted by propaganda as the true Lancastrian heir and the last legitimate claimant standing. The official Tudor version comes down to us today in the words of our greatest dramatist, William Shakespeare. Here are the key phrases of the final speech of his play *Richard III*, delivered on the field of Bosworth by its victor, Henry VII as Earl of Richmond:

> We will unite the white rose and the red:
> Smile heaven upon this fair conjunction,
> That long hath frown'd upon their enmity!
> What traitor hears me, and says not Amen?
> England hath long been mad, and scarr'd herself …
> … All this divided York and Lancaster,
> Divided in their dire division,
> O, now let Richmond and Elizabeth,
> The true succeeders of each royal house,
> By God's fair ordinance conjoin together!
> And let their heirs, God, if thy will be so,
> Enrich the time to come with smoothed-faced peace,
> With smiling plenty, and fair prosperous days!
> Abate the edge of traitors, gracious Lord,
> That would reduce these bloody days again,
> And make poor England weep in streams of blood!

Written in the 1590s, more than a century after the event, these lines with their starting point of the symbolic Tudor rose, stressed both the legitimacy of the Tudor dynasty and its essential role as a provider of peace and a bulwark against anarchy. Henry was presented as the true heir and restorer of 'this fair land's peace'. The reality was rather different. Henry's position was weak. His claim to the throne was extremely questionable.

Henry's bloodlines on both sides, though royal, were compromised by bastardy, as Richard III's Proclamation against him had stated forcefully.[1] His father's royal blood was not English but French. Henry's paternal grandmother was Catherine de Valois, the French Queen and widow of England's Henry V. His paternal grandfather, Owen Tudor, was of no higher status than a Welsh squire and said to be bastard-born himself.[2] The two had secretly married in 1428 or 1429 in complete contravention of a parliamentary statute instigated by the Council of Henry VI, Catherine's child by her royal marriage. The sons of the Tudor marriage, Henry VII's father Edmund and his uncle Jasper, were not even formally recognized as Henry VI's legitimate uterine brothers until 1453.

Henry's English blood came from his mother, Margaret Beaufort, and descended from a marriage of John of Gaunt, Duke of Lancaster. This was not Gaunt's first, which produced the House of Lancaster and Kings Henry IV to VI; nor his second, which produced Kings of Spain and Portugal; but his third, to his mistress Katherine Swynford, who had already given him children out of wedlock. These children were legitimized by Richard II, but through Letters Patent issued by Henry IV in 1407, they were debarred from the throne.[3]

Henry was not the only non-Yorkist claimant. There were the Stafford Dukes of Buckingham, descended from Gaunt's younger brother Thomas of Woodstock. Henry was, however, through his mother, the sole quasi-Lancastrian contender, because the Wars of the Roses had extinguished the main Lancastrian line and killed the male Beauforts as well, and it was as the Lancastrian heir that he was determined to reign.

Henry brought to his rule the same sort of shrewdness and rigour that had enabled him to survive a decade and a half as a continental exile, when first Edward IV and then (insistently) Richard III had sought – with a likelihood of success – to persuade his hosts-cum-gaolers to give Henry up.[4] The new King Henry tried, at least initially, to reconcile all but the seemingly most irreconcilable of Yorkists. He even gave men who had fought directly against him at Bosworth an opportunity to prove their loyalty. Some, such as Thomas, Earl of Surrey, did so. Yet Henry knew that mere protestations of support would not suffice. Sustained and strenuous effort would be required to maintain his grip on power, backed up by deployment of military force and administrative efficiency. Even then, it would take something extra to assure his powerful subjects and the ambassadors of foreign nations of his permanence. Thus the King and his ministers made Henry himself and, from 1486 his son Arthur, figures of royal destiny. He was assisted in this by his new fellow countrymen's ignorance of their own history.

For it hardly needs stating that modern access to information, whether written, visual or archaeological, gives us a far better grasp of our past than that given to our ancestors. The gaps in the historical record created by the inaccessibility of evidence were often filled by myth. Thus we know perfectly well, in the twenty-first century, that the Tower of London was begun in the reign of William the Conqueror; but as late as the seventeenth, it was generally accepted to be the work of Julius Caesar.[5] During the same period, so the architectural historian John Goodall tells us, Inigo Jones thought that Stonehenge was a Roman Ionic temple.[6] Rome certainly had a grip on the imagination: it was important to English medieval chroniclers that Brutus, Britain's supposed ancient founder was, like Romulus, descended from Aeneas.

There was another figure, who may have been Roman, perhaps British, or Romano-British: King Arthur. So far as our fifteenth- and sixteenth-century forebears were concerned, Arthur had existed and so had Camelot. There was even physical proof of Camelot, in the form of the Round Table and the site of its original location. It can still be seen today, in the Great Hall of Winchester Castle. But the difference between now and then is that in 1485 it was seen, experienced and believed. It was no whimsy that Henry's eldest son should be called Arthur, no accident that he should be born at Winchester, the ancient capital, first of Wessex and then of England. Through the choice of name, Henry was signalling that the boy's birth foreshadowed the rebirth of the nation, as enshrined in the description of the earlier Arthur as 'the once and future king'. The second coming of Arthur was an obvious secular equivalent to the second coming of Christ and the Christian resurrection, even if it was not openly articulated and perhaps only subliminally understood as such.

The Arthurian legend was a powerful one to harness and Henry VII was following in the footsteps of his predecessors by doing so. Henry II and Edwards I, III and IV had all gained or secured their throne through battle or coup and all had used Arthur and Merlin in their court display and in propaganda. Henry II came to the throne roughly two decades after Geoffrey of Monmouth's imaginative histories had propagated the myth of Arthur to England's secular reading class;[7] Edward I attended the reburial of Arthur at Glastonbury and created a new Round Table which was soon believed to be the original; under Edward III, there was a flowering of heraldry to articulate the knightly virtues at the core of the legend;[8] and Edward IV, who came to the throne as a vibrant and towering youth of nearly six foot four inches, identified himself with Arthur and was certainly projected as Arthurian by contemporary chroniclers such as John Hardynge, who beseeched him to add Scotland to England and Wales in order to make Albion entire again.[9]

Henry VII was typically thorough in exploiting King Arthur to serve his purpose. Whereas Edward IV had given the name to a bastard son, Henry VII had chosen it for his heir. He even, perhaps showing a lighter touch, had a greyhound called Lancelot.[10]

Arthurian symbolism was not the only propaganda card Henry brought into play: drawing on his Welsh origins (he was born in Pembroke Castle), he invoked the legend of the messianic Welsh prince 'revealed by a heavenly voice to Cadwallader, last king of the Britons', a mythical figure of eight centuries before, who was told 'that his stock and progeny should reign in this land and bear dominion again'.[11] Henry projected this association through the symbolic propaganda of heraldry: with the Red Dragon of Cadwallader taking its place opposite the White Greyhound of the Honour of Richmond as joint supporters of the royal arms.

In addition to these heraldic beasts, he made use of a device that had been created specifically for him: the red rose of Lancaster. As David Starkey has recently pointed out: 'for the sixty-odd-year rule of the house of Lancaster, from 1399 to 1461, not a single convincing contemporary use of the red rose as a royal dynastic emblem has been found. Instead it appears, out of the blue, at the battle of Bosworth.'[12] After his victory, it featured as one of Henry's principal badges. This was sheer genius. It created symmetry with the much-used white rose of the Yorkists, simultaneously projecting Henry as the true Lancastrian heir, rather than a mere offshoot of the main branch, while choreographing the expectation of a permanent peace in the union of the two houses through Henry's marriage with Elizabeth of York. This was demonstrated by the merging of the York and Lancaster emblems in the Tudor rose – remembering of course that the red rose surrounded the white.

The use of these symbols was stark and straightforward. For all that Henry had married the heiress of the House of York – a marriage which the Pope had 'approved, confirmed and established' as a means of bringing an end to 'the long and grievous variance, dissensions and debates that hath been in this realm of England between the house of the duchy of Lancaster on the one part and the house of the duchy of York on the other'[13] – the new King was crowned alone. His coronation thus made it clear that succession was through the heirs of *his* body. The red rose and the Beaufort portcullis were there as primary symbols, but the presence of the Tudor rose was a visual reminder to would-be followers of the traitorous heirs of Edward IV's brothers,[14] that the incumbent Queen was Edward IV's daughter and living heiress.

Symbols and display, in peace as in war, were there to project power and to command obedience. Nonetheless there remained, in Shakespeare's parlance, 'traitors … that would reduce these bloody days again, and make poor England weep in streams of blood!'

The first major challenge came quickly, from John, Earl of Lincoln, Richard III's nephew and designated heir. Following Henry's early efforts to accommodate his Queen's Yorkist cousins, Lincoln had seemed reconciled, but in 1487 he did exactly what Henry himself had done and landed with a mercenary army. His force was largely an

unlikely combination of Irishmen and Germans, with the latter commanded by Martin Schwartz, a former Augsburg shoemaker turned
ruthless battlefield commander.[15] That said, it was a well marshalled
force and only with difficulty were Lincoln and Schwartz defeated
and killed at the Battle of Stoke Field, particularly as the brunt of
the fighting was borne by the vanguard of Henry's army – under the
command, as at Bosworth, of the Earl of Oxford.

Lincoln had not, openly at least, advanced his own claims, but
those of his young cousin Edward, Earl of Warwick[16] – or rather, the
man who purported to be him. In reality, 'Edward' was an imposter
by the name of Lambert Simnel. Henry had the real Earl of Warwick
under lock and key in the Tower of London and was therefore able to
expose the imposture. All the same, Simnel posed a threat. It showed
the vulnerability of Henry's position, when a fake pretender could
present such a challenge.

Another would do so even more forcibly in the next decade, having
been given creditability by the King of France, Emperor of Germany
and James IV, King of Scots.

⊰ ✝ ⊱

Despite his symbolic elevation as King on 24 June 1488, the anniversary of Bannockburn – an auspicious date somewhat undermined by
the fact James III's corpse had not yet been buried – fifteen-year-old
James IV was in no hurry to assume power. For the next seven years,
he concentrated on enjoying the sport of kings, hunting and hawking,
the ritual taking of life expected of the medieval monarch.[17] He even
allowed his twenty-first birthday (17 March 1494) to pass without
taking control. He could afford to take a leisurely approach towards
ending his minority, for the three mutually antagonistic groups that
might have been expected to vie for control of the realm during this
period had instead been brought into the fold.

The three factions consisted of those nobles who had supported
James III; those who had opposed him; and a third group who had
risen up in 1489 because they felt that they had been inadequately
rewarded for their support of the new regime. The latter group had a
strong case, given the keenness of Patrick Hepburn, the new Earl of
Bothwell, to reward himself, his family and his supporters with the

fruits of victory. However by 1490 Bothwell had managed to curb this enthusiasm, and the leaders of the discontented faction, Lords Lennox and Lyle, had taken their place in the King's Council, along with James III loyalists such as Bishop William Elphinstone.

With the demise of James's first Chancellor, the Earl of Argyll, in January 1493 the post was gained by Archibald Douglas, Earl of Angus, to whom posterity has erroneously given the wonderful soubriquet of 'Bell the Cat' – a colourful name to suit a colourful personality.[18] Though Angus had been a continual plotter against James III, he had not initially taken a position in the central government of the former King's son, having fallen foul of Bothwell and his Hume allies in the Borders and thus of James IV himself. However, over many hours in James's company and many games of dice and cards he had re-established a rapport with the young King.[19] It would have done his cause no harm that his niece, Marion Boyd, became James's first mistress; part of the reason for Angus's subsequent fall from grace was Marion's replacement in 1496 by Margaret Drummond.[20] A further deterioration in relations between Earl and King followed in 1498, when Angus involuntarily provided James with another mistress – his own: Janet Kennedy.

Angus may have assisted James in taking those early steps in government, but in 1495 the twenty-two-year-old King finally took control. Given the calamitous reign of his father, his first priority was to demonstrate sound judgment. He did so by pursuing a policy that was bound to win the approval of his nobles and his people: conflict with England and its new, unstable, Tudor dynasty.

3

1496 and 1497
War on the Border

In late 1495, James IV began harbouring the imposter who presented a remarkable challenge to the English throne. Claiming to be Richard, Duke of York, the younger of Edward IV's two sons – immortalized in history as the Princes in the Tower – Perkin Warbeck carried out his grand pretence with sufficient plausibility that some of the great European powers accepted his story at face value. Or at least, they deemed it useful to do so, recognizing Warbeck's potential as a lever for extracting concessions from the insecure Henry VII.

From March to November 1492 Warbeck had been at the court of Charles VIII. At that time it suited the French King to promote the Pretender's nuisance value, as King Henry, himself a former French royal guest, was using an expedition in Brittany to act in the style of a more established English monarch. But by the end of that year Henry, just like his predecessor Edward IV, had been bought off by the French, thereby demonstrating the limitations of his military might, the unfinished nature of his business at home and France's more pressing business elsewhere.

From France, Warbeck moved to Mechelen in the Duchy of Burgundy,[1] where the Dowager Duchess, Edward IV's sister Margaret, received him as the long-lost nephew he purported to be. Late the following year, with Margaret's blessing, he travelled to Vienna and was treated royally by Emperor Maximilian.[2] Their support for the Pretender seriously alarmed Henry, for he understood all too well the danger posed by a claimant – however precarious the claim – who enjoyed the backing of foreign powers. After all, for the best part of a decade and a half, Henry had been just such a claimant himself.

Most dangerous of all would be one who, again like himself, was able to make common cause with malcontents at home. In January 1495, after months of evidence gathering by his ministers and agents, Henry exposed a conspiracy that included men at the very heart of his regime – even the titular heads of the 'upstairs' and 'downstairs' of the King's own household, his Chamberlain (Sir William Stanley) and his Steward (Lord Fitzwalter). It seemed that they had weighed their chances with the King against those with Warbeck and, remarkably, decided for the latter; particularly so for Stanley, whose late intervention at Bosworth had been so crucial. Both men were removed, but despite Henry's success in rooting out malcontents and his strenuous diplomatic efforts,[3] foreign support for Warbeck persisted. Maximilian sponsored both a rebellion in Ireland and an attempted invasion of England, and though neither enterprise succeeded, Warbeck did gain a place on the British mainland: on 20 November James IV received him at Stirling Castle.

James was promised that the frontier town of Berwick would be returned to Scotland when Warbeck became king, but it is extremely doubtful that he viewed his guest as anything more than a counterfeit gambling chip in the game of European diplomacy. That, however, was exactly what made him such an asset. In giving Warbeck token support, James could strengthen links with Emperor Maximilian and gain recognition from Ferdinand and Isabella of Spain.

Warbeck's prospects duly featured as the first part of the discussions when a Scottish embassy was received by Maximilian. But as soon as they tactfully could, the ambassadors, led by James's senior minister, Bishop Elphinstone, introduced the Scots' main business: a possible marriage between their master and the Emperor's daughter, the widowed Margaret of Austria.[4]

In their turn, the Spanish joint rulers sent an embassy to James.[5] The aim was to offer him false promises and persuade him to break with Warbeck, thereby neutralizing the threat to Henry. With the English throne secure, they would be in a position to proceed with the marriage of their daughter Katherine to Henry's heir, Prince Arthur.[6] The task of the ambassadors, Don Martin de Torre and Garcia de Herrera, however, was made all the harder by their arrival being delayed;

as a result, their instructions from Spain arrived at the court of King James before they did. Not hesitating to open the correspondence, James learned that he was to be flattered and deceived. Thus when Torre and Herrera eventually arrived, the tables were turned: they rather than the king were 'in the dark'. James received the ambassadors with Warbeck at his side, and took the opportunity to give a full theatrical performance, no doubt insulting both the ambassadors and the name of Henry VII. Certainly the meeting was sufficiently remarkable for Ferdinand and Isabella to write to their permanent ambassador in England expressing dismay 'for what the King of Scotland did in the garden of the Castle, especially as our ambassadors were present'.[7] This was not mere oafish rudeness by James – that was not his style at all. In a character sketch given to Ferdinand and Isabella soon afterwards, the Scottish monarch was described as 'of noble stature, neither tall nor short, and as handsome in complexion and shape as a man can be. His address is very agreeable.'[8] James's behaviour in Stirling Castle's garden was calculated to gain a reaction. His aim was to be noted and acknowledged by Europe's rulers.

For, paradoxically, what the fake King of England gave the real King of Scotland was the opportunity for continental recognition of his kingdom's independent identity. This would be one more step, perhaps even the final one, towards ensuring that Scotland's monarch was seen as a fully independent ruler of a fully independent country.

Warbeck spent the first few months of his stay in Scotland near the King. James was an outgoing, sociable man, possessing the ability to charm ambassadors as well as to insult them. He may even have considered Warbeck congenial company. Certainly the Pretender must have had something about him to have been so well treated at so many royal courts. The two men were around the same age, given that James was just five months older than the man that Warbeck claimed to be.

A sort of marital alliance was agreed, with Warbeck wedding Lady Catherine Gordon, a royal relative, if a distant one and then only by marriage.[9] In the autumn of 1496 James stepped up his support with a military intervention, notionally on Warbeck's behalf, which crossed the Tweed into England on 20 September. The would-be

King of England stayed in his kingdom for all of one day, during which time he took exception to the killing and pillaging of his 'subjects'. The King of Scots responded mordantly that the 'subjects' in question had failed notably in welcoming their new ruler.[10] With Warbeck back in Scotland, the Scottish forces continued what was in effect a major cross-border raid aimed at plunder and, just possibly, the taking of Berwick by force. For Warbeck it was a failure, but for James it proved a startling success. Enough booty was grabbed for the campaign to pay for itself,[11] and in a fortnight of campaigning in the Tweed and Till valleys, he had demonstrated the effectiveness of his artillery and in the process destroyed the towers of Twizel, Tillmouth, Duddo, Branxton and Howtel.[12] James was in the process of completing the job by reducing the Border stronghold of Castle Heaton to rubble,[13] when scouts informed him that an English relieving army was advancing from Newcastle. Showing strategic wisdom, the King immediately took his own forces back over the border. He could always return the next year to continue the work.

James may have acted cautiously on behalf of his army, but that was not the case on his own behalf. James was accompanied on his foray south of the border by the newly appointed Spanish Ambassador, Don Pedro de Ayala, who it seems was much more to James's liking than his predecessors. No sooner had Ayala arrived than the King invited him to join the English expedition – for the ride.[14] Though an attack against England was contrary to his country's interests, Ayala was sensible and sophisticated enough to accept. He did not go alone but took a retinue of servants: there were at least seven, because he later reported that four had been killed and three wounded. The King plunged into the heart of the action, leaving Ayala with no choice but to follow. As part of the detailed character sketch of James, sent to Ferdinand and Isabella in 1498, Ayala included the following observations:

> The King is twenty-five years and some months old … He is courageous, even more so than a king should be. I am a good witness of it. I have seen him often undertake most dangerous things in the last wars. On such occasions he does not take the least care of himself. He is not a good

captain, because he begins to fight before he has given his orders. He said to me that his subjects serve him with their persons and goods, in just and unjust quarrels, exactly as he likes, and therefore he does not think it right to begin any warlike undertaking without being himself the first in danger. His deeds are as good as his words. For this reason and because he is a very humane prince, he is much loved.[15]

Safely back over the border, James could reflect on his successful campaign. His relations with Warbeck may have cooled on a personal level, and he now saw little of him, but James still considered it politically useful to subsidize the Pretender's entourage and to keep him in Scotland.

Henry had regarded James's invasion preparations with anything but equanimity. In spite of the arrests of 1495, there were still more than enough former Yorkists of doubtful loyalty to keep Henry's network of spies fully occupied. Hoping to stave off conflict, he tried hard to negotiate with James. In May, he even proffered the hand of his six-year-old daughter Margaret for a future marriage. This was an offer of a quite different order to that of a mere knight's daughter,[16] suggested by Henry in 1492 and, unsurprisingly, rejected outright.

Unswayed by the offer of the infant Princess, James proceeded with his 1496 expedition. That in doing so he had broken a seven-year truce negotiated in 1494 was reason enough for Henry to declare war, but it was James's open military support for Warbeck that provoked an extreme reaction from Henry. In late October it was agreed by the Great Council that a grant of £120,000 should be duly ratified by Parliament to counter James by land and by sea. This was an incredible sum. It was equivalent to more than twenty times the entire annual ordinary revenue of the Scottish King.[17]

When James's 'Maister Spyour' arrived from England on 5 November and made him aware of the English plans,[18] he changed his usual arrangements for the winter months, including Christmas, and arranged to stay in the Borders. But he did not back down. On the contrary, he himself led a January foray into England known as 'The Raid of Hume' after the major Border family who took part. Nor did he seem deterred when he learned further details of Henry's plans.

He was happy to send the Earls of Hume and Angus to a conference in May, but his steadfast refusal to give up Warbeck made this a pointless exercise. James must have known that Henry was in earnest, but nonetheless he pressed on.

And Henry VII was indeed in earnest. Too much so. As a result he was destabilized, not by James but through his own extraordinary overreaction to the Scottish threat. The huge army that was raised to march on Scotland necessitated an equally enormous tax to pay for it. This provoked a major popular rebellion in May 1497. It began in the West, far from the Scottish border and also far from the bulk of the newly raised English army mustering in the Midlands.[19] Soon unrest began to spread as the rebels spilled out of Cornwall and began advancing on London, picking up new recruits along the way; by the time they reached the capital, their number had swelled to 15,000.[20]

The threat was sufficiently serious for Henry's Queen, Elizabeth of York, to take refuge in the Tower of London with her daughters and her second son, five-year-old Henry. This young child had recently been given a new title to enable him to be presented as the *real* Duke of York in contrast to the imposter Warbeck. The Queen and her children seemed safe within the Tower, but for the best part of a week they were unsure what turn events might take outside. Finally King Henry's troops crossed the Thames and forced an engagement at Blackheath, five or so miles from Tower Bridge. The rebels were defeated, but only after a major battle on 17 June. It was one more traumatic lesson for Henry VII, but, as ever, one from which he learned. It was to lead to a complete change of policy towards Scotland.

There was someone else who was bound to be marked by this episode, particularly in light of his experience of being confined with his anxious mother inside the walls of the Tower. That was the boy prince who was later to become Henry VIII.[21]

꘎ ✝ ꘎

It cannot be known whether James would have pulled back if Henry's massive attack had gone ahead. Certainly he never gave any indication that he would. In the event, the time and cost of putting down the Western Rising did more than delay Henry's plans: it drastically changed them. In July, one of Henry's most important ministers,

Richard Fox, Bishop of Durham, was sent to James with peace proposals.

James, however, did not want to come to terms, certainly not yet. This was no longer about Warbeck; the Pretender had by this time exhausted his political currency and spent too much of the physical kind. At Ayr, earlier in July, Warbeck and Lady Catherine Gordon had been put aboard the appropriately named *Cuckoo*, which immediately sailed to Ireland. From there Warbeck departed for southwest England at the beginning of September, gained some support from irreconcilable rebels and was then defeated and finally captured by Henry, all within a month. He needed only light persuasion to reveal his true Flemish identity both to Henry and foreign ambassadors, before eventually being sent to the Tower.

There may have been some half-hearted plans to coordinate military actions with Warbeck, but the Scottish King could satisfy his political aims in other ways. James had already started raiding in June. Determined to supplement his reputation of the previous year and impress both an internal and external audience with a demonstration of military power, he found the perfect instrument in Mons Meg, a giant bombard siege gun that had been built for his grandfather, James II. Boasting the ability to fire 330 lb. stone cannonballs with a diameter of around eighteen inches the best part of a mile and three quarters.[22]

Some planning was required to transport the eight-and-a-half-ton monster, travelling at a maximum speed of three miles per day, the forty-two miles from Edinburgh Castle to the north bank of the Tweed and opposite the Bishop of Durham's frontier fortress of Norham Castle.[23] No fewer than one hundred workmen and five carpenters were needed for this single weapon.[24] The carpenters were pressed into action almost immediately as the gun carriage collapsed on the outskirts of Edinburgh and it took two and a half days to repair. At the beginning of August Mons Meg, along with the remainder of James's artillery and an army that included many of his nobles, took up position opposite Norham. With the giant bombard and the other guns pounding the castle walls, the King of Scots could impress a three-fold audience. Firstly, his nobles were able to see James fulfil what in their view was his most important role, as the leader of his warrior class. There too was Ayala, this time a safe distance from the action in the company of his fellow Spanish ambassadors on the Scottish side of the border, drinking wine and playing cards with the King, while the siege guns did their work.[25] Lastly, Henry VII's senior councillor and negotiator, Richard Fox, Bishop of Durham, could not have failed to take note of the giant stones thudding against the walls of Norham, trapped, as he was, inside the castle and aware of the Scottish troops now close to its walls.

James did not capture Norham. But that may not have been his intention. We know from his accounts that he anticipated a short campaign, in order to display military might rather than fully exercise it.[26]

By the time the Earl of Surrey arrived from Yorkshire with Northern Army troops to relieve Norham, the siege party had departed. James arrived back in Edinburgh on 12 August after a two-day journey[27] to discover that Surrey was on the march. Instead of stopping when he reached the River Tweed, the Earl had crossed it and was laying siege to the Humes' castle of Ayton, a few miles north of Berwick. By the 16th, James was on the move again, accompanied by a small force. But neither side sought a long campaign. Surrey's troops in the field far outnumbered James's hastily re-gathered army and there were certainly too many for James to risk a set-piece battle. On the other hand, Surrey had problems of his own, with many of his soldiers falling sick in bad weather.

Physically, the Earl of Surrey was not a big man. His memorial brass showed him to be small and lean, with a long face, aquiline nose and long straight hair.[28] Small he may have been, but he had a commanding presence: Polydore Vergil described him as 'a man endowed with prudence, dignity, and firmness'.[29] It was enough to hold a sickening army together. Even so, he knew he could not linger long in Scotland.

The result was a brief stand-off between the two forces, enlivened by a great deal of posturing between them. James stayed about fifteen miles away at Cattleshiel near Duns: far enough from Surrey to keep out of striking range while retaining the ability to threaten the Earl's line of communications and Berwick. The two commanders were also sufficiently close for their messengers to travel between them with challenge and counter-challenge. James offered to fight Surrey in single combat, which the Earl – who was thirty years older than his twenty-four-year-old opponent – wisely declined on the grounds that, as a mere lieutenant of his own monarch, he could not fight the Scottish King.[30]

Nothing happened because further action suited neither party. Besides which, warfare was not cheap and both sides had spent heavily in relation to their resources. James was withdrawing towards Edinburgh by the 20th, and Surrey, after destroying the castle at Ayton, moved back over the Border.[31]

James was delighted with his work. His treasury might have emptied, but then he had also directly (himself) and indirectly (through the Western Rising) given Henry vast expense and a major threat to his throne. Ayton had fallen, but it had no strategic value. Unlike Norham, which had extraordinary symbolic significance, having been the venue where Edward I began his adjudication on the rights of contenders to the Scottish throne and received the homage of 'King' John Balliol.

It was no accident that James chose Norham to demonstrate his authority both to his own nobility and to admiring Spanish ambassadors. With James having already rejected peace terms from Henry's leading councillor, Richard Fox, it was surely all the sweeter that the Bishop was inside Norham Castle as Mons Meg's enormous gunstones bashed its walls.

James was very pleased with himself. It was with good reason that Ayala was to write of him the following year: 'I can say with truth that he esteems himself as much as though he were Lord of the World.'

Now with his prestige enhanced in Britain and in Europe, it suited James to begin negotiating a lasting settlement with the English.

4

The Common Condition

It was a sign of James IV's authority and ambition and of Henry VII's continuing insecurity that the negotiations began. But it was symptomatic of the long-standing relations between the two countries that the bargaining continued for years. The Kings and their ministers might wish to stabilize relations, but that view was not shared by their subjects – both high and low. No one was in a better position to comment on this than Ayala. He remarked in 1498 that only King James among the Scots desired peace and that it was done against the wishes of most of his subjects. And he also knew the views of the English and that he was thought noteworthy for having spent a whole year north of the border and for being able to hear the word 'Scotland' without losing his temper.[1] Age-old perceptions ran deep.

Mutual hostility between the Scots and the English and instability in the Border region had been a constant over many centuries, as was noted by Aeneas Silvius Piccolomini, later Pope Pius II. In the 1430s, decades before attaining the papacy or even becoming a priest, he served as a diplomat and in that capacity visited Britain. When he penned his memoirs – the only pope ever to have done so[2] – it was clear that the passage of time had not dimmed his recollection of the experiences and various misfortunes of his visit. Circumstances had dictated that, far from associating with only the highest ranks of society, he mixed with a variety of people; and the deep insight he offers into the lot of the common people (which had changed little by the time James IV came to the throne half a century later) makes him worth quoting at length. The majority of the comments of Aeneas, as he dubs himself in his third-person account, are illuminating, if sometimes a little dyspeptic:

About Scotland the following facts seem noteworthy:

It is an island [sic] joined to England, stretching 200 miles to the North and fifty miles across. It is a cold land, of few fruitful plants and is, for the most part, barren of trees. In the earth there is a sulphurous rock which they dig up to feed their fires. Their communities have no surrounding walls and their houses are most often constructed without mortar and have roofs covered with turf, while in the countryside the doorways are shut off with ox hide. The people, who are poor and uneducated, fill themselves up with meat and fish but only eat bread as a delicacy. The men are short in stature but brave; the women fair, beautiful and highly sexed. In Scotland, the kisses of women mean less than handshakes do in Italy. They do not have wine, other than what they import. All their horses have small bodies and are by nature only walkers. They usually keep a few for breeding and castrate the rest. They do not rub them down with iron brushes nor comb them with wooden combs, nor even control them with bridles. The oysters there are larger than those in England and many pearls are found within them. Hide, wool, salt fish and these pearls are all exported from Scotland to Flanders. There is nothing more pleasing to Scottish ears than curses sworn against the English. It is said that there are two Scotlands, one cultivated, the other wooded and without fields. The Scots that live in the wooded part speak in a different tongue and sometimes eat tree-bark. [3]

It is unlikely that Aeneas got close to the Highlands, so some of his talk of the 'second' Scotland is highly speculative. Presumably he travelled as far as Perth to see the Scottish King James I, but certainly he ventured far enough north to attest from personal experience that 'at the winter solstice the day in Scotland is not more than four hours long'.[4] As for the Scots 'stuffing themselves with meat and fish', this may have been true of the higher echelons and wealthier members of society such as merchants, but those lower down the pecking order would have made do with poorer fare.

Aeneas may have been less than enamoured of Scotland, thanks to the many difficulties he encountered during his winter visit, but that does not negate the interest of his factual descriptions. He had hoped to travel there through England, but for political reasons he was deported and forced to make the journey by sea. It was not a happy one. His ship, battered by gales and leaking badly, looked set to founder far out from shore until a sudden change of wind blew it back towards the coast and into the safety of Dunbar harbour. Determined not to return by ship, Aeneas was forced to risk travelling without the proper authority. Accustomed to being feted by cardinals and kings in his capacity as a diplomat, he now found himself supping with less exalted folk while disguised as a merchant – and fortunately for posterity, his passage across the border into Northumberland left quite an impression.[5] In describing this episode he captures the uncertainty of life on both sides of the border in the fifteenth century:

> There is a river,[6] flowing from its source on a high mountain, which determines the boundary between the two countries. Aeneas crossed this river in a small boat and deviated from the course of his journey into a large village, where he called at a country cottage and there had dinner with his host and the local priest. They served up a multitude of relishes, chickens and geese but there was no wine or bread. Afterwards, all the men and women of the village came running as if to some unusual spectacle, and just as we wonder at Ethiopians or Indians, so they stared in astonishment at Aeneas, imploring the priest to tell them who he was, with what intention he had come and whether or not he was of the Christian faith. But Aeneas, who had learnt that his journey was lacking in certain regards, had acquired some loaves of bread and a measure of bramble wine at a monastery en-route. When he set them out, a greater admiration held the locals, who had seen neither wine nor white bread before. But pregnant women and their husbands began to approach the table, to touch the bread and smell the wine and even to ask for a portion so that he had no choice but to share it all among them.
>
> The feast went on until the second hour after sunset, when the priest, host and all the men and boys together left Aeneas and hurried out, explaining that they were fleeing to a tower a safe distance away. They did this, they said, out of fear of the Scots, who often crossed the river when the tide was low and came marauding at night. But they were not willing to take Aeneas with them, despite his begging entreaties, nor did they take any of the women, although there was a good deal of

beautiful young wenches and matrons. For, since they do not count rape
as a crime, they do not believe their enemies can do the women harm.
Thus Aeneas remained there with two attendants and the guide among a
hundred women who sat in a ring around the fire and passed their sleep-
less night cleaning hemp and conversing eagerly with the interpreter.

After much of the night had passed, two girls led Aeneas, who was
now heavy with sleep, into a chamber strewn with straw. They would
sleep with him, such was the custom in their part of the world, if they
were asked. But Aeneas had his mind less on women than the maraud-
ers, who he feared would be coming at any moment. He pushed the
girls back despite their complaining, for he was afraid that if he committed the sin, he would pay the penalty for this choice when the robbers
arrived. He therefore remained alone with the cows and goats, but the
animals prevented his sleeping by stealthily picking out the straw from
his bed.

But after midnight there was a great racket of barking dogs and honk-
ing geese. At this all the women scattered, and the guide also took flight,
and the most frenzied commotion arose, as if the enemy were upon us.
But Aeneas thought it best to await his fate in his room (which was the
stable), since, if he was to run outside, he might become the booty of the
first person he ran into, not having knowledge of the road. But the women
returned after a short time with the interpreter and they announced that
nothing was wrong and it was friends rather than enemies who had come.
Aeneas judged this to be a reward for his earlier restraint. At daybreak
he began his journey once more, and came to Newcastle, which they say
was built by Caesar.[7] There for the first time he felt he was returning to
a recognizable world and a habitable country again. For Scotland, and
the part of England which borders it, has nothing in common with the
country in which we live,[8] being as it is rough, uncultivated and inacces-
sible to winter sun.

The future Pope's generalizations about Scotland and the Anglo-
Scottish borders are supported by other visitors, though they take
a less jaundiced approach. A fellow Italian, this time a Venetian diplomat, visiting Britain in c. 1500,[9] took the summer solstice as his
starting point for discussing the hours of daylight in Scotland: 'many

persons of veracity tell me, and assure me that it is a positive fact, that at the furthest extremity of Scotland, at the time of the summer solstice, one may see to read and write at any hour of the night'. However he does go on to say that 'the days in winter are short in the same proportion'.[10] The same visitor gives the Scottish a better report than the English:

> The English are, for the most part, both men and women of all ages, handsome and well proportioned ... the Scotch are much handsomer; and the English are great lovers of themselves, and of everything belonging to them; they think that there are no other men than themselves, and no other world than England.[11]

Impressionistic as this may be, there are two sentences in particular that strike home. The first sets out a fundamental difference in the way that the English and Scots viewed their relationship: 'All the English chroniclers insist that their King is the supreme Lord of Scotland, and that they have changed the Kings of Scotland at their pleasure; and the Scotch, on the other hand, pride themselves on having always repulsed the English.'[12] The second sets the position in 1500: 'The English could muster a very large army, were they as devoted to their crown as the Scotch are; but from what I understand few of them are very loyal. They generally hate their present, and extol their dead sovereigns.'[13] This goes to the heart of the matter: the Venetian diplomat confirms Ayala's statement that James, a strong Scottish king, could take his people with him, even though the Scots as a whole were, in the words of another Venetian visitor at around the same time, 'always enemies of the English';[14] whereas Henry VII, as proved in 1497, could not rely on popular support for his position at home in England, let alone when it came to making any traditional assertions over the border into Scotland.

This seems to have been a view that diplomats from the Italian states shared. In December 1497 Raimondi de Soncino, Milanese Ambassador to England, wrote home to his master, Ludovico Maria Sforza, Duke of Milan:

> The English are more restless than any people of Italy. For this reason the affairs of Scotland are more formidable to the kingdom than they would

otherwise be; and although the peace has been made, yet the king there is no more than twenty-six years of age and very spirited, and the Scots, who have nothing to lose, are always willing for a war with England.[15]

⚜ ✝ ⚜

There was, though, one element of occasional collaboration at a level of society far below that of kings and, normally if not always, below that of their administrative representatives. It did not bring stability but rather the opposite: it criss-crossed the border and brought together the most lawless individuals in the very area that was the cockpit for ongoing Anglo-Scottish hostility. This was a world of alliances, sometimes temporary and sometimes long-standing, between raiders of the sort Aeneas's hosts had gone into their pele (or peel) towers to escape. These were the Border Reivers, whose activities bedevilled commerce, administration and the basic operation of the law from the fourteenth century to the seventeenth in a region that might be called Scotland's 'wild south' or England's 'wild north' in the manner of America's Wild West.

The Reivers were already well established when James IV became King in 1488, and they had made their mark on the landscape on both sides of the Border. The Preston pele tower, built in the 1390s between Alnwick and Berwick, was one of seventy-eight in Northumberland alone by the time of Agincourt in 1415.[16] It is still impressive today with its two storeys, but it would have been even more so with its original four. The reasons for the spread of these towers varied from place to place; certainly they were not always constructed as places of shelter for the law-abiding. Their stone solidity, reinforced by roofs of turf and earth, and their storage space at ground level for as many as forty cattle meant that they provided a secure centre of operations for raiding parties as well.

Border outlaws organized themselves mafia-style in wider family groups known as 'surnames'. On the Scottish side were the likes of the Burns, Scotts and Irvines; on the English there were the Fenwicks, Charltons and Musgraves. Then there were 'surnames' with members on both sides of the border, such as the Grahams, Halls and Nixons.[17] To complicate matters, allegiances were in a constant state of flux with opposing surnames sometimes collaborating, or members of previously hostile families intermarrying. Most confusing of all, family groups or individuals occasionally gravitated away from law-breaking and instead became law enforcers at the highest local level. Thus the early sixteenth century saw a Dacre and a Ker installed as Wardens of the Middle March, the former for the English, the latter for the Scots. Quite naturally, there would always be a suspicion that at least a toe, if not an entire foot, of such a man would remain in the camp of the lawless.

Much of the negotiation at national level was dedicated to ensuring that escalating suspicions and confusions arising from border disputes did not escalate into a full-scale war that would embroil the Scottish and English monarchs. Thus sporadic incidents and incursions needed to be explained away as the action of rogue elements or as uncharacteristic ill discipline on the part of more trusted forces. In no way could such forays be seen as condoned or sanctioned by the king of the injuring party. And there were good reasons why the treaty, when it was eventually agreed, had to incorporate a safeguarding clause that sanctioned one king taking remedial action should the other king have failed to do so:

> That if anything contrary to this peace be done by the subjects of either, the peace shall not on that account be considered to be annulled; and if either prince, yet holding by the treaty, neglect to make redress within six months for the wrong done, the other may grant letters of reprisal, according to the extent of the wrong.[18]

There were fundamental reasons for the turbulence on the border. The wars of William Wallace and Robert the Bruce had been followed by further eruptions throughout the fourteenth and fifteenth centuries.

That tramp of armies across land that, at the best of times, produced poor yields was one factor in prompting a move away from arable farming. But another, even greater, they shared with most of Europe: the Black Death. It crossed the border with English troops in 1349 and was dubbed 'God's judgment on the English,'[19] by Scottish soldiers who saw the enemy struck down by disease. But the plague proved far from partisan. As Scottish soldiers returned to their homes, they took the plague with them and around a third of their countrymen died.[20] And on the pattern of the rest of Britain, the overall population number would not begin to increase again until the sixteenth century.[21]

The depopulated areas, though still far from verdant, encouraged animal husbandry. But livestock was vulnerable to theft, with Reiver cattle-rustling at its height as the nights darkened between Michaelmas (29 September) and Martinmas (11 November). Fattened up from summer pastures, stolen cows and sheep were driven long distances by raiders on horseback until they reached the Reiver strongholds.

From the fourteenth century onwards the Reivers enjoyed a secure base, ideally situated for raids, in a depopulated area of the West March known as the Debatable Land. About twelve miles in length, stretching from north of Carlisle to Langholm, and only three and a half to four miles in width, the name derived from continuing uncertainty as to which parts fell within Scotland and which in England. The Debatable Land defeated numerous coordinated Anglo-Scottish attempts to bring it to order as its Reiver occupiers, most notorious of whom were the Armstrongs of Liddesdale, melted away on their hardy ponies into the inhospitable boggy scrubland of Tarras Moss just to the north.[22]

Reiver daring could be extraordinary: during James's 1497 campaign they even succeeded in stealing two of the King's own horses.[23] However, in times of war they might serve a purpose for a kingdom defending itself: their nimbleness kept food and forage away from the invaders – if sometimes also from their own countrymen. Either way, in troubled times, their activities could create a form of 'cordon insanitaire' of up to thirty miles on each side of the border.

The Reivers have been romanticized in the Border Ballads and in the works of Sir Walter Scott – who shared his name with sixteenth-century men who were Reivers and officers, sometimes both at the same time. The reality is that these were rustlers and thugs, no more heroic than Billy the Kid or Jesse James. They sought to operate outside the law and if some were not actually outlawed – and thus subject to the savage punishment that capture could bring

– it was only because it was in the predatory self-interest of the local men in authority who were tasked with suppressing them, but who often aided or even organized their activities.

Loyalties on the Border could be suspect. That was why so much effort was made by the high-ranking Anglo-Scottish negotiators to create such firm guidelines for ensuring that local disputes did not turn into cross-border ones. All that was then needed was a spirit of goodwill.

5

The Treaty of Perpetual Peace

With both sides set on talks in the late summer of 1497, the wheels of diplomacy initially moved rapidly. Barely two weeks after the end of hostilities, Henry asked his senior councillors to make contact with the Scots. A high-level meeting was arranged at a place which, with diplomatic finesse, suited both sides: in Scotland, but at Ayton. The Scottish delegation included Bishop Elphinstone, Sir Patrick Hume and Andrew Forman, Bishop of Moray; leading the English side were Bishop Fox and William Warham, the Master of the Rolls. We know that the Earl of Surrey was also back at Ayton on 30 September, because it was there that he knighted his two elder sons, Thomas and Edward, both of whom had been with him on his punitive raid the month before.[1] This action could not have been taken amiss by the Scots, because they agreed a seven-year truce on the same day. The Truce of Ayton, as it was called, was to prove the foundation document of a more lasting settlement.

There is one element within the peace accord that is particularly striking and which shows the seriousness of intent on both sides: paragraph after paragraph anticipates the likelihood of continued cross-border raiding and how it should in no way be allowed to be seen as officially condoned and thus undermine the agreement. This was wise, because the negotiators knew that they could not guarantee to control the Reivers, whose activities were a focus for mistrust between the two sides. But so were any unexpected groups of men on the 'wrong side' of the border, so entrenched and long-standing was the mutual suspicion. In 1498, when 'certain young men of the Scots came armed unto Norham Castle'[2] on two consecutive days, the peace threatened to unravel completely. The near contemporary albeit Anglo-centric historian Edward Hall gives an account of what happened on that second day:

> The keepers of the said castle, suspecting some fraud to lurk in their looking, demanded of them what was their intent, and why they viewed and advised so the castle. The Scots answered them proudly with many disdainful words, insomuch that, after their blustering and blowing answers made, the Englishmen being moved therewithal replied to them with hard and manly strokes; and after many a sore blow given and taken on both parts, and divers Scots wounded and some slain, the Scots, oppressed with the multitude of the English people, fled as fast as their horses would carry them. When they came home and certified the King of the same, he was therewith sore moved and angry; and swore by sweet Saint Ninian[3] that there was nothing to him more inconstant and unsteadfast than the observing of the league by the King of England, and sent word thereof to King Henry in all haste by Marchmont, his herald.[4]

The situation was sufficiently grave for Henry to send Bishop Fox to meet James. Fox was not chosen because he was the absentee owner of the castle, but as one of Henry's chief counsellors. James may well have been 'sore moved and angry', but he was, more generally, in a very different mood from early the year before. He did not want to break the peace. This we can gather from letters to Ferdinand and Isabella, written by ambassadors a month or so apart. They are striking in their consistency, particularly as the first was by Ayala and the second by his London-based rival, De Puebla.

On 25 July, Ayala wrote:

> It has been a very difficult task to conclude the peace between Scotland and England, because the old enmity is so great. It is a wonder that the peace is not already broken. The King of Scots has borne the injustice committed by the English only because the peace has been made by Spain. The English have committed new murders and robberies in Scotland, before satisfaction has been given for the former murders. The King of Scots has sent to England, and declared, that, if satisfaction be not given without further delay, he will not consider himself any longer bound by the treaty of peace.[5]

Followed on 25 August, by this from De Puebla:

> The peace with Scotland is not yet broken; it even seems to improve. The
> King of Scots 'has seen the ears of the wolf', and is now endeavouring to
> 'make a bed of roses' for the King of England. Two or three months ago
> the English killed a great number of Scots, but King James would not
> permit the Scots to kill an equal number of English. He only wrote a
> letter to Henry, full of compliments and courtesy, as though he had been
> a son writing to his father. The King of England, in consequence of it,
> sent the Bishop of Durham to make reparations.[6]

The general tone of these letters is striking. Each also contains a sentence of particular interest. From Ayala: 'The King of Scots has borne
the injustice committed by the English only because the peace has
been made by Spain.' And from De Puebla: 'He only wrote a letter to
Henry, full of compliments and courtesy, as though he had been a son
writing to his father.'

The former had more than an element of truth, as James had
authorized Ayala to act as *his* ambassador to negotiate with the
English in London. What an affirmation it was for James, that the
new mighty nation of Spain – forged through the union of Isabella
of Castile with Ferdinand of Aragon and by their conquest of the
Moorish south – now regarded Scotland as a completely independent
entity. Yet King Henry also saw the benefit for himself and England
in the Scottish–Spanish diplomacy. The defeat of Warbeck and peace
with James seemed to have finally made the English throne secure for
the Spanish marriage with Henry's heir, Prince Arthur, and that, with
God's blessing and the provision of children, should finally confirm
the Tudor inheritance.

Spain had mediated in Anglo-Scottish affairs in order to procure
the diplomatic coup, sealed by a royal marriage, that would complete a defensive ring against the burgeoning power of France. But
they had been the midwife rather than the progenitors of the British arrangement. Both the Scottish and English monarchs were keen
to give up ancient hostilities to achieve permanence for something
they each wanted. The prize for James was England's final recognition, after centuries of challenge, of Scotland's independent kingship;

for Henry, very simply, it was the permanence of his dynasty.

As to De Puebla's statement, James, once so hostile to Henry, was indeed now prepared to be filial. According to Polydore Vergil (writing just a decade or so later) it was James who took the initiative in the meeting with Fox. He ardently raised the possibility of his marrying Princess Margaret, the King of England's eldest daughter.[7]

᪲ ✝ ᪲

Margaret, like the Peace itself, was not sufficiently mature in 1498. Over three years would pass while interested parties waited to see if the Ayton agreement would hold and whether the new Anglo-Scottish relationship would prove stable. Finally, on 24 January 1502, Henry VII's most senior ministers sat down with their Scottish counterparts at the magnificent new Tudor palace of Richmond. The English negotiators were led by Henry Deane, who was the successor both as Archbishop of Canterbury and Lord Chancellor to Henry's long-standing chief minister, Cardinal Morton. He was accompanied by Richard Fox, now Bishop of the rich See of Winchester, and Thomas Howard, Earl of Surrey. They were matched by men who had the full authority of the King of Scotland: Robert Blackadder, Archbishop of Glasgow; Patrick Hepburn, Earl of Bothwell; and Andrew Forman, who from Ayton onwards had been the recurrent negotiator on the Scottish side. These appointed commissioners signed three treaties. One was a practical administrative measure for the extradition of robbers and murderers on the Anglo-Scottish border, but the other two were even more critical. The first agreed the marriage between James IV and Margaret Tudor with a generous dowry of £10,000.[8] But even this was but an adjunct of the second, which was a treaty of perpetual peace between the two countries. It was the first permanent peace treaty between them – rather than a succession of fixed-term truces – since 1328.

The intended permanence of this 'Treaty of Perpetual Peace' resonates from every clause. Those of ongoing relevance and of greatest importance are as follows:

1. That between the Kings of Scotland and England, their heirs and successors, their kingdoms and subjects of every degree there be a good, real

and sincere, true, sound, and firm peace, friendship, league and confederation, to last all time coming.

2. That neither of the said kings nor their successors shall make war or cause war to be made against the other and his heirs, nor give aid, either openly or secretly, for the urging on of war.

3. That neither of the said kings shall receive, or allow to be received, any rebel, traitor etc.; and, if any rebels shall have fled into the other territory, the prince of the same shall neither give nor cause to be given any aid or favour, but shall imprison them, and within twenty days shall hand them over, if requested to do so.

4. That if any prince, of whatever dignity, attack the realm of one of the aforesaid princes, that prince whose realm has not been attacked shall assist the other with such forces as are requested, and with all speed, and shall be paid for the same by the other prince; nor shall any former treaty be allowed as an obstacle to this arrangement.

There were additional clauses specifically inserted to ensure that nothing and no one, past or future, would knock the new arrangement off course.

Not Berwick:

5. That the town of Berwick shall remain unmolested by the King of Scots and his subjects; and that the King of England's subjects of Berwick shall not attack the King of Scots or his vassals.

Nor existing allies, which were listed, followed by the words:

6. Either king may give aid to his ally, but not by an invasion of the other's territories.

Nor would the misdeeds of their subjects. This was of extraordinary importance. It was a recognition that lawlessness could undermine everything:

7. That if anything contrary to this peace be done by the subjects of either, the peace shall not on that account be considered to be annulled; and if either prince, yet holding by the treaty, neglect to make redress within six months for the wrong done, the other may grant letters of reprisal, according to the extent of the wrong.

Nor future monarchs:

8. That the successors in either kingdom shall within six months ratify the treaty.

Finally there was one clause that, above all others, was designed to make the agreement stick:

9. That the sanction of the Pope be obtained before 1 July 1503; and that he who breaks the treaty of peace be excommunicated.[9]

Should a king violate the treaty, he risked a punishment far worse than anything that might occur on Earth – that of damnation in the life eternal. Should the offender die while excommunicate, he would be considered 'out of grace' with God and therefore be denied burial in consecrated ground. As a result he would not be clothed in new flesh ready for resurrection at the Day of Judgment. Instead of eternal bliss he would suffer everlasting damnation.

The papacy had another role to play, in giving their blessing to James's and Margaret's marriage. Formal permission was needed, as for all royal marriages where there was consanguinity (a shared ancestor) within seven generations. In James's case it was four, in Margaret's five. But this, among all things, had been easily obtained; Alexander VI, the Borgia Pope, relished the opportunity to detach the Scots from a default alliance with the French. The first part of the marriage, the betrothal, could and did proceed without delay. On the day following the treaty signing, a solemn High Mass was celebrated at Richmond, with Bothwell acting as proxy for James and with three archbishops (Blackadder, Deane and Thomas Savage of York) and four bishops officiating.[10] All the signatories were there, along with the King and Queen of England, their children (bar Prince Arthur), the greater nobility, the higher clergy, and the ambassadors of Europe. Among the latter was Ayala, whose diplomacy had helped to clear the way for the marriage of Katherine of Aragon and Prince Arthur the previous November.

Margaret's betrothal was a magnificent state occasion. The Mass was followed by a procession to the Queen's Great Chamber for the 'fyancells' or vows to take place, as explained to the assembled company by the Earl of Surrey 'well and right solemnly in a very good manner', according to an expert observer, one John Yonge or Young,[11] Somerset Herald.[12] This was followed by a splendid banquet, with Elizabeth of York dining at one table with Margaret, her daughter and now fellow queen. With Arthur Prince of Wales long apart from his younger siblings and running a separate establishment at Ludlow in the Welsh Marches, ten-year-old Prince Henry, Duke of York, had lately enjoyed a prime position as the principal male in the Queen's household, an establishment mainly of women. Now he had to take his place after the new Queen of Scots. A Scottish queen certainly trumped an English duke, even the younger son of a king. Henry would have to walk one step behind.

Margaret was not to journey to Scotland for another seventeen months. Not because her parents thought her unprepared for travel or socially incapable, but rather because they feared that her under-developed twelve-year-old body was not yet ready to accommodate the highly sexed King James – the proud father of a bastard brood of seven, openly installed in the Scottish royal nursery.[13] No one was in any doubt about the dangers of childbirth, both for mother and child, but it was also believed that there were perils in the exertions of sex itself. The death of Katherine of Aragon's brother being attributed to an eagerness to procreate with his wife, Margaret of Austria, and his placing a fatal strain on a weak teenage constitution.[14]

Any apprehension that Henry and Elizabeth may have felt would have been heightened on 4 April, little more than two months after the celebrations for Margaret, when news reached the court that Prince Arthur, in whom Henry had vested so much hope, had died two days earlier at Ludlow. Henry held himself accountable, as David Starkey writes: 'it seems clear that Henry blamed himself for giving his eldest son Arthur the premature sexual experience to which con-temporaries attributed the boy's early death.'[15]

On 11 February the following year came the second major blow in the most troubled period of Henry VII's turbulent life: Elizabeth of York died on her thirty-seventh birthday, nine days after the birth of a baby girl who also died. This loss was devastating not only for King Henry but for his son and namesake. In a letter to Erasmus written some years later, Prince Henry was to describe news of his mother's death as 'hateful intelligence'. He was emotionally close to his mother[16] in a way that was never replicated with a father who had been completely focused on Arthur. In his teenage years, Prince Henry, as the sole surviving son, was brought much nearer to the King – physically at least.

⊰ ✝ ⊱

Elizabeth of York's account books show that she spent much of the final year of her life with Margaret, setting her an example of queenly behaviour in preparation for the long journey north.[17] On her mother's death, Margaret's redoubtable paternal grandmother took a much greater role, making up in organizational ability for any lack of affection, the latter being a gift which Lady Margaret Beaufort – officially titled 'My Lady the King's Mother', but who could sign herself 'Queen' – saved for her only child, the King himself. It was thus to her grandmother's recently enlarged manor house at Colly-weston in north Northamptonshire that Margaret, her father and the English court set out on 27 June 1503, arriving there on 5 July. After a few days' rest she said farewell to her father and grandmother and departed for Scotland with a cavalcade of English courtiers, led by the Earl and Countess of Surrey, together with some from Scotland, including Andrew Forman, Bishop of Moray.

This was not merely a matter of taking Queen Margaret to her new kingdom. It was a royal progress through England and southern Scotland that was planned with military precision and funded at vast expense. The purpose of its magnificence, from an English perspective, was to demonstrate the power and permanence of the Tudor dynasty. For the Scots, it was an opportunity to show that their King was no longer a client of his English counterpart but an equal.

Some nobles would join the procession, then leave and later re-join as it moved along the Great North Road. Sheriffs along the way would provide a ceremonial escort through their entire county right up to the northern border, whereupon they would hand over to their neighbouring counterpart. Everything was organized, everything choreographed. In the words of John Yonge, Somerset Herald, who was part of this moving assembly:

For the conveying of the said Queen throughout England, there was appointed many great Lords, Nobles, Knights, Ladies, Squires, Gentlewomen and others, to convey her from place to place, some further than others, as they were ordained by the King.

Likewise, of the nobles of the country, governors of towns, other officers of the lordships, mayors, sheriffs, aldermen, burgesses, and citizens of the great towns through which she would pass, to make her all honour and reverence.[18]

Margaret herself rode a 'fair palfrey' and there was also a litter for her, which she could use for grand entrances into towns or when she was tired. Her clothes and the attire of the accompanying lords and ladies – not to mention the coats of her footmen, embroidered with the Beaufort portcullis, the tabards of the heralds, the uniforms of the sergeants at arms with their maces aloft, the banners and bannerets, down to the trappings of the horses – were a feast for the eyes.

Each day the baggage wagons went ahead of the main party. They alone would have brought people to line the roads and look on in wonder: Margaret's carriage with its covering of green and white – the Tudor colours – and decorations bearing the arms of Scotland and England combined and surrounded by the red roses of Lancaster and Beaufort portcullises; and those of her accompanying lords and ladies, all displaying their arms, which Yonge thought a magnificent sight 'for very noble was the convoy'.[19] For most of the people, however, Margaret herself was the main attraction. This was a spectacle not just for the great and well-to-do, it was for all the king's subjects. And the people came out in their droves, eager for a sight of the English Princess, now Scottish Queen, as she went by:

Through all the fortunate towns and villages where she passed, all the bells were rung. And by the road came all the inhabitants of the country to see the noble company, bringing great vessels full of drink.[20]

They were rewarded with an extraordinary visual extravaganza, accompanied by the music of the royal party's minstrels, drummers and trumpeters.

The entourage made its way north in steady daily stages: from

Collyweston to Grantham, then to Newark and on to Tuxford, followed by a night stop at a country manor of the Archbishop of York; from there to Doncaster, then Pontefract and on to Tadcaster. From Tadcaster, the next step was York, the second city of England.

The arrival there is still commemorated in the name of Queen Margaret's Arch, through which the procession entered the city. York put on its proudest face. The Mayor dressed in crimson satin; his aldermen, resplendent in scarlet gowns and with their chains of office around their necks, greeted the Queen 'very meekly' and rode before her to the Minster. The occasion was watched from the street by an appreciative but respectful crowd dressed in their 'best array'. In addition, 'all the windows were so full of nobles, ladies, gentlewomen, damsels, burgesses and others, in such great numbers that it was a fair sight to see'.[21] The streets were so packed with spectators that it took Margaret's litter two hours to get from the gateway to the Minster. From there it was a short ride to the Archbishop's Palace and rest.

Margaret remained in York for the next day, a Sunday, and attended a High Mass at the Minster followed by a procession. Somerset Herald, much taken with the frequent extravagant costume changes and brilliant horsemanship of the Earl of Northumberland as he made his various entrances and exits during the journey,[22] again turned his attention to Margaret. The Queen, preceded by the Archbishop and bishops, earls and lords, heralds and sergeants at arms was at the heart of the spectacle:

> Richly arrayed in a gown of cloth of gold with a rich collar of precious stones and a girdle reaching down to the ground made from spun gold. The Countess of Surrey carried her train, a gentleman usher helping her. After her came the ladies and gentlewomen, very richly dressed in goodly gowns, great collars, great chains, girdles of gold and other riches.[23]

As the focus of this magnificent pageant, Margaret exhibited a golden radiance that makes modern celebrities seem very tinny indeed. No effort had been spared to create an impression on York. The Earl of Surrey, who had overseen Margaret's entire expedition, understood better than anybody the particular importance of the city. He was aware that York had owed a special loyalty to Richard III and had been at the heart of his power base, first when Richard had been Edward IV's trusted brother, and then as King. A former Yorkist himself, Surrey had proved his new loyalty in 1489 by putting an end to a major disturbance in Yorkshire and hanging the leaders in York. He had spent ten long years as Henry VII's lieutenant in the North. The wondrous pomp of the ceremonials had been planned for a full-blooded purpose that went beyond pageantry. This was a demonstration that, almost eighteen years after Bosworth, Henry and his dynasty were here to stay. Underlying everything else was a show of strength. Margaret might now be a Scottish Queen, but on her journey to the border, and in York especially, she was first and foremost a Tudor Princess.

For Margaret the day's events did not end with the procession; afterwards she attended a banquet at the Archbishop's Palace. The following day, after the attendance of the Archbishop, sundry other bishops, the Lord Mayor, sheriffs and aldermen, she was back on the road north with her long-standing supporters and a number of new additions to her entourage, more than sufficient to replace any departing nobles and gentry. That night they rested at Newburgh Priory, the next at Northallerton, then Darlington, then moved onward to Durham.

Margaret stayed at Durham for three days, lodging in the castle, where she was 'well cherished' by the Bishop, William Senhouse. But this was hardly a rest cure, as her presence was timed to coincide with the formal enthronement of the new Bishop. Among other festivities, he served a 'double dinner and a double supper for all comers worthy of being there.'

Thence to Newcastle and more crowds for two days, with the second spent in special celebration of St James's day. After that it was Morpeth and on to Alnwick and the seat of the Earl of Northumberland, where she hunted in his park and killed a buck with her own bow.

The following night she reached Belford. As a sign that she was nearing journey's end, it was Sir Thomas Darcy, Captain of Berwick, who ensured that her dinner was made ready there 'very well and honestly'.

Finally to Berwick, where her entrance was announced with gun-fire and two days of festivities and sports, including bear baiting. She was joined by Thomas, Baron Dacre, the Warden of the West March and Surrey's successor as Henry VII's trusted 'strongman' on the Borders. Then on 1 August, with a party of between 1,800 and 2,000 she crossed the border into her new country.

Bearing in mind traditional Scottish suspicions, the welcome that Margaret received at Lamberton was truly impressive. James was not there to meet her, but, as her prospective bridegroom, he was not expected. In his stead the reception committee was led by the Archbishop of Glasgow. The Bishop of Moray, back on his native soil, joined him and they knelt before their Queen.

Margaret was escorted to a grand pavilion that was reserved for the noblest from each country, so that our Herald correspondent was only able to sneak a glimpse from outside. But there were three other pavilions, serving as pantry, buttery and kitchen, and everyone including Yonge himself 'was able to make good cheer and drink'.[24] Yonge estimated that there were a thousand Scots at the gathering. Of Margaret's own party, as many as six hundred continued towards Edinburgh, stopping en route with the Humes at Fast Castle, at an abbey to the east of Haddington, with the Earl and Countess of Morton at Dalkeith Castle and finally at Newbattle Abbey. At every opportunity the common people of her new country crowded to see her.

It was on the 3rd, at Dalkeith, that she received an unexpected visitor, one who was not scheduled to meet her until Edinburgh. Fol-lowing a romantic tradition of diverting from a hunting expedition to pay his bride a surprise visit, the King arrived, met and charmed his young Queen. James welcomed Surrey, his old adversary, 'very heart-ily', but his focus was completely on Margaret and he stayed late.

The next evening he arrived again and found Margaret playing cards. When she saw him she rose to meet him, 'receiving him very gladly and happily kissing him'.[25] James also gave the Archbishop of York and Bishop of Durham a cordial welcome, but quickly relaxed

the company and called for music. After an introduction by the paid
professionals, it became an evening of music-making by talented ama-
teurs: including James on the clavichord and lute; the Earl of Derby's
son, Sir Edward Stanley, singing ballads; and Margaret dancing with
the Countess of Surrey. The next evening, James visited again and this
time it was Margaret's turn to show her skills on clavichord and lute,
with the King kneeling at her side.

Two days later, when the couple finally met officially outside Edinburgh, Margaret no longer saw the King as a stranger. Indeed, as
Yonge records, on each encounter she received him with increasing
affection. Scarcely more than a child, she was happy to trust him and
to go along with his playful suggestion that they enter the city on one
horse. This crowd-pleasing act received rapturous applause from the
citizens. It was the beginning of many days of festivities, embracing
the marriage service and the celebrations that followed. All was a triumph of display and symbolism, captured in the poem 'The Thistle
and the Rose', written by the Scottish court poet William Dunbar to
celebrate the occasion and definitely 'on message' for both countries.[26]
The thistle had become the Scottish royal symbol, introduced on to
coins by James III and established as a badge by the end of his reign.[27]
The 'fresh rose of colour red and white' was most definitely that of the
Tudors.

For the prime organizers, Thomas Howard the Earl of Surrey and
Andrew Forman the Bishop of Moray, the series of events that began
at Collyweston and ended at Edinburgh were a triumph. However,
the collaboration at the top table may not have been shared lower
down, if Edward Hall's account, written in the reign of Henry VIII,
is accurate. Unintentionally, he shows the English in a poor light. It
seems that English visitors typically viewed James's lavish hospitality
as 'deliberate prodigality',[28] and thought that the jousts and other pastimes provided for them were merely the best that this rough country
could provide. On returning to England, 'they gave more praise to the
manliness than the good manners and proper breeding of their Scottish hosts.'[29]

But such cavilling could be ignored by the two major players: James
and Henry. As it was later to be reported in the parliamentary record

of 1504, King Henry had acted to 'secure a perpetual peace with the realm of Scotland, and many other countries and regions, to the great weal, comfort and peace of all his subjects'.[30] For his part, James felt secure in the belief that he had won recognition of his sovereign status both within Britain and at royal courts abroad.

He showed himself very happy with this new state of affairs throughout the time the party from England were with him and seemed particularly to favour Surrey's company, which upset his young wife. Margaret wrote to her father that same month, commending 'all your servants who have by your command given right good attendance on me at this time and especially all those ladies and gentlewomen who have accompanied me here'. But then a grumbling tone enters the letter:

> Sir, as for news I have none to send, except that my lord of Surrey is in great favour with the King here and he cannot bear to be without his company at any time of the day. He and the Bishop of Moray order everything to please the King. I pray God it may be for my own benefit in time to come. They do not call my Chamberlain to see them, though he knows my wishes better than anyone. And if he speaks anything on my behalf, my Lord Surrey speaks to him in such a way that he dares speak no further.[31]

One can only sympathize with the young Queen, barely into her teens, who must have been exhausted after weeks of taking centre stage in the many activities and festivities since leaving London, and who was now so busy trying to fulfil her new role that she dictated all but the last few scribbled lines of the letter, asking 'to be excused for not writing myself to Your Grace, for I have no leisure at this time'.[32]

Surrey, on the other hand, having discharged his duties so successfully and with military precision, both in accompanying Margaret to Scotland and in the ceremonies that followed, was no longer at the Queen's beck and call but that of her husband, the King. It was certainly not Surrey's fault if James valued his company and the Earl would not have doubted for a moment that bolstering that relationship was the best way of serving Henry's interests and thus his own.

As for James, as much as he may have been delighted with the young Queen, he must have decided she could keep. In contrast, he had only a short time to spend in the company of this military man, more than four times older than Margaret and twice his own age, who had decades of campaign experience and had fought – and been wounded – at two of the major engagements of the Wars of the Roses: Barnet in 1471 and Bosworth fourteen years later. Indeed, the Earl was so seriously hurt at the second, where he fought on King Richard's losing side, that, fearing he would have been vulnerable to any cut-throat looter scavenging the battlefield, he begged his direct knightly opponent Gilbert Talbot to finish him off.[33] Instead Talbot showed mercy and commanded that he be taken to safety. Surrey survived his wounds and spent the next three and a half years in the Tower of London, at the end of which he was given the opportunity to prove his loyalty to Henry VII. This he had done through long and dedicated service north of the Trent.

James, being interested in all things military but having yet to participate in a pitched battle himself, was fascinated by Surrey. The two opposing commanders of six years before exchanged war stories from their own campaign. What better time to do so than now, over drink and over cards, in the new age that had been created, one of 'Perpetual Peace'. Surrey well appreciated that James had 'entertained him as thankfully and favourably as could be thought'.[34] When at last he had to depart, he did so with 'great gifts' from the King.[35]

6

A New Monarchy

It was customary for Scottish kings to reward their brides with a 'morrowing gift' the day after their marriage and James's to Margaret was the burgh of Kilmarnock,[1] this being just the first of his gifts of dower lands and palaces. The latter included two of his five great Renaissance establishments, which would be built or rebuilt within a few years to a new standard of magnificence and for a cost that was hitherto unparalleled. These two were Margaret's in name alone, yet much of the decoration in all five palaces was designed to reflect her as well as James himself.

John Yonge (Somerset Herald) tells us that the painted glass of the windows in the Queen's apartments at Holyrood showed 'the arms of Scotland and England combined and surmounted with a crown decorated with thistles and roses'; and when a month after her marriage James took her to her own palace of Linlithgow she could not have missed the message of the decorative effects. James I's towered and crenellated east façade, on a promontory which gave stunning views over its own loch on three sides, would have made Linlithgow Palace romantic enough. But James IV ensured that the palace had been refurbished and that there were added touches, including 'tiled pavements decorated with the initials J and M, surrounded by chains of love knots',[2] and vaulting bosses similarly decorated with 'entwined initials IRM in roman capitals'.[3] From Linlithgow they travelled north to the second of Margaret's palaces: the castle of Stirling with its new forework or gatehouse that, though still in the early stages of completion, provided a magnificent entrance to the royal residence. We do not know how favourable was Margaret's first impression of the place; we do know that as soon as she reached the Royal Nursery the most unholy row broke out. Extraordinary perhaps, but it nevertheless seems that both her parents and James had neglected to tell the young bride of the castle's Royal Nursery, or rather of its occupation by the King's several illegitimate children. James may have thought that Margaret would be more accommodating; but she had been brought up in the comparatively strait-laced atmosphere of her parents' court. The children, though still treated most royally, were then moved elsewhere.[4]

James had a succession of mistresses, whose presence in the royal bed helped their families prosper, and he acknowledged five illegitimate progeny. He had four successive, more or less open favourites: Marion Boyd, Margaret Drummond, Janet Kennedy and Isabel Stewart – all of whom bore him children. There was a later story that James's advisers had Margaret Drummond poisoned in 1502, together with the two sisters with whom she was dining; in order, so it was claimed, to remove her from the King's affections and clear the way for Margaret Tudor. This was, however, a late-seventeenth-century invention of William Drummond, made 1st Viscount Strathallan by King James II and VII,[5] and nothing more than an attempt to 'sex up' the family history. Whatever the cause of Margaret Drummond's death, James had already begun his long-standing relationship with Janet Kennedy four years previously, having imprisoned Janet's former lover, Archibald Douglas Earl of Angus.

James may have tactfully housed Janet away from court, but he did not give her up after his marriage. However, for all that he was certainly a sexually charged being, he was also an intelligent one. Henry VII's and Elizabeth of York's fears that James might damage their daughter by demanding his conjugal rights before her full maturity seem to have been misplaced. Whether or not it was due to continued abstinence on James's part, Margaret did not give birth to a child – sadly a short-lived son – until 21 February 1507, a good three and a half years after the marriage. Margaret was there for duty; as for pleasure, he could take that elsewhere, involving, not exclusively, Janet Kennedy, to whom he had given Darnaway Castle, in northeast Scotland. Janet was thus close by when he went on his regular pilgrimages to the shrine of St Duthac at Tain. Margaret's role was to produce heirs for Scotland and also, should fortune that way incline, for England too.

Siring living heirs gave confidence to kings. In one sense James had done that already, because Alexander Stewart, his son by Marion Boyd, had been legitimized and could, should there be no children by Margaret, become his successor – though this was very much a back-up position.

The other thing that gave kings confidence was the exercise of power and, to an increasing extent across Europe in the late fourteenth and early fifteenth centuries, its display.

✣

For many years, some historians struggled to define the nature of Renaissance kingship; not so much in seeking to capture its 'big bang' moment, but in defining exactly how it marked a break from its medieval predecessor. In fact, there wasn't any identifiable break, because this was an evolution and not a revolution. Then again, others tried to dismiss Renaissance monarchy as merely a cultural phenomenon, and by so doing missed the extraordinary enhancement of monarchical power.

In fact, this change was so coherent that, as Dr Glenn Richardson argues in his comparative study, *Renaissance Monarchy*, it placed Renaissance kings, right across Europe, on a different plane to their subjects and it did so because it built on the traditions of monarchical rule that were understood and valued by those they ruled.[6] In his essay 'Renaissance Monarchy?',[7] Professor Roger Mason pins this down in a paragraph:

> In the course of the late fifteenth and early sixteenth centuries, traditional ideas of kingship, deriving from a blend of Christian, chivalric and classical sources, were reworked in ways that signalled a subtly different style of governance – and a redefined vocabulary to describe it – in which princely 'virtue', 'honour' and 'reputation' were underwritten by self-conscious displays of 'magnificence'. The result might be described as a form of 'enhanced' medieval kingship in which princely majesty was increasingly a matter of conspicuous public consumption

and performance. Yet such ostentatious displays of wealth and power not only masked more profound changes in the nature and extent of royal authority, but also served to advance them. And it was in precisely this, the public projection of political power and prestige, that Renaissance Monarchy came both to differ from the forms of kingly rule that had preceded it and to redefine the nature of sovereignty itself.[8]

Medieval monarchs had the protection of divine sanction through anointing at their coronation. They extended their rule through executive efficiency. Their Renaissance successors had new resources – material, technological, cultural and intellectual – at their disposal; and the successful ones ensured that they not only used them, they flaunted their use.

Due to the complicated interweaving of forces that sparked the Renaissance itself, 'the finest of everything' was available in a profusion and a variety that was completely new. This was an age of extraordinary cultural change, which, in the second half of the fifteenth century, was accelerated exponentially by the way that it was wholeheartedly embraced by Europe's rulers. They advanced it because they had the resources to take advantage of the new technology. They also looked favourably on the revival of classicism, which they confidently took as giving support for imperial rather than republican values. They valued Erasmian humanism as liberating intellectual thought from the confines of the monastic cloister and taking it out into the wider world. This was something that, at this stage at least, was prized by royal courts across Europe. In contrast, there was a development they were not keen to share. This was the production of powerful siege artillery. It was sufficiently expensive to lend itself to royal monopoly, but vigilant kings such as Henry VII and James IV ensured that they reinforced the economic argument with a legal one. Over a century, these large guns had been completely transformed from the basic tubes used by Edward III in the Hundred Years War, which became so hot that they could be fired just a few times a day and even then were prone to blow apart and kill their own gunners.

Of course, on occasion, that once might be sufficient for more primitive artillery: in 1405, one shot against the town walls from the giant cannon deployed by Henry IV was enough to persuade Berwick to surrender.[9] Half a century on, although there were still explosive ruptures such as the one that killed James II in 1460, they had become less common. By this time it was possible for even the gargantuan Mons Meg to be fired safely eight to ten times – before it was given the rest of the day to cool down[10] – and smaller guns could be used far more often.

When harnessed effectively, siege artillery could make or break nations and empires. The confusingly named Hundred Years War had already extended over 112 years when Charles VII of France deployed powerful new guns against England's fortresses in Normandy and effectively ended the war within months. Similarly, it was Queen Isabella's adroit and relentless use of artillery against the citadels of Andalusia that brought the European empire of the Moors to a close and proved a major step forward in creating Spain as a great power. It was with good reason that other rulers, including James IV and Henrys VII and VIII as notable examples, put such trust in their large guns.

A second European technological innovation, on a par with the twentieth-century invention of television and the worldwide web, was printing. The written word had hitherto been reproduced in medieval manuscripts, but these were luxury items which, especially in their most highly illustrated form, were intended to be viewed as much as read. Printing made the written word far more accessible, bringing it to a wider range of people: to the town burgess and the country squire as well as to kings and queens, clerics and courtiers. There was a market for books for pleasure and leisure, in addition to writings that were spiritually improving: William Caxton's first publication in English in 1473–74 was *The History of Troy*; the second, which swiftly followed, was a book on how to play chess.[11] Importantly – and this is something that has changed with the impermanence of web pages – printing made people's writing fixed and permanent. The danger of error through copying was removed. To the increase in quantity of the written word was added the assurance of quality.[12]

The printers had no shortage of literary material at their disposal. In the years immediately preceding the fall of Constantinople in 1453, what had previously been a trickle of Byzantine scholars entering Italy became a flood. Scholars of Ancient Greek poured in, bringing with them texts unknown to Western Europe in the hope that possession of these treasures would help them to find a lucrative position in what had become a very competitive market. Knowledge and understanding of Ancient Greek had declined over the centuries, but it was rekindled through retranslation, and complemented the study of Latin, Europe's common scholarly language. Interest in classical art was fired by a new passion for archaeology and the excavation of ancient sites, which unearthed striking examples such as the *Laocoön* marble statue. There was support for these activities at the highest level of the Roman Catholic Church; far from seeing classicism as challenging their position, successive Popes embraced it. When Julius II heard in 1506 that the *Laocoön* had been discovered in the area of Nero's Domus Aurea, as a classical enthusiast he rushed to acquire it.

Indeed, the classical revival underpinned Christian humanism and was to make bestsellers of works by Erasmus and his English friend Sir Thomas More. This interest in the myths of the ancient world did not, however, turn people away from 'the dark age' myths of King Arthur. They were accommodated in print, just as they were accommodated in the forework of Stirling Castle. Caxton published Sir Thomas Malory's *Morte d'Arthur* in the summer of Henry VII's victory at Bosworth in 1485 and it would have been published much earlier had Caxton not feared the wrath of Edward IV, who viewed Malory as the Lancastrian ne'er-do-well he had imprisoned in the Tower of London.[13]

Even in printing's earliest days, monarchs kept a close eye on printers. In the wrong hands the dissemination of the printed word could be extremely dangerous. But in the right ones, print could be used to provide an entire country with the essential 'truth' about its very existence, as endorsed by the monarch himself.

Printing came rather later to Scotland than it had to England. It did so in 1507 at the instigation and under the patronage of James IV

himself. Among the earliest commissions of the royal printers Chepman and Myllar were books designed to amplify James's chivalric per-
sona, a national liturgy to replace the English Sarum rite and, most
importantly of all, chronicles designed to propagate the independent
history of the Scottish nation with its roots in the classical past.

7

Renaissance Monarchy – Power

James IV and Henry VII were highly successful executive kings. Once James IV began to direct matters himself, he did so with tremendous energy, verve and dexterity. He moved around the country personally dispensing the law through Justice Ayres, prepared for a major offensive against rebel forces in the Isles and planned to rally his nobility and people behind him through that initial aggressive stance against England. Unlike his father, James was able to delegate, giving power to nobles and to clergy administrators. Those who applied themselves successfully, and who appeared to put the King's interests ahead of their own, did well; some, such as the Earls of Bothwell and Huntly, did very well indeed. But those who failed, as Archbishop Blackadder did in a diplomatic mission to Spain,[1] or appeared to take a different line (and a major reason for Angus's fall from the Chancellorship was that he was seen as pro-English at the time of the Anglo-Scottish wars of 1496–97) suffered the consequences through loss of preferment. They might also be forced to pay heavy financial penalties.

James's authority was increased because the late-medieval Scottish monarchy was the focal point for Scottish national pride and identity: 'the crown also acted as the glue which held Scotland together as a political society, acting as the accepted source of legitimate power and judgment in a diverse realm.'[2]

This statement might seem open to challenge, given that both James I and III were murdered in just over half a century – James I stabbed to death by a small group of assassins in the sewer through which he tried to escape, and James III after Sauchieburn. Together with James II's hot-blooded killing of the 8th Earl Douglas, the evidence seems to point to decades of struggle between a weak monarchy and mighty subjects. But while these violent deaths might on the surface appear to echo events over the border in England, any similarity is superficial.

In Scotland there was no clash of rival royal houses, no aim to replace the House of Stewart with another. The assassination of James I was instigated by his own half-uncle, Walter Stewart, Earl of Atholl; that of James III was the end result, if not necessarily the intended one, of the rebellion of his own son. Even the rebellion of the 9th Earl of Douglas against James II, in revenge for the death of his brother, aimed at James as his lord and not as his king.[3] In each case the attack was personal, striking against the individual monarch as opposed to the Stewart monarchy. In fact the position of the crown was inherently stronger as a result of these reigns: the bloodletting of James I and II against mighty subjects heightened the difference in power between the king and his strongest nobles. James III increased the symbolic nature of that difference, being portrayed on his coinage wearing not the open crown of a king, but the closed crown of an emperor.[4] James III's downfall was not due to the inherent weakness of his position but due to a personal failure, a vindictiveness which caused subjects such as the Humes and his own nearest and supposedly dearest to fear for their very existence. If a comparison of James III to an English king is to be made, it is to the aloof and vengeful Richard II.

Like their predecessors, these Stewart rulers described themselves not as kings of Scotland but as kings of Scots. They were at the apex of a pyramid of respect and obligation based on actual or assumed kinship that went from the bottom of society to the very top and made the king the 'father' of his people.[5] His subjects looked to him to give general direction to the nation and to be the ultimate decider of disputes, either directly or through his servants. The most crucial test of the king was to be both authoritative and impartial; or, if partiality was needed, then to have his judgment respected or at least to appear to stand above the fray. This was a test which James III failed dismally, but one that his successor passed with distinction. Thus bitter rivals at the local level, such as the Montgomerys and the Cunninghams in Ayrshire, served their king together against the English in

1496; similarly, the nobility followed him en masse to Flodden. Even John Ramsay, favourite of James III and conspirator with the English in 1488, who had been stripped of his title of Earl of Bothwell by the young James IV, was on the Scottish side in north Northumberland in 1513.

James IV was extremely hard working and his was a highly-effective personal government. Where his father had sought to centralize power on Edinburgh, James was happy to delegate it to trusted lieutenants and support them on the ground, bringing summary justice in his wake, when required. Parliaments were not called, as they were in England, primarily to raise money; they were used for codifying the criminal and civil law as the highest court in the land. Parliaments served as an extension of the King's Council and only three were called in the last seventeen years of James's reign. More important on a regular basis were meetings of the Privy Council, which were small and uncluttered and normally had quorums under ten.[6] But the best decision-making process of all was when the king's 'natural counsellors',[7] his nobility and higher clergy, talked with him directly at court. Five minutes with James himself being far more productive than umpteen meetings of the council.[8]

This combination of application and charisma ensured that James was able to raise far larger sums of money from his subjects than his father and be more forceful in doing so than the elder James had ever been. James III revoked royal grants, and to much consternation, just the once; James IV did so no fewer than five times.[9] Reminiscent of Henry VII to the south, James made vast profits from royal justice, which was sometimes very harshly applied; his rights as a feudal superior were monetized and rentals of crown lands were exploited vigorously.[10]

He also increased the monarchy's control over the appointments of the Scottish Church and claimed a larger share of its revenues. He nominated first his brother and then his legitimized son as archbishops of St Andrews. Such appointments were allowed by popes who themselves had no aversion to nepotism. James also stood firm against any reassertion of the Archdiocese of York's traditional claim of hegemony over St Andrews and the Scottish Church, the archdiocese being an ecclesiastical echo of ancient Northumbria at its fullest extent.

While James's demonstrations of belief seem genuine enough, he nonetheless displayed a talent for using the Church for practical purposes. In one instance, this extended to its very fabric: Ladykirk, which still stands opposite Norham Castle, was built by James, so legend has it, as a mark of thanks for his surviving a near-drowning in the Tweed in either 1496 or 1497. There is, however, no record of such an event. More to the point, certainly in the opinion of Ladykirk's current minister,[11] is that the tower gave a clear view of the fords for crossing the Tweed on either side of it, and that, being a church building, this observation post was safe from potential enemy fire. It is an explanation that would certainly accord with James's interest in military matters.

With additional funds from the English, with Margaret's dowry and with some French support for his massive shipbuilding programme, James created for himself far greater resources than those enjoyed by any of his predecessors. This allowed him to go some way towards meeting his huge expenditure. It is estimated that the Treasurer's annual receipts increased from £4,500 in 1496–97 to £28,000 in 1512.[12] However, if one includes money from church properties, profits from justice, the king's feudal rights and better exploitation of crown lands and lordships, total annual revenue by the end of the reign was possibly as much as £44,500.[13] This was still £7,000 short of expenditure, but it could be covered by the likes of the 'spiritual tax' of the clergy, which amounted to nearly £7,000 in 1512 alone.[14]

As he expanded his financial basis, so James, at least in name, increased his territorial one. James engendered something else not given to the Kings of Scots who had gone before him: royal title over the landmass and islands of what we now know as Scotland. The islands to the north of the Scottish mainland, Orkney and Shetland, had come as the dowry of his mother, Margaret of Denmark, and were under Scottish crown authority.[15] Those to the west, the traditional power base of the Lords of the Isles, were not so secure. The Lords had come under the full overlordship of the Kings of Scotland in 1263, after Alexander III defeated their previous overlord, King

Haakon of Norway, at the Battle of Largs. The Lords gained additional lands on the mainland as a reward for their support of Robert the Bruce, but they had still resisted integration into the polity of Scotland. Their successive challenges to the first three Kings James had weakened them and led to a civil war and the Battle of Bloody Bay in 1480. The Macdonald and allied clans continued to defy Scottish royal power until 1493, when Parliament was used to forfeit their lands and title. 'Lord of the Isles' now became a Scottish royal title. It still is one today, the present incumbent being Prince Charles.

Insurgency in the Islands and parts of the Highlands continued during James's adult rule. He personally directed campaigns there in 1495 and 1498, but he also delegated to the 2nd Earl of Argyll and then – following Argyll's failure – to the 3rd Earl of Huntly the task of 'Daunting the Isles'. He backed them up in person, through his administrative and judicial capacity, and by sending his newly powerful navy to destroy the sea bases of the rebels. The task was not completed by 1513, but James had wider control of Scotland than any of his predecessors. For the bulk of his subjects – those not at the mercy of the raids of the Reivers or the rebels in the Isles – this was a time of lawfulness. And that meant the King himself had more personal freedom. James was able to cover vast distances extremely quickly on horseback with just a few companions. He could, and did, demonstrate kingship of the most active kind, travelling in person to trouble spots, but more importantly, he was able to show himself to his people.

⊰ ✦ ⊱

Henry VII needed to be effective in order to survive. Early in his reign he had tried more traditional methods to retain the acquiescence of his Yorkist nobility – both those who had joined him against Richard III and many of those who had actually opposed him. Like Edward IV, he had offered them the martial opportunity of a short-lived expedition against France. In Henry's case unwisely so, as the expedition teetered towards humiliation before being rescued with the face-saving and generally remunerative Treaty of Étaples,[16] buttressed by payments from the French King to Henry's own councillors to win their support for English neutrality.

As his rule took root, Henry increasingly reinforced it through intimidation. One means was military: he adopted the French practice of having a royal bodyguard and created the Yeomen of the Guard; he maintained the monopoly of artillery power within his kingdom; and he introduced a Statute of Livery and Maintenance to preclude the recreation of the 'bastard feudal' armies of the Wars of the Roses.

Henry also introduced a tighter control of his subjects through legal and institutional reforms: the creation of the Court of Star Chamber early in his reign strengthened royal control of the administration of the law. He used the law aggressively, making wealthy subjects pay bonds guaranteeing future good behaviour; in some cases these were so high as to prove ruinous. Then there was the notorious 'Morton's Fork': compulsory 'benevolences' or gifts of money to the King, named after Henry's Chancellor, John Morton. In fact, in this as with some other policies of increased royal control, Henry was following in the footsteps of Edward IV's later years;[17] and Morton, far from being the mastermind, had urged caution. According to Polydore Vergil, after Morton and his fellow long-standing councillor of Henry VII, Sir Reginald Bray, died, 'it was obvious to all that these two were above all responsible not for aggravating royal harshness against the people, but for restraining it'.[18]

Even before their deaths, in 1500 and 1503 respectively, Henry's administration had been based on his own quarters, his Privy Chamber,[19] while still taking counsel from his old advisers. Afterwards his government became more direct and personal, a form of legal and fiscal tyranny, keeping his subjects 'in danger at his pleasure'.[20] It was exerted through relatively low-born administrative servants such as Richard Empson and Edmund Dudley, who used the law to exact fines and pour money into the Privy Purse.

As an outsider, Henry had no scruples about changing the nature of government. During his exile in France he had observed at close quarters the more arbitrary style of the French monarchy and briefly sat on the royal council – and impressed the King's ministers.[21] Pedro de Ayala even remarked later that Henry 'would like to govern England in the French fashion'.[22] But Henry was no ideologue. All was in pursuit of one overriding ambition: survival, first of himself and then of his dynasty.

This was not an aim achieved quickly. Henry felt acutely vulnerable, as he showed by the measures he took against the fake pretenders Simnel and Warbeck – with his regime destabilized by his reaction to the latter, rather than by the man himself. There were also real pretenders, such as Edward IV's passive nephew Edward, the genuine Earl of Warwick; and, following the death of John, Earl of Lincoln, that of his younger brothers Edmund, Earl of Suffolk, and Richard de la Pole.

Perhaps because of his affection for his cousin the Queen,[23] Suffolk seemed initially to acquiesce in Henry's rule, but Henry's financial bonds on the family were so repressive that Suffolk chose first temporary and then, from 1501, permanent exile at Maximilian's court, together with his brother Richard. As Suffolk was shuttled between Maximilian, his son Philip of Burgundy and their allies, Henry spent vast sums – far larger than those he had previously extracted from Suffolk – in trying to recover him. In 1505, for instance, Henry 'lent' Philip a mind-boggling £138,000.[24] The following year Suffolk was returned and imprisoned in the Tower, but only because Philip, en route to Spain, was forced ashore on England's South Coast and it was made clear that Henry's months of generous hospitality would not end until Suffolk was handed over. But Henry did not rest with Suffolk's imprisonment. In June 1508, the year before his death, Henry concluded a three-hour meeting with the Imperial Ambassador by handing him a list of English rebels on the Continent. His previously measured tone became maniacal as he outlined his plans for bringing them to book, causing the Ambassador to lament in a letter home: 'God knows how much I was ashamed, and what things he said to me about it, and certainly I should like to be elsewhere, if ever I were to meddle much with such a thing.'[25]

Perhaps Henry was right to fear conspiracy from all quarters. Calais, England's gateway to the Continent and a possible springboard for invasion from it, was full of conspiring Yorkists in high places.[26] Henry created a network of spies to counter them. He also entrusted work in this crucial area to his most talented ministers.

Thus it was Sir Thomas Lovell – whose offices included Treasurer of the King's Chamber, Lieutenant of the Tower and many more besides – who was sent to unravel one conspiracy, which he achieved by threatening to have one suspect thrown off his ship and into the sea.[27]

There were also dangers closer to home. One of Henry's Calais spies happened to be at court in May 1501, when Henry had been gravely ill, and later reported that there had been talk 'among many great personages' of the possible succession and that some of them 'spoke of my lord Buckingham saying that he was a noble man and would be a regal ruler'. Others had put the case for Suffolk – but not a single one had spoken up for fourteen-year-old Prince Arthur.[28]

The dominant portrait of Henry VII down the ages, fostered by his seventeenth-century biographer Sir Francis Bacon,[29] has been that of a miser. Certainly, when health allowed in his later years, he was often to be found personally signing accounts in the 'counting house' of his Privy Chamber, separated from his nobility, England's traditional warrior class. Henry raised massive sums of money from a range of sources: better administration of the crown estates; tax revenues expanding with the increase in trade and manufacture; parliamentary grants; and from the crown's more dubious schemes of bonds and fines. But far from hoarding these revenues, Henry spent on a scale unprecedented in peacetime. It is estimated that as much as £342,000 went to the Hapsburgs in the last few years of his reign,[30] which perhaps makes Henry's irascibility towards their ambassador the more understandable.

Henry also spent lavishly on his court, on festivals and on tournaments. He encouraged jousting for the nobility and those with noble bearing in the saddle. In former times jousting had functioned as practice for war; under Henry it became a replacement for it. 'By nature he preferred peace to war', was Polydore Vergil's judgment of the King.[31] In so doing, Henry was changing the traditional relationship between king and nobility. Unlike an Edward III or Henry V, he did not seek to be the warrior leader of a warrior class; indeed, at his major battles of Bosworth, Stoke and Blackheath he was, at least initially, to the rear of his forces. Though, according to Vergil, this was in no way due to any lack of personal bravery: 'his spirit was so brave and resolute that never, even in moments of greatest danger, did it desert him'.[32]

Henry VII set out to do something that Richard II had tried and failed to do before being replaced by Henry IV: to separate himself physically from his nobility and to raise the crown to another level above them. According to Vergil, Henry 'well knew how to maintain his royal dignity, and everything belonging to his kingship, at all times and all places'.[33] Indeed so. Instead of spending vast sums of money on the hazard of war to secure himself and his dynasty, he lavished it on symbolic display. His purpose was not merely to impress foreign ambassadors – for all that 'his hospitality was splendidly generous: he liked having foreign visitors and freely conferred favours on them'[34] – but to project an enhanced monarchy. In order to achieve this he took every opportunity to exploit economic growth and technological innovation.

8

Renaissance Monarchy – Display

Renaissance monarchs were not only expected to act like kings, but to dress and disport themselves regally. Edward IV differentiated himself from his enfeebled and poorly dressed predecessor, Henry VI,[1] by spending huge sums of money on clothes, jewellery, furniture, tapestries and manuscripts.[2] Henry VII did the same. His clothes in his later years may often have been sombre (see colour plates), but they were of the richest and most expensive fabrics.

There was one critical difference between the sovereign and his subjects: so far as the king was concerned there existed no stipulation governing what might be spent in order to act in accordance with his rank. In fact, so long as he did not bankrupt either himself or the country, there was no limit. Thus if Henry wished to spend £2,000 (80,000 times the daily pay of an archer) on decorating his helmets and horse harness with gold, pearls and precious stones for the 1492 French campaign, then he did so. A king could, and indeed should, dazzle all around him. Literally so, when it came to jewels. It has been estimated that Henry spent £110,000 on jewellery between 1492 and 1507,[3] a sum only £10,000 less than the 1496 onerous loan against taxes that precipitated the Western Rising.[4] It was also more than the massive £90,000 grant that Henry requested – and failed to get in full – from the Parliament of 1504, using Margaret's marriage as one of the reasons he needed the additional funding.[5] Parliament might cavil at such a demand outside time of war, but it was Henry rather than they who followed the spirit of the times, as expressed in royal courts across Europe.

This was a new age: a time of vastly increased wealth, growing trade, new technology, of the explorations of the Portuguese and of the two Genoese – Columbus from Spain and Cabot from Bristol

– that had expanded the physical horizons of Europe. This was a time of magnificence, of Renaissance courts with Renaissance princes. Culturally, the progenitor was the fifteenth-century Duchy of Burgundy and the court of Philip the Good. It has been described as a 'theatre state',[6] where ritual and display could be more effective than military means for furthering ducal interests.[7] The Duchy was a centre of chivalry, with its illustrious Order of the Golden Fleece comparable to England's Order of the Garter, as well as one of expanding wealth thanks to its being the hub of the European cloth trade. The two came together in sumptuous and extravagant ceremonial, not only in form – Philip liked to dress up as King Arthur[8] – but also in substance. Burgundy set the standard for other northern European Courts, including those in Germany, especially after Emperor Maximilian married Charles the Bold's heiress. Burgundian court culture was fostered in England by Edward IV, who had time to study it in person during his interregnum months and who used Burgundy as the model for court ceremony.[9] It also strongly influenced France and Brittany, where Henry VII lived out his exile. Indeed, it strongly influenced Henry himself.

Many of his most costly jewels were incorporated in an impressive new crown, whose design is implied by its name: the Imperial Crown.[10] Money was lavished on court ceremony and there were vastly expensive tournaments and pageants. Indoors were pageant cars, a new concept, and from Burgundy, naturally. The outside events were extraordinary, none more so than that which in 1501 greeted Katherine of Aragon, when she emerged from St Paul's at the end of her three-hour wedding ceremony to Prince Arthur. She was accompanied by young Prince Henry, Arthur having gone ahead to the Bishop of London's Palace, there to be ready to welcome her to the next stage of the extended festivities.[11] What she saw was no less than a pageant mountain. This 'Rich Mount' had to be enormous in order to accommodate its many spectacular features. The English Privy Council had agreed to a wine fountain, traditional for such occasions, but then Sir Reginald Bray had taken control of the project. Bray had been one of Henry's organizers and fundraisers for the Bosworth campaign and he remained a close adviser, financial enforcer and general 'Mr Fixit' until his death in 1503.[12] He knew as well as the King himself that this supreme moment of triumph, the marriage of Henry's son and heir to the daughter of one of Europe's great powers and with it full recognition of the Tudor dynasty, needed something more than a wine fountain, albeit one that would 'run divers sorts of good wines'.[13] Rich Mount matched that triumph. It was, as its name implies, a rich and verdant green from its herbs and trees, with the greenery interspersed with rocks and coarse stones. This decorative effect must have been impressive, but it was completely secondary. For mixed among the coarse stones were jet, amber and coral. And at the side, the base rocks gave way to bright ones of metal ore. This was a staggering display of wealth, but it was mere stage dressing for the crucial elements of Rich Mount, the three separate tableaux on the very top of the mountain, each with its own prominent green tree. To the left, in honour of Katherine, the tree bore oranges and the lion of Leon and, before it, the King of Spain was depicted standing inside the castle of Castile. To the right, reflecting England's historic claim to France, was a tree of golden fleurs-de-lis and Lancastrian red roses; from one of the latter 'grew' a white greyhound of Richmond (in case anyone was slow to realize the 'rich mount' pun), with the King of France to the fore. Finally, centre stage, was the tree of England and its King, who with sword aloft and demonstrably King Arthur,[14] was rising out of England's ship of state. On this central tree were the red roses again and, complementing the greyhound, the other royal supporter – the ferocious red dragon of Cadwallader.

The decorative effect must have been extraordinary, but the wealth of symbolism was there to transmit a simple message: Henry VII and his son were a true continuation of the House of Lancaster and as such were immovable. The throne was rightfully theirs: God had ordained it. 'History' had predicted it. Besides which, they were now fully recognized by their fellow monarchs and no knavish challenger could possibly match their wealth, resources and the entrenched nature of their support.

The marriage of Arthur and Katherine was a matter of national rejoicing and Henry's subjects were invited to celebrate the fact. And they could do so, because at the bottom of Rich Mount, not forgotten, was the wine fountain.

Magnificent as Rich Mount was, it was a transient spectacle to be dismantled after the festivities. It paled into significance alongside the King's real and permanent Richmond, newly built beside the Thames, and described as 'this earthly and second Paradise of our region of England'.[15]

๚ ☩ ๛

Like Henry VII, James projected the majesty of his monarchy through building, with the most striking work at the five royal palaces that included: Edinburgh Castle and Falkland, as well as Holyrood, Linlithgow and Stirling.[16] The forework or gatehouse at Stirling was much more than just an entrance to a set of buildings. In the manner of its design, construction and decoration and in the way that it was themed, it was in itself a projection of the authority, legitimacy, the right to rule by God and history, and the very independence of the Scottish monarchy. The forework as it now stands is impressive enough, with its two circular towers on each side of the entrance gateway; however this is but a small remnant of the structure built in the 1500s. Then it had four towers – two on either side of the gate, which rose to twice their current height and were surmounted by steep conical turrets, stepped gables and gilded stone lions and unicorns. To see something similar today, one would have to go to France, to the medieval fortress towns of Carcassonne or Fougères. Further features added to the whole: the flanking of the large central gateway with pedestrian entrances had the effect of making it seem like a triumphal arch of Ancient Rome, except that above it, instead of an inscription, was displayed the brightly painted lion rampant royal arms of Scotland. And a final element transformed it in its entirety, deliberately making it a processional entrance worthy of Camelot itself: the coating of the stonework in 'king's gold', a golden-yellow limewash. The echo of Camelot was intentional, because Ancient British myths about this hilltop fortress had over the course of a century and a half crystallized into something much more. Stirling had been explicitly identified as Snowdon (or rather Snawdoun), the site of Arthur's court, with that status being confirmed to the French chronicler Jean

Froissart in 1365 by no less a person than the then king, David II, himself.[17] James I had created a Snawdoun Herald in around 1433, an office that still exists today.[18]

The gold of the forework heralded the gold of the Great Hall. On state occasions the King would sit beneath a canopy on a raised platform, carefully situated so that light pouring through the new-style tall windows of glass would illuminate him like an actor on a stage set. This was a setting for the theatre of monarchy and the exercise of power through heightened ceremony. There was a deliberate quasi-religious element, reminding onlookers that here was a being who had been rendered semi-divine through anointing at his coronation; as such it provided a secular complement to the more overtly religious element that was enacted in one of Stirling's two chapels or in the King's private oratory.[19]

The royal palaces gave physical expression to James's Renaissance kingship. The existing and newly created 'medieval' features they contained, the crenellations, parapets and conical towers, were no longer there for defensive purposes but as a decorative backdrop for displays of chivalry and the assertion of power.[20] These were integrated with appealing architectural and design elements from across Europe provided by talented and expensive master craftsmen armed with new materials and techniques. Thus James employed a full-time French plasterer and it was an Italian mason who contributed the elegant Italianate classical roof corbels of Edinburgh Castle.[21] The South Tower and Queen's gallery that James commissioned at Holyrood might be described as Anglo-Burgundian because they imitated Richmond Palace in honour of James's English bride;[22] but James's palaces also echoed the revival of the Scottish Romanesque of the fifteenth century – fostered in opposition to English Perpendicular Gothic – and were adorned with classical motifs.[23] The Scottish Renaissance under James IV was not a rejection of what had gone before but a heightening and adornment in step with the rest of Northern Europe. James II's Burgundian marriage and chivalric interests had integrated Scotland more firmly into European culture.[24] James IV took matters further in projecting an independent, outward-looking and majestic monarchy – with its proper place among Europe's rulers.

⊰ ✚ ⊱

Henry VII's magnificent palace at Richmond was a building in two
parts. The first, dominating everything else, was the stone keep with
its many turrets and onion domes and a vast expanse of glass in the
hugely tall bay windows. The keep housed the royal living quarters
and was equipped with a moat, not for defence against outsiders but
to maintain a symbolic distance from royal 'insiders': the courtiers.
The second part, comprising the outlying buildings, was constructed
of red brick, itself revolutionary. The place was a riot of ornamenta-
tion; everywhere there were symbolic red roses and Beaufort portcullises, lions and dragons. The grounds covered over thirteen acres[25]
with numerous courtyards, orchards, gardens and a vineyard. The
country's first long gallery looked out upon the King's own privy
garden and orchard. There was even 'most clean and pure water' on
tap.

As for recreation, the palace had been designed to accommodate
a complete range of indoor games, with special facilities for bowling
and tennis in addition to the usual archery butts. Intellectual pursuits
were honoured by the provision of the first royal library. It was here
that Henry VII charmed the young Katherine of Aragon at the time
of her wedding to Arthur by showing her a selection of rings and telling her to choose one.

Like Edward IV before him, Henry furnished his palace with
rich tapestries and furnishings. All was inspired by Burgundy – a
Burgundy now in the full flood of the Northern Renaissance and
welcoming a revolution in building techniques and decoration. Richmond even outdid Burgundy itself: so impressed was Duke Philip
during his enforced stay in England that he declared it would be the
model for his next palace.

Richmond was a demonstration that no English noble, not even
the Duke of Buckingham or the Earl of Northumberland, could get
anywhere near to competing with the crown at this level of expenditure. By 1501, at the time of Arthur's marriage to Katherine, Henry
believed he had finally made the crown secure for his dynasty.

It was a new kind of monarchy, one based on unassailable financial
strength and a diplomacy aimed at relentlessly pursuing all potential

usurpers and avoiding foreign wars. As Polydore Vergil noted from his direct knowledge of Henry: 'by nature he preferred peace'. After all, war was expensive and, above all, unpredictable.

Completed in haste, so as to be ready for Arthur's wedding to Katherine of Aragon, Richmond was a fitting new Camelot for Arthur Prince of Wales, Henry's son, heir and protégé.

Then in 1502 Arthur died.

9

Henry VIII – The Protected Prince

The historical record offers few glimpses of Arthur Tudor, Prince of Wales. There is just one contemporary portrait[1] of him at the age of thirteen or fourteen and a scattering of written observations, although we learn from the Milanese Ambassador Soncino that Arthur, just before his eleventh birthday, was 'taller than his years would warrant, of remarkable beauty and grace and very ready in speaking Latin.'[2] We know that he was intelligent, that his teachers included scholars such as Erasmus's friend Thomas Linacre and that he was familiar with the works of twenty-four classical authors, in Latin.[3] These small snatches cannot tell us what kind of king he would have made, how different he might have been to his younger brother Henry.

What we do know is that Henry's life as Prince of Wales was to be very different to his brother's. Eleven-year-old Henry did not receive the title until February 1503, ten months after Arthur's death and in the same month his mother died. Part of the reason for the delay was the need to discover whether Katherine of Aragon was pregnant with Arthur's child – a striking point, considering later questions about the consummation of the marriage.

Henry was not to have a separate household, not in terms of bricks and mortar anyway. One witness, a Spanish ambassador, Fuensalida, describes Henry in his teenage years as a virtual prisoner, living in quarters off his father's Privy Chamber 'in complete subjection to his father and grandmother,'[4] adding that he didn't 'say a word except in response to what the King asks him.'[5] But this picture is probably overdone, as Fuensalida needed to provide an excuse for his inability to get a clear answer from anyone at the English court about the future of the widowed Princess of Wales, Katherine of Aragon. It

would, however, have been contrary to everything we know of Henry
VII's character as revealed by his previous actions, if the young
Henry had not been put under some sort of constraint. Henry VII's
energetic policymaking had always been monomaniacally directed at
the succession. This was not purely a matter of ensuring the continuation of the dynasty; the King had a more personal stake in making
sure his son inherited, as only one's own kin could be relied upon to
ensure that the appropriate Chantry Masses were said to guarantee
the salvation of one's very soul. Thus in the last half-dozen years of
his life the old King, suffering repeated bouts of ill health, focused
on the survival of his remaining son. One thing was certain: much
as King Henry favoured jousting as an essential part of courtly pageantry and promoted it as a suitable pursuit for the scions of his
Yorkist nobility, he considered the tiltyard far too risky an environ-
ment for the Prince.

This was a major limitation on the younger Henry. Particularly
as he had met someone who ticked all the boxes of early sixteenth-
century celebrity, the ruler of the most chivalric court who excelled
at the most chivalric sport of jousting: Duke Philip the Fair of Burgundy. During Philip's enforced stay in England, fourteen-year-old
Henry had spent time in his company and been star struck. The
modern equivalent would be for the world number one in a teenager's
favourite sport coming to stay for the entire summer holidays and
giving coaching lessons into the bargain. The effect on Henry can be
seen in the letter he wrote to Erasmus the following year, describing his reaction on learning of Philip's death from illness aged just
twenty-eight: 'never, since the death of my dearest mother, has there
come to me more hateful intelligence.'[6] Bearing in mind Henry's love
for his mother this was 'hateful intelligence' indeed.[7]

Henry would have liked the chance to emulate his hero at jousting.
Instead he was forced to 'ride at the rings', an exercise which called for
skilful horsemanship and poise; but using a lance to skewer a ring
on a cord was a poor substitute for using it to thump an opponent's
shield. At the age of sixteen, Henry V had fought and nearly died
at the Battle of Shrewsbury; at the age of eighteen, Prince Henry's
grandfather Edward IV had secured his throne at the horrific Battle

of Towton.[8] At almost eighteen, Henry was still 'riding at the rings', and although he was very good at it, it wasn't enough.

The extraordinary thing was that, even after the greatest change of his young life, by order of the Privy Council, he continued to be restricted in this matter – in public, at least. That change, in April 1509, was the death of his father.

᪥ ✝ ᪥

When Pedro de Ayala had written to Ferdinand and Isabella that Henry VII 'would like to govern England in the French fashion',[9] he meant that Henry wanted to rule by diktat, without recourse to Parliament or the advice of his own Council. He had concluded with the words 'but he cannot'.[10] That however was in 1498. During the last few years of his reign, Henry had been very 'French' indeed. There had been no Parliament since 1504 and government from the Privy Chamber was matched by money into the Privy Purse. The King's policy of 'fiscal terror'[11] had sustained him, but in early 1509, during the final months of his life, he was overtaken by a terrible anxiety. He feared death, or rather what might come after death: namely the everlasting damnation of his soul. Thousands of pounds began to be spent on Masses;[12] and in the very last weeks – according to John Fisher, Bishop of Rochester, who heard his confession – the King promised 'a true reformation of all those that were officers and ministers of his laws'.[13] There is no reason whatsoever to doubt Henry's sincerity of belief, but he was also intent on securing the succession of his son by placing him in the control of the 'old hands' of Warham, Fox, Surrey and Bishop Ruthall of Durham and by throwing his newer agents of repression – Empson and Dudley – to the wolves. Thomas Penn in his recent *Winter King* suggests that a February meeting between Henry and Fox may have been the time when these plans were made.[14]

The sequence of events after Henry's death was acted out with exemplary precision.[15] Henry VII, King of England and founder of the Tudor dynasty, died at 11 p.m. on Saturday, 21 April 1509. But his rule did not end then: not officially at least. For a full two days his long-standing councillors, including Fox, Warham and Surrey, went in and out of the King's most private apartments, his Privy Chamber, acting as if the King, though gravely ill, was still very much alive. It was important that no one else knew the real situation, not even the new King – especially not the new King. This was not a case of excluding the seventeen-year-old Prince Henry, soon to be Henry VIII. It was for his own protection. Thus it mirrored the pattern of policies of Henry VII's entire reign: to protect himself and to ensure the succession of his dynasty.

Fox needed to speak to the young Prince alone. He did so at Evensong in the Chapel Royal, and thereafter Henry obediently played the part directed by Fox and Surrey. The old King's death was announced later that evening and the new King rode through the City to the Tower of London the next day, to be closely followed by the arrested Empson and Dudley. To popular approval, a general pardon was issued and widely propagated using the marvellous method of printing. The new King's grandmother, Lady Margaret Beaufort, was made official Regent, to serve for the two months until young Henry reached eighteen. Henry VII's long-standing senior ministers continued to serve his son.

Did Empson and Dudley present a real threat? Certainly they had been equipping their households with weaponry and hiring the men to use it, but it seems unlikely that they could have succeeded in making young Henry a captive of their policy. There were, however, nobles with royal blood who could have seized the opportunity to strangle the new reign at birth, had they known that the old King was dying. The caution of Henry's ministers was therefore understandable. There had been many threats to Henry VII's life before he came to the throne and they had continued throughout his reign.

Inevitably, there would be changes with the passage of time as and when Henry VIII learned to exert his will, or to get others to do it for him. In the meantime, existing policies such as the Perpetual Peace were formally renewed without question. Henry needed time to master the different elements of kingship, just as James IV, his brother-in-law across the border, had done before him.

When all these elements came together, Henry's sense of power and the effect of its exercise on Britain and on Europe would, with all the force of a suddenly uncoiled spring, be all the greater. The difference is amply demonstrated by a comparison of two regencies: the first, of Henry's grandmother; the second, of Katherine of Aragon, governing during Henry's absence in France in 1513.

The first regency came to an end on 24 June when, four days before his eighteenth birthday, Henry was anointed and crowned in a glorious coronation ceremony alongside Katherine, whom he had chosen as his Queen. She was spared the imperiousness of her new grandmother-in-law, because Lady Margaret was to die on the 29th. She had been in poor health and maybe it was, as some thought, eating a rich dish of cygnet at the coronation banquet that led to her demise.

In the weeks between the late King's death and his burial in Westminster Abbey on 11 May there had been two households.[16] The first was at Richmond, where as part of established etiquette, the late King, or at least his coffined body, was treated with the pomp and display worthy of his royal rank. There Lady Margaret had presided over the Council with Richard Fox, the Lord Privy Seal, and Thomas Howard, Earl of Surrey, the Lord Treasurer. The second household was that of the new King in the Tower of London; with him was a much smaller executive body including Thomas Ruthall, soon to be enthroned as Bishop of Durham, and William Warham the Lord Chancellor. This separation was important because although the new King's name was on the final letters patent that assigned the perquisites of power – lands, offices and titles – all such documents had to go through a three-stage process. These were the Sign Manual (through Ruthall), the Privy Seal (through Fox) and finally the Great Seal (via Warham).[17] This procedure had been instituted to cope with the adult incompetence of Henry VI in the mid-fifteenth century, to prevent him being suborned by one official or one person acting through that official and then agreeing, it was feared, to virtually anything.[18] The procedure was now reintroduced during Henry VIII's minority. Of course an active King could cut through the process – the various seals had been introduced to help expedite matters, not to delay them – but the teenage King did not yet have the inclination or the confidence to challenge his ministers' advice. It was a position that would continue after his majority. The unprecedented levels of administrative control exercised by Henry VII were to be denied to his son.

There had been no real physical threat to the new regime. Empson and Dudley were never in a position to mount one. Far more importantly, neither the proud Duke of Buckingham nor his ally the Earl of Northumberland presented a problem; the arrest and short-term Tower imprisonment of Buckingham's younger brother Henry Stafford had doubtless served as an effective warning. As Henry VIII knew from his childhood experience, the Tower could provide protection as well as imprisonment. And he was in safe hands: firstly the captaincy of the Tower had been given to John de Vere, Earl of Oxford, commander of the vanguard in Henry VII's major battles at Bosworth, Stoke and Blackheath; secondly the Captain of the Guard was Sir Henry Marney, a veritable strongman in his fifties who now took on for the new King the same responsibility he had held in the Prince's household. He was by no means the last to make that transition.

The vast majority of the citizens of London would have had no knowledge or understanding of what was going on behind the scenes. It was not their concern. What they welcomed, what made them rejoice, as they stood in their delirious thousands watching the processions leading to the coronation, was the new age heralded by the proclamations of young King Henry. They also welcomed his youthful, virile presence. He was almost exactly the same age as his maternal grandfather Edward IV had been when he came to the throne; and Henry VIII would have towered over the citizens just as Edward (who stood six foot three and a half inches tall) had done. His physique was seen as a major advantage and for years young Henry lived up to the image. Edward IV had been popular with the citizenry of London and they saw an echo in Henry. As Polydore Vergil put it: 'for just as Edward was the most warmly thought of by the English people among all kings, so this successor of his, Henry, was very like him in general appearance, in greatness of mind and generosity and for that reason was the more acclaimed and approved by all.'[19] Henry had the Earl of Suffolk, his father's Yorkist spectre, safely under lock and key in the Tower. He also had the Yorkist legitimacy denied his father: he was the heir of Edward IV's surviving heiress, Elizabeth of York, whereas Suffolk was merely the son of one of Edward's younger sisters. To anyone pining for the reign of a Yorkist king, Henry VIII could be presented as the real thing: the Yorkist centre of the Tudor rose.

10

Henry VIII – A Liberated King

Though Henry took up the reins of kingship in stages, there was one area in which events moved forward with startling speed, considering the previous delays. This was his marriage to Katherine of Aragon. After the death of Arthur and the subsequent realization that Katherine was not pregnant with Arthur's child, it seemed reasonable to the two key decision-makers – Kings Henry VII and Ferdinand – to substitute the new Prince of Wales for the old one. Not immediately, of course, for young Henry had a few years of growing to do. The fact that papal permission would be needed for Henry to marry his brother's wife did not pose a problem. Far more troublesome were various complications over the dowry.[1] At long range and via their ambassadors, the two kings squabbled. Katherine was a mere puppet in these exchanges, as was Prince Henry; no sooner had the couple been betrothed than he was instructed to abjure her publicly. Katherine was in limbo. She was also in dire financial straits, starved of money by both her father and sometime father-in-law. This was the position when the older Henry died. Within a few weeks she was not only wife but crowned Queen, the previous obstacles having been brushed away.

We do not know the level of Henry's involvement with the initiative. He said that he was obeying his father's dying wish, but that may have been intended to absolve the old king for his previous behaviour. It may also have been because Henry believed, as was later suggested, that it was God's will that he take Arthur's place.[2] Perhaps this was not just as King, but as husband too. What was soon clear was the new King's and Queen's mutual affection.

Katherine became pregnant in the first year of marriage, but the initial joy gave way to the despair of a miscarriage, followed by an infection that caused a phantom pregnancy similar to the one, so many years later, experienced by her daughter Mary. Hopes were raised only to be dashed again. Then Katherine quickly became pregnant once more and on 1 January 1511 she gave birth to a healthy boy.[3] Celebrations for the baby, named Henry, commenced. The country was overjoyed and so was the King, on whom the event had a liberating effect. At a tournament that took place 12–13 February at Westminster, King Henry not only participated in the jousting, he was its star performer, joyously enjoying feats of horsemanship and fighting. This was no covert disguised appearance, such as one he had made the previous year in order not to flout his council's wishes.[4] He now jousted openly because that was what he wanted to do.

Henry had shown his will and with impressive effect: according to a contemporary chronicler, he displayed 'the excellency of person, which never before that day, as I think, was seen'.[5] It seems his jousting companions did not need to hold back, as Henry could take as well as give 'hits'. As the chronicler relates: Henry 'broke in those six courses four spears as well and as valiantly as any man of arms might break them. And such as were broken upon him, he received them as though he had felt no dint of a stroke'.[6] During the day the young King made courtly displays of chivalry towards 'his lady', the Queen, who presided over the tournament from her grandstand; and at its conclusion he openly showed his affection, 'kissing and hugging her in most loving manner'.[7] Katherine was someone Henry both loved and trusted.

Just ten days later, joy turned to sadness when baby Prince Henry suddenly died. The King and Queen were devastated, Henry so much so that the French Ambassador, some weeks later, was advised by Fox and the Council 'not to present the [French] King's letter touching the death of the Prince or say a word about it at present, as it would only revive their King's grief'.[8] But for Henry life did not go back to how it had been before. Having shown his will in his personal conduct, he was within months to show it in government through a new chosen instrument. That instrument was Thomas Wolsey.

⁂ ✝ ⁂

Wolsey had been a scholar at Magdalen College Oxford, then a don, college bursar and briefly Master of Magdalen College School. In 1500 at about the age of thirty, he became Dean of Divinity. He resigned the post in 1502, having started on another career path, supported successively by the Marquess of Dorset, then Archbishop Henry Deane and finally Richard Nanfan, the Treasurer of Calais. Having proved his worth as a chaplain administrator, in 1507 he became a royal chaplain to Henry VII. Wolsey was used in diplomatic missions to Emperor Maximilian and, notably, James IV. He was rewarded by Henry VII in February 1509 with the deanship of Lincoln.[9] His position in the early months of Henry VIII's reign is unclear, but in November 1509 he was appointed Royal Almoner – responsible for the Crown's charitable works – and a Privy Councillor. Within eighteen months he had become its dominant force.

Two reports almost exactly twelve months apart show the nature of the change. The first, on 29 May 1510, was sent to King Ferdinand by the Spanish Ambassador in England, Luis Caroz De Villaragut. Later that day Caroz wrote a second letter, this time addressed to his minister, in which he admitted to naivety in dealing with the English,[10] but the account he gave Ferdinand of his dealings with Henry and with Fox and other Councillors makes clear the nature of his difficulty. Firstly, he recounts his meeting with Henry and the proposal for a new and closer Anglo-Spanish Treaty:

> He [the King] does not like to occupy himself much with business. All was, therefore, very soon concluded with the King, who told [me] to arrange the details with his councillors. The councillors are very different from the King. They are slow in concluding anything.

Having learned that the English had signed a treaty with the French, Caroz was anxious to discuss the matter. This was his conversation with Henry and its outcome:

> Caroz said to Henry: 'I beg, therefore, your Highness to tell me which of them [the English councillors] are the most trustworthy, because suspicions are rife in all quarters.' The King answered: 'Do not speak with anyone except with the Bishop of Winchester about French affairs.'

When Caroz asked: 'Do you confide in him?' The King replied, 'Yes, at my risk. Here in England they think he is a fox, and such is his name.'

Caroz further elucidates and describes his meeting with Fox:

> The Bishop of Winchester is Privy Seal. On speaking the first time to the King about the affairs of the King of France, and asking him what his intentions were in case the King of France should entirely destroy the Venetians, the King told me to confer on that subject with the Bishop [of Winchester]. The Bishop, on his part, declared that the affair was a difficult one, and that he would give his answer after the Feast of Easter. Easter has passed away, but the Bishop has not given his answer.

But Caroz did get an explanation for the French treaty from the councillors:

> They declared, however, that no other choice had been left them than to conclude the treaty of peace with France, because the King being young and not having a son, it would have been dangerous to engage in a war with France. Besides, they said, he [King Henry] had not yet concluded any alliances with his friends and relations. As soon as he had concluded such alliances and God had given him a son, he would be more at liberty to do what he wished. [11]

Caroz was pleased to hear this, but he was being fobbed off. Henry VII's old councillors were continuing the dead king's peace policy. However their words turned out to be strikingly accurate.

Henry's son, born seven months later, may have been short lived, but the King's 'liberty' was not. At the joust in February 1511, Henry was to free himself from restrictions on his activities as a man and just over three months later he was to remove those which had constrained him as a ruler. David Starkey pinpoints the moment exactly.[12] It was on 26 May 1511 that Wolsey presented a 'signed bill' to Chancellor Warham to grant a minor office. It was stated that this was sufficient to issue the Letters Patent and the use of the Great Seal and was thus a direct challenge to the now established 'three seals' route which had kept the Council in control of patronage and administration. Warham baulked. Wolsey exercised his will, or rather the

King's, and stated that these letters were being presented 'by royal command'.[13] This, Warham could not refuse, but just in case Wolsey did not really have Henry's backing, he made sure that there was a note on the enrolment grant. It was written in Latin and stated, in translation: 'as the said Master Wolsey claimed'.[14]

Henry had gained control through Wolsey.

A number of explanations have been offered for Wolsey's rise.[15] He may have had the support of Fox and Sir Thomas Lovell, or, as a member of Henry's household he may have gained notice on his own account. Once he had come to Henry's attention, he showed his talents. Given the opportunity, they would have served him well in any age, for he had an appetite for hard work matched by a mastery of detail and an extraordinary efficiency. These were qualities noted by all observers – including extremely hostile ones such as Polydore Vergil – and Henry VIII realized their value. The new King, unlike his father, had no patience with the minutiae of routine administration, though he would apply himself diligently to matters of particular interest and concern. But there was much more to the relationship than that. Henry and Wolsey did not just form an administrative partnership, they had an intellectual one as well, for Wolsey was different in one important respect to the other clerical councillors. Fox, Warham and Ruthall were all graduates in law; it was the standard route for administrative preferment.[16] Wolsey, however, was not trained in law but in theology and had become an academic expert and teacher. In Henry he found a ready student, for though the young King may have liked to spend day after day in hunting or sporting pastimes, he had a good brain, the benefit of a rounded humanist education and an intellectual capacity commended by Erasmus himself.[17] Most importantly, theology was to remain a particular interest of Henry's throughout his adult life.

The fact that both men, when they so wished, could be charming, eased the relationship, as they spent increasing amounts of time in each other's company. It enabled Wolsey to know what the King wanted, and further, through growing intuition, to anticipate it. This was the major difference between Wolsey and the old guard of Henry VII's council: unlike them he did not lecture Henry on what his duties might be. In the words of George Cavendish, who was to be Wolsey's first biographer as well as having been his gentleman usher in the 1520s: 'He was most earnest and readiest among all the council to advance the King's only will and pleasure, without any respect to the case.'[18] In short, like an amiable, hardworking and interesting genie, Wolsey was there to do Henry's bidding.

Now that the repressive influence of Henry's father had been removed, Wolsey would help the young King to be what he wanted to be. In the words of Cavendish again: 'All [Wolsey's] endeavour was only to satisfy the King's mind ... Thus [he] ruled all them that before ruled him.' And with the eclipse of the influence of Henry VII's prominent councillors, so went the late King's entire peace policy. Having mastered what had become a substitute for war, the world of the tiltyard, young and vital Henry VIII now sought the real thing. He wanted to do what his namesake Henry V had done: he wanted to invade France. Wolsey was there to make it happen and Henry completed his transformation from being a compliant king to becoming an extremely demanding one.

The consequences would affect all Europe. And what, closer to home, of the new 'perpetual peace' between England and Scotland? Would a personal meeting influence the matter? For though Henry may not have met James, Wolsey had done so, and it had not gone well.

There is nobody more charmless than a normally charming man who is deliberately rude. That was James's approach to Wolsey in March and April 1508, as Wolsey reported back to Henry VII from his embassy to the Scottish King.[19]

James was certainly not showing the courteousness and bonhomie he had accorded Surrey and the English delegation in 1503. In other circumstances, perhaps, he might have enjoyed Wolsey's company, but not in 1508.

Wolsey was made to wait at Berwick for the best part of a week before receiving James's permission to proceed. He arrived in Edinburgh on 28 March, but, in spite of the good offices of Queen Margaret, he was not able to see James himself until 2 April. The excuse given was that the King was too busy shooting guns and making gunpowder. Then 'in [Wolsey's] attempts to deliver his credentials he saw James once every day till 10 April; during which time he encountered such inconstancy that he could not conceive what report he could or should send'.[20]

There were complaints aplenty from James, arguments about the granting or non-granting of the safe conducts necessary for the subjects of one country to travel through the other. There were problems in the Border region, north and south; though Wolsey's view was that 'with regard to raids, murders, and robberies, the English have suffered four hurts to the Scots one' and 'said so plainly, and perceived that Lord Hume was somewhat abashed'. However Wolsey gave no weight to the worst infraction: the murder of Sir Robert Ker, Warden of the Scottish Middle March. James was utterly appalled by this act and by the fact that the malefactor – the illegitimate son of a prominent Northumberland family, known as the Bastard Heron – had been allowed to remain free in England. This was truly scandalous: James quite rightly regarded 'injuries done to his subjects, who are always ready to live and die in his service ... as injuries done to his own person'. The crime was of a completely different order to mere 'raids', which both James and Henry agreed were a matter for the wardens on both sides being too small a consideration for the concern of Princes.

It is clear however that in spite of James's discontent, he was at this point merely threatening a renewal of the 'Auld Alliance' with France, although Wolsey reported that 'all his subjects except [Andrew Forman] the Bishop of Moray call on him daily to do so'. It was Forman himself who rammed the last point home by telling Wolsey that 'no one was ever less welcome in Scotland', as people knew Wolsey was arguing against the alliance. Wolsey could not have had a pleasant time of it; as he himself bitterly reported to Henry VII, 'they keep their matters so secret here that the wives in the market knoweth every cause of my coming'.[21]

James was asserting his independent status, based on compliance with the terms of the Treaty of Perpetual Peace. A Scottish alliance with France for mutual defence did not breach those terms and, as

Wolsey reported from Scotland, 'various members of council had said in conversation that the two alliances could stand together'. All the same, that is not what James himself said, as the threat of an alliance with France, rather than its realization, would be far more effective in giving him the diplomatic space and additional time he needed to strengthen his negotiating hand. James recognized that in a new Europe of kingdoms and empires of ever-increasing size and power, chivalric and cultural propaganda would ultimately not be enough. Though he had a keen interest in military weaponry, James's pre-occupation with guns and gunpowder was not just a hobby. Scotland needed to be able to display intimidating force. James and his commanders had used naval power to impressive effect against the rebels of the Isles, but he also saw a wider international potential. James was not intent on small measures, he was building the biggest ship in Europe, in effect a gigantic gun platform, designed – should it prove necessary – to fight a new kind of naval war.

The question was whether England would see this as a deterrent or as a declaration of intent. Chaplain Wolsey, when reporting to the elderly Henry VII, seemed, even after his own dusty treatment, to be giving King James the benefit of the doubt. But the Wolsey of the summer of 1511 was to be a very different creature.

11

James IV and the 'Realization' of Scottish History

A pragmatic approach for an English king intent on a serious invasion of France would be to neutralize any potential threat from Scotland before crossing the Channel. Edward III did so with the slaughter at Halidon Hill in 1333. Henry V at least partially did so by taking the captive James I with him to France between 1420 and 1422, thereby making the Scots engaged in fighting his forces traitors against James as well as himself.

Henry VIII was in a position to secure his northern border through fair words and paying lip service to the Treaty of Perpetual Peace: by in fact demonstrating the devious 'realpolitik' of King Ferdinand and Emperor Maximilian, who shared an exceptional political deviousness as well as a grandchild in the future Charles V.

'Fair words', however, would not sum up Henry VIII's approach to Scotland at all.

From the summer of 1511, the English policy was one of belligerence, threat and accusation. It might be argued that this merely rivalled James's own approach to England. But there was a fundamental difference: James was determined to display to his people and to his fellow monarchs that peace with England did not mean subordination to it. Whereas the new English policy seemed directed at achieving that very thing.

⁂

In the time he spent with James, Pedro de Ayala saw a statesman who would always seek advice but then decide the best course of action himself:

He lends a willing ear to his counsellors[1] and decides nothing without asking them; but in great matters he acts according to his own judgment, and, in my opinion, he generally makes a right decision. I recognize him perfectly in the conclusion of the last peace, which was made against the wishes of the majority in his kingdom.[2]

This was written in July 1498, in the year following the Peace of Ayton and during the five years of 'stress testing' before the Treaty of Perpetual Peace.

Reliance on English constancy was a dangerous course, as James III had found. His successor needed to be certain that England would maintain the peace, because he sought nothing less than a permanent change of Scottish policy. But it is a sign of James IV's personal authority, after just three years of active kingship, that he had ignored the traditional Scottish hostility towards England to further a far more pressing ambition: a final settlement with the southern neighbour at a time of Scotland's strength. In so doing he had substantiated the centuries-old assertion that Scotland was an independent entity because its ruler, the King of Scots, was ultimately answerable only to God himself.

England, the enemy for hundreds of years, was the one country that might subsume Scotland. Though there had been long periods of peace through previous treaties negotiated by strong Scottish kings, none had been permanent. But with Henry VII, in James's mind, things were different. He had helped Henry to secure his throne by making peace with him and withdrawing his support for potential usurpers; he had given recognition to the newly arrived Tudor dynasty by marrying Henry's eldest daughter. This validation was made all the stronger for Henry by virtue of coming from an independent entity. Here was the nub of the matter. For James, the key word in the phrase 'Treaty of Perpetual Peace' was 'perpetual'. By giving Henry one type of recognition, James had grasped another: an understanding that the King of Scotland was in no way a vassal of the King of England but someone separate and autonomous.

The definition of this relationship had been at the very centre of Anglo-Scottish disputes; now, for James, the problem was solved. In a new age of stronger national identities, of the creation of Spain and extension of France, the King of Scotland had gained his own place. Whatever happened subsequently, he saw that change as 'perpetual'. If the 'majority in his kingdom' continued to harbour suspicions about England, that did not matter to him; he was confident in his ability to take his people with him. In James's own mind the main point had been won. His was the reign when all of Scotland had been brought under the sway of its king; and as that king he had also won acknowledgment of his kingdom's independent place in the world.

The importance of this cannot be over-emphasized. Scotland's right to complete self-determination had its affirmation in its own official history, the *Scotichronicon*, which had been completed by Walter Bower in the reign of James II. By the time of James II's grandson it was seen as definitive, with copies made for every church and monastery. It was the orthodox view, neither to be queried nor questioned,[3] but it was also the popular view. Professor Roger Mason is in no doubt that when James IV licensed Chepman and Myllar in 1507 to print chronicles 'it was presumably a version of Bower that he had in mind'.[4] The universal dissemination of the *Scotichronicon* was intended to make permanent, in print, Scotland's glorious independent past as the King and his people willed it and understood it to be. As Walter Bower had himself justifiably said with pride: 'Christ, he is not a Scot who is not pleased with this book.'[5]

James had made an impressive continuing display of independence through maintaining strong diplomatic ties with France. This had been highly effective with Henry VII. But Henry VIII and Wolsey had wilfully chosen to interpret it otherwise: as heralding a renewed Scottish alliance with France against England. Their brutal repudiation of James's self-determination was something he could not ignore. It undermined his position as Scotland's King and threatened both his country's future and its 'past'.

❧ ✝ ❧

The monarchy was a focus for Scottish nationhood long before Scotland had anything even resembling the geographical or cultural identity that defines it today. As Dr A. A. M. Duncan puts it in *The Kingship of the Scots 842–1292*, 'Scotland was put together first as a kingdom and then as a community.'[6] Indeed, kingship was regarded as so important in Scotland's 'history' that the country's two most notable medieval chroniclers had conjured up a whole host of imaginary kings to take that 'history' from the reign of Kenneth I (Macalpine), its first credited king in the ninth century, right back to its earliest, most mythical, times.

The need for such an act of creativity derived from the fact that Scotland's real history was unclear. The Scottish past is now far better known and understood than it was in the medieval period. Then, there were vast gaps, but these presented an opportunity for establishing a desired national story that could offer an 'authenticity' which, in the words of Professor Mason, 'endowed the ethnically diverse and polyglot subjects of the Scottish crown with a common ancestry and a sense of belonging to a single ethnic community'.[7] Most importantly, it also gave the Scots a pedigree and antiquity far more impressive than the English could boast.

The differences between the 'real' and the 'imagined' past are both striking and illuminating. The 'imagined' past was essential for the purposes of fifteenth- and sixteenth-century Stewart kings because it served their contemporary political needs. It was all the more powerful as it was a past they personally believed in. And this belief was shared by their subjects, who unquestioningly understood Scottish history to have been as they wanted it to have been.

⁂

The ancient history of Scotland is a remarkable one. But it has only been properly reconstructed through the brilliant work of historians over the past century and a half. It is now generally accepted that the tribe that gave Scotland its name, the Scotti, first arrived from Ireland around AD 500. Their precursors in Scotland were the 'Picts', so called by the Romans because they painted their bodies. The Picts were a fierce and fearsome people. They may have been defeated in battle by Agricola, one of Rome's greatest generals, in AD 84 at Mons Graupius in north-east Scotland,[8] but that was the fullest extent of the mighty empire's success against them. Agricola himself was recalled to Rome before he could capitalize on his victory and the Romans were only able to establish their furthest *Limes* or frontier line in the next century, and that lay many miles to the south at the Antonine Wall. Crossing the landscape at its narrowest point – the thirty-nine or so miles from modern Bo'ness on the Forth to Old Kilpatrick on the Clyde – the Wall was built and consolidated in the dozen or so years following AD 142.[9] The intention was to pen the Picts on its far side, within the area the Romans named Caledonia, but it was deserted in a generation. From pottery artefacts discovered at the Wall, now a World Heritage Site,[10] there is no evidence of Roman occupation after the AD 160s.[11] Nor has anything ever been found of the Roman Ninth Legion, sent to relieve the garrison from Pictish attack but which apparently vanished without trace. The Romans retreated to Hadrian's Wall. The Picts had seen off the most powerful empire in the world. Further imperial sorties followed, such as those under Septimius Severus in the early third century, but there was no conquest[12] either then or in the following fifteen or so decades before the Roman empire collapsed, with its armies leaving Britain at the beginning of the fifth century.

When the Scotti arrived around a hundred years later, they settled on the Argyllshire coast in a place they called Dalriada. This was the same name as their homeland in Ulster and at first the settlers were merely a colony of their mother country. The Scotti were one of five main groups who lived in Scotland in the centuries between the departure of the Romans and the arrival of the Normans. As well as the Scotti and the long-standing Caledonian Picts, two of the other peoples were the Welsh Britons of Strathclyde and the Angles who occupied the Lothians – having spread northwards as the kingdom of Northumbria expanded between the sixth and ninth centuries – and bringing the English language with them.[13]

The Scotti were a small group but their very Irishness made them culturally important, as their western islands and then the mainland itself were the entry point for Celtic Christianity from across the Irish Sea. It was from the Dalriadan island of Iona that St Columba set out later in the sixth century on his missionary journey to convert the Picts to Christianity, which apparently included his giving a ferocious monster at Loch Ness a lesson in obedience. Then it seems that the Scotti and the more numerous Picts lived in relative harmony until the mid-eighth century, when a series of wars broke out between them.

The Scotti faced another threat to their kingdom of Dalriada, one so disruptive that it finally divided the lands to the east of the Irish Sea from the mother country on the west. This came from the fifth and less settled group of inhabitants of what is now Scotland: the Vikings. Their pillaging attacks on Iona began in AD 794 and continued until 849, when the island's monastery was abandoned. Incursions inland affected Picts as well as Scots, and it is possible that a massive Viking defeat of the Picts in 839 made them vulnerable to Kenneth Macalpine, king of the much less significant area of Dalriada. It was in 842 that in the words of the ancient *Scottish Chronicle*, King Kenneth 'came to Pictavia'.[14] In just over half a century he and his successors had established total control. Pictavia disappeared from the historical record, along with Dalriada. By AD 900, following the death of Donald II and the accession of his cousin Constantine II, a new name is used for the enlarged kingdom: Alba, the Gaelic word, then as now, for Scotland.

Constantine's long reign of forty-four years was important in other ways. Within four years he had decisively defeated the Scandinavians; and there were no more incursions for half a century.[15] In AD 906 a ceremony, if not an actual coronation, took place at Scone, with Constantine sitting on the Stone of Destiny.[16]

As King Constantine and his successors imposed their authority over territories such as Strathclyde and Lothian, they established a greater kingdom but one that was nonetheless incomplete, lacking as it did suzerainty over the Highlands and Islands. Yet consolidation to the south gave them a common border with the English and set the crucial centuries-long double conundrum which James IV believed he had solved, but which still has an echo to this day: namely, that in the seemingly relentless aggregation of territories under single authorities within the island of Britain, how could a King of Scots ensure he brought all of the northern half of the island under his control while at the same time preventing himself from being subsumed by his mighty southern neighbour? How could he be a strong independent ruler of Scotland and not just a client of England and a subordinate British lord?

It was a problem that Constantine himself faced.

⊰ ✞ ⊱

It came in the form of Athelstan, grandson of Alfred the Great of Wessex and the first clearly documented monarch who could claim to be King of Britain.

The significance for the Scots and for Constantine their King was that they now shared a border with a capable ruler fully able to harness England's resources. Moreover, having successfully acquired kingdoms within England, Athelstan was eager to gain the subservience of the remaining kings within Britain.[17] On 12 July 927, at Eamont near Penrith in modern Cumbria, his pre-eminence was recognized by the kings of the West Welsh and Strathclyde and by Constantine II, King of the Scots. The significance of the occasion being marked by Athelstan becoming godfather to Constantine's son.[18] The contemporary poem, *Carta dirige gressus*, summed up the agreement from Athelstan's perspective as '*ista perfecta Saxonia*' or 'England made whole'.[19] Athelstan was intent on maintaining it by force; so when Constantine rebelled in 934 Athelstan successfully invaded Scotland by land and sea.[20] Worse was to follow for Constantine, when he joined ranks with the Kings of Dublin and Strathclyde; their joint army was crushed in 937 by Athelstan at the Battle of Brunanburh. Constantine's son was among the many thousands killed.

The Norman chroniclers that followed rejected any notion of Scottish independence and thus Athelstan's settlement was portrayed as permanent. This was to be Athelstan's lasting significance for Anglo-Scottish relations; he gave the successive Norman kings – William the Conqueror, William Rufus and Henry I – the precedent for their campaigns against Scotland. These, if not designed to turn the Scots into a subject people, were certainly intended to maintain their king as a subject lord.

The King of Scotland at the time of the Norman Conquest of 1066 was Malcolm III. A commanding figure, he sought to take advantage of England's upheaval following the Conqueror's victory at

Hastings and to extend the boundaries of his kingdom southwards. William's reaction to any challenge was unstinting. His 'harrying of the North' in 1069 and 1070 brought devastation to the area between the Humber and the Tees and the deaths of an estimated 100,000 – one in twenty of the entire English population.[21] He then turned his attention to the ally of his northern rebels, King Malcolm.

Malcolm had reinforced his support for Edgar Atheling, the Saxon heir to King Harold's English throne, by marrying Edgar's sister Margaret. In William's eyes, this gave Malcolm far too close a formal connection with his English enemies. The Conqueror invaded Scotland in 1072 and after a short campaign brought Malcolm to terms at Abernethy near Perth. The agreement has been variously referred to as a pact, treaty or a submission by historians, though Malcolm did pay homage to William and thereby became, in the words of the Anglo-Saxon Chronicle, 'his man'.[22] But what exactly did that obeisance mean? Cecily Clark, acclaimed commentator and translator of the Chronicle, noted that 'the significance of this homage has been much disputed'.[23] This is a magnificent understatement. Different interpretations of the homage were not merely important in relation to Malcolm and William but fundamental to disputes between their successors for half a millennium.

Abernethy introduced a further complication: as part of the agreement, Malcolm and his heirs were granted lands in England. So when subsequent kings of Scotland paid homage to English kings, did they do so for their lands in England, or for the kingdom of Scotland itself? If just for the former, the Scottish king would expect to be treated by his English counterpart as of the same rank in all their other dealings. When the time came that he no longer had estates in England, it would therefore follow that he should be regarded by the English king and his subjects as a totally independent monarch. If, on the other hand, the Scottish monarch was the ruler of a client kingdom, then the King of England could demand the personal attendance of his Scottish 'subject'. He might even assume the right to interfere in the internal affairs of Scotland. Equally, the English nobility would not look upon such a king as a superior of an entirely different rank, but rather as an equal.

Two further factors came into play in the relationship between English and Scottish kings. Firstly, the readiness and ability of English monarchs to enforce compliance; secondly, the extent, if any, to which the rulers of Scotland felt compelled to comply.

The situation was always potentially volatile. The nature of the relationship was open to fluctuating interpretation, as was the demarcation of the border and the level of respect paid to the lives and property of the subjects of the other king.

When the very first 'his man', Malcolm III, raided England in 1079, a mere seven years after Abernethy, William had more pressing concerns. Believing the incursion was not sufficiently serious to require him to intervene in person, he sent his little-valued eldest son Robert Curthose on a short campaign the following year.[24] However, just over a decade later in 1092, matters escalated after the Conqueror's son and successor, William Rufus, occupied the disputed town of Carlisle. That action in itself was enough to give Malcolm a grievance, but the following year he received an insult that far overshadowed a matter of territory; this time honour was at stake. Having agreed to travel as far as Gloucester to meet King William, Malcolm took the deepest umbrage when Rufus refused him an audience. He returned north, gathered troops in Scotland and invaded, only to be ambushed and killed, along with one of his sons, outside Alnwick in 1093.

This would be the first of many Scottish actions from the eleventh to the sixteenth century that would be centred on territory or recognition, or a combination of both. Scottish kings had to be prepared to fight over land – actual or potential – and for their dignity, in order to reinforce their position within Scotland itself. The role of the king within his country and the nature of his kingship required it.

Malcolm's actions, both submissive and aggressive, were repeated down the centuries. So were those of William the Conqueror. With a few notable exceptions, English kings did not look to conquer and govern Scotland directly. They tended to be more reactive and to defend what they believed to be defensible; for instance, the late eleventh century saw the construction of castles at Carlisle and on the Tyne, paralleling Hadrian's Wall, but these defended a line across the narrowest part of the country rather than the border itself.

To the English, the relationship with Scotland was important, but it was not a concern of the first rank. The priority that William's Norman and Plantagenet descendants gave to the interpretation of Abernethy and successive treaties crucially depended on the authority they could command within England itself and the level of their preoccupation with events to the south – in France. What they sought on their northern border was a degree of security. Some English kings achieved this by raising large armies to deter or even defeat the Scots. Other English rulers, not always the weaker ones, won Scottish complaisance through negotiation and apparent agreement to increased Scottish self-determination, if only as a short-term expedient for more immediate advantage in England itself or across the Channel.

A series of precedents was created in the relationship of the kings, a position given a degree of complexity during the twelfth and thirteenth centuries as Norman aristocratic families gathered lands on both sides of the border.

Then, on 19 March 1286, a freak accident altered the entire position. As King Alexander III hastened home through stormy conditions to join his young new wife, his horse stumbled near Kinghorn in Fife and he was thrown to his death. Alexander's first wife and all three of his legitimate children had predeceased him, leaving just his infant granddaughter Margaret to inherit.[25]

Though the role of a native Scottish king was well recognized within his own country and the Scots had prior experience of a minority, they had no precedent for a three-year-old potential Queen designate whose soubriquet, 'the Maid of Norway', reflects that her father was King Erik II.[26] Later that year, Alexander's counsellors set about marrying their late King's granddaughter to the son and heir of Edward I of England.

The warlike Edward had restored royal authority within England through force of arms on behalf of his lack-lustre father, Henry III. He had conquered Wales. But in 1290, with the betrothal of his six-year-old son to the Maid of Norway, it seemed that the English king had, on this occasion, triumphed through diplomacy. He had persuaded King Erik of Norway to give up his daughter, and let her sail south, in exchange for his financial support. He had also gained a grudging sort of Scottish acquiescence.

Scotland seemed destined to become an inalienable part of a greater kingdom of Britain that would be dominated by England. It only required the marriage to take place for the course of the kingdoms to be set; the couple would not even have to produce children for this to be so. For should Margaret die young and without heirs and Edward remarry, the children of that later marriage would inherit Scotland as well as England.

Many of the Scottish nobility did not trust Edward and they were right not to do so. Edward may have 'offered to protect the independence of Scotland and the liberties of its prelates and magnates',[27] but he also 'demanded control of their castles'.[28] And it was on the basis of the assurance underwritten by treaty, rather than the aggressive demand, that young Margaret set sail the following month. But, taken ill at sea, she only reached Orkney. There, in the comforting arms of a bishop, she died at the end of September.[29] With that death, the expected futures of both countries changed.

Though Edward may have been denied the opportunity to deliver Scotland to his son, he was not going to allow the child Margaret's demise to deny his successors control. His ambitions were aided by Scotland's six guardians, who fatefully invited him to Norham to adjudicate between the thirteen claimants to the empty throne. He was happy to do so, in exchange for the recognition of his overlordship by John Balliol, the successful candidate, who was proclaimed at Berwick Castle at the end of a much-adjourned process in late 1292.

Having made Balliol King John, Edward unmade him in 1296 for refusing to support English action against France and embarked on a swift campaign of retribution, treating any opposition as treason. He removed the Stone of Scone to London along with vast numbers of Scottish documents and he destroyed the Great Seal of Scotland, noting its passing with the words: 'a man does good business when he rids himself of a turd'.[30]

However, the English interpretation of Scotland's position was not clarified until 1305, when it described Scotland not as a kingdom but as a dependant 'lordship' like Wales and Ireland.[31] The intervening years had seen the rise and then defeat of William Wallace, but also an English policy that veered between crushing military campaigns and short-term conciliation due to Edward's need to focus on other priorities – principally English interests in France and the desirability of lessening the burden on the English taxpayer.

In 1307 Edward I died and a strong English king was replaced by a weak one: the Maid of Norway's intended husband, Edward II. He in turn faced a would-be strongman in Robert I (the Bruce), who in 1306 had claimed the kingship and been crowned at Scone (without the stone). Bruce's triumph in securing his throne in conditions of war against England and civil war against the supporters of the Balliol claim is one of the most celebrated periods of Scottish history, principally because of the Battle of Bannockburn – a Scottish victory which, albeit set up by English military incompetence, demonstrated King Robert's brilliant leadership, personal example and ability to exploit boggy ground.

Bruce provided posterity with a glittering model of successfully deployed active kingship. He followed Bannockburn with the statute of Cambuskenneth of November 1314, which instructed all holders of Scottish lands to do homage to him or lose them. Of course, any who did so were seen as traitors by Edward II and lost any lands in the Plantagenet dominions. It marked the beginning of the end of a cross-border aristocracy. One that had included the Bruces. No longer could landowners hold land in both countries and have dual or divided loyalties; they had to choose whether they were English or Scottish.[32]

Bruce's achievements were crowned in the last eighteen months of his life by the seemingly final English recognition of Scottish independence through the Treaty of Edinburgh of 17 March 1328, ratified by the English Parliament as the Treaty of Northampton on 4 May. From the English side, this agreement was made in the name of the fifteen-year-old King Edward III; but it was the initiative of his regent mother Queen Isabella and her lover Roger Mortimer. They had forced Edward II from the throne in January 1327 and were keen to come to a settlement with Scotland to secure their position. King Robert showed his strong negotiating hand early with a symbolic surprise attack on Norham Castle on 1 February, the day of young Edward's coronation; it was further strengthened through the shambles of an attempted retaliatory raid by the English that summer.[33]

As part of the 1328 Treaty, an Anglo-Scottish royal marriage was agreed between Robert's heir David and Edward's sister Joan. Crucially, not only would English overlordship cease to be claimed but all official English documents suggesting the fact would be sent north for destruction.[34] In addition, the Scots' own documents would be returned to them.

Papal recognition of Scottish independence, following its articulation in the Declaration of Arbroath of 1320, was supplemented, after Robert's death, by agreement that his son, aged seven in 1331, could receive the full rite of coronation.[35] He was duly crowned and, most importantly, anointed with holy oil. The coronation of Kings of Scotland was now akin to that of Kings of England and France. It gave the new King an authority granted by God himself.

However, the Stone of Scone was not used in the coronation: it had remained in Westminster. Nor had the Scottish documents been returned, because Edward III replaced his mother and Mortimer by coup in 1330 and rejected the treaty negotiated in his name. That rejection was underlined by one of the worst Scottish defeats at English hands: Halidon Hill outside Berwick, on 19 July 1333. The Scots were decimated by the power of the Anglo-Welsh longbow. For Edward it was a pacification exercise which cleared the path for his far more important war against France. It marked a return to the long-standing English policy of subduing the Scots in the north in order to facilitate the war against the cross-Channel enemy.

On reaching adulthood, David conducted a series of raids with diminishing success. In 1346, he agreed with Philip VI of France that he would assist him in derailing Edward's invasion of France through an incursion into northern England, only to be wounded and captured at the Battle of Neville's Cross outside Durham on 17 October 1346. David II spent the best part of the next eleven years as a prisoner in England, until, after the payment of a vast ransom, he was returned to his kingdom.

⊰ ✞ ⊱

There were eruptions of warfare between Neville's Cross and Richard of Gloucester's invasion in 1482, but in comparison to the five decades before 1346 the near century and a half that followed was a period of comparative peace. Granted, there were successful large-scale Scottish attacks in the 1370s and 1380s, and English invasions in 1385 and 1400. But, particularly after Hotspur's defeat of Douglas at Homildon Hill in 1402 and Henry IV's defeat of them both at Shrewsbury the following year, this was generally a more peaceful period between the two nations, even if this did not always extend to their Border subjects.

For the Scots, however, these were not times of guaranteed monarchical independence. Certainly not in the case of James I, an 'honoured guest' – that is to say, a captive – of his English counterpart from 1406–24. When James, from the English side, saw his Scottish subjects captured by Henry V in France, he could not spare them a traitor's death because, as Henry saw it, they were fighting against their overlord: not James, but himself.

However, during this long period, taking in the Hundred Years War against France and the thirty-five years of Wars of the Roses upheaval that followed, English attention was not on Scotland but turned first to France and then in on itself. It was a time when, with the border generally fixed, Scotland could focus on its own affairs – on its present and also its past.

⊰ ✞ ⊱

Edward I had sought to annex Scotland's history, just as he had the Stone of Scone, and with similar unintended consequences. Through removing the latter to Westminster he believed he had prevented Scotland from crowning kings; instead, the Scots merely abandoned their former tradition of seating kings on the stone at coronation. From David II onwards, with the blessing of the papacy, they were crowned and anointed.

In removing Scottish documents by the cartload, Edward had sought to erase Scotland's independent identity. Instead he

created even larger gaps in their history and gave two highly crea-
tive writers the opportunity to fill these with a tale of independent
destiny that was, moreover, older and more distinguished than that
of their southern neighbours. These 'historians' were John Fordun, a
fourteenth-century priest, and his early-to-mid-fifteenth continuator,
Walter Bower of Haddington, the Abbot of Inchcolm.

Their version of the national story was a complete rebuttal of
England's view of its dominant role within Britain, as concocted by
another great fabricator, the twelfth-century Geoffrey of Monmouth,
who 'traced' the founding of Britain to Brutus – the great-grandson
of Aeneas – who gave Britain its name. Geoffrey may have borrowed
from earlier sources, but whenever he drew a blank, he created. To
add to Brutus, he included other mythical figures such as Arthur and
Merlin, King Lear and Cymbeline.[36] Importantly for the various parts
of Britain, he and his continuators gave Brutus three sons: the eldest,
Locrinus, inherited England; the second, Kamber, was given Wales;
and the third, Albanactus, received Scotland. Thus, through primo-
geniture, England's domination was there from the start, but it was
entrenched through Arthur, King of all Britain (with Scotland as a
tributary kingdom), Scandinavia and Gaul.[37] Yet the *Brut* tradition,
as it became known, was about far more than storytelling; for the
Scots it proved the stuff of nightmares, because the *Brut* was to the
fore when Edward I sought to justify his attempted annexation of
Scotland to Pope Boniface VIII.[38]

The *Brut* had its answer, both in the Scots' counter to Edward's
papal submission and in the Declaration of Arbroath,[39] projecting the Scots as a homogenous native people with 'one hundred and
thirteen kings of their own royal stock, the line unbroken by a single
foreigner.'[40] Scottish 'history' had required finessing. Rather than the
Kingdom of Scotland deriving haphazardly from an agglomeration
of other kingdoms and forged by kings with an ancestry from beyond
its shores, it had to have been better planned. The story of Scotland's
kings and their kingdom had to appear both destined and immutable
through having stemmed not from man but from God. It needed a
coherent account, and that is what Fordun and Bower provided.

Encapsulating Scottish resistance to the Romans and their superior lineage to the Roman-based 'Britains' of the English story, the Scots were shown to have descended from the Greek Prince Gaythelos (or Goídel Glas), a superior ancestor to Brutus and Aeneas, the defeated Trojan. Yet there was an even better thread, because Gaythelos was the husband of the Egyptian Princess Scota, whose ancestor was Noah. Thus the Scots could be traced back to Adam and to God himself.

From Egypt the 'Scottish' descendants had made their way to Spain and then Ireland, and they had established their domination both there and over uninhabited Caledonia, which they gave permission to the late-arriving Picts to inhabit, shortly before settling themselves in unoccupied Dalriada under their first King of Scots, Fergus I, in 330 bc. Many centuries follow of Scot–Pict collaboration, which included their sending a joint letter to Julius Caesar telling him to leave Britain.[41] Then, due to the supposed dire treachery of the Picts, warfare broke out leading, over the centuries, to the point when Kenneth Macalpine 'came to Pictavia' and became the first King of all Scotland.[42] But this was no ordinary mortal, this was a supercharged Kenneth who fought and won seven battles in one day.[43] The extermination of the Picts had begun.

Returning to the words of the Declaration of Arbroath, it was under Kenneth and his successors that 'the Picts they utterly destroyed, and, even though very often assailed by the Norwegians, the Danes and the English, they took possession of that home with many victories and untold efforts; and, as the historians of old time bear witness, they have held it free of all bondage ever since'.[44]

To the modern reader, it is far-fetched, but no more so than Geoffrey of Monmouth and his Arthurian legends – which the Scots, from the time of David II in the fourteenth century, annexed to themselves.[45] Most importantly, the finished work known as the *Scotichronicon* was something that the Scottish kings and their people could celebrate as their unbridled history, from their earliest times right up to Bower's own day, finishing in 1437.

The *Scotichronicon* was supported by the Scottish Kings James because it served their purposes exactly. It showed that the king led his subjects in a relationship that stretched back to time immemorial.

It was 'proven' that the Stewart kings ruled over a homogenous people within Scotland, just as their forebears had done, and in a direct succession that reached back three hundred years before Christ and then back to God himself. It was essential that the kingship of the then reigning king and of all his predecessors and successors should be seen as part of God's design. This served both to give foundation to their primacy within Scotland and to stress Scotland's independence from all other realms, most notably England.

12

Their Renaissance Majesties

Many people today think of Henry VII as an extremely successful king. Here was a man with a highly questionable claim to the throne, who had first gained and then consolidated his position, and who had brought extraordinary wealth to the crown and raised regal display to unprecedented levels. He planned a fine monument in Westminster Abbey. His executors, who included Warham, Fox, Ruthall, Surrey and Christopher Bainbridge (the Archbishop of York),[1] ensured that he had one: a magnificent chapel containing what John Pope-Hennessy has rightly described as 'the finest Renaissance tomb north of the Alps,'[2] by the Florentine master Pietro Torrigiani. There was one thing that Henry requested that he did not receive: a gold-plated kneeling statue of himself in full armour at Bosworth and holding the crown, as if God himself was blessing his victory. This was to have been placed on top of the shrine of Edward the Confessor. Henry was seeking to reserve for himself the very best and most sacred spot for any English monarch.[3] Perhaps it did not happen due to the cost; or maybe it was thought to be a step too far.[4]

Henry's pursuit of dynastic stability before all else had worked to the advantage of England's traditional foes. Peace with England allowed Charles VIII and Louis XII of France to look south with ambitions of conquest; it enabled James IV to view himself as a monarch of equal status. But peace went against the grain for the more martial of the English nobility. To them, as for their ancestors, the king was expected to be the warrior leader of their warrior class, not the appeaser of England's enemies.[5] In their eyes Henry VII had failed in his most important duty. Henry VIII's policy of belligerence against France was much more to their liking.

Henry VIII, like his father, identified with Arthurian chivalry.

But for him it was a cue for action, with himself taking the foremost role. The famous Round Table hanging on the wall at Winchester Castle was painted in 1516 with the red-and-white Tudor rose at the centre and, prominently at the top, a depiction of King Arthur on his throne. Contemporary onlookers would have been struck by the close resemblance of the ancient king to the current one.[6] Henry gathered round him fellow young bloods in a youthful chivalric brotherhood reminiscent of Edward III and was, in David Starkey's words, a 'participatory monarch' rather than one who believed in 'keeping distance' like his father.[7]

That said, certain elements of his father's way of ruling continued. For one thing, the financing of the King through the Privy Purse was taken to even greater heights by William Compton, Henry VIII's Groom of the Stole; for another, there was vast expenditure on display.

Henry VIII might move more readily among his people, but in terms of demonstrating his status, he was ever increasingly 'above' them. Gone were the dark fabrics of his father, replaced by glorious colour. The Sumptuary Laws of 1509, like their predecessors under Edward III and Edward IV, were extremely detailed and designed to ensure the proper stratification of social position by appearance. Thus only those of the rank of knight and above could wear foreign woollen cloth; only earls and above could have sable; but only the King and his immediate family could use in their apparel 'any cloth of gold of purple colour or silk of purple colour'[8] – the imperial purple, no less. Perhaps unsurprisingly, no one below the rank of baron could wear any form of gold or silver, including gold or silver thread.[9] However, according to at least one witness, the Venetian Ambassador Sebastian Giustinian in 1519, even his fellow kings could not compete with Henry in one respect, declaring that 'he was the best dressed sovereign in the world. His robes were very rich and superb.'[10]

Kings were, however, expected to be more than commanding figures in sumptuous outer packaging. To be a brilliant Renaissance monarch a king had to be a brilliant Renaissance man. This was not merely a question of whom you brought to your court – though

Francis I of France's employment of the elderly Leonardo da Vinci as a consultant sage was a spectacular coup – it was a matter of who *you* were. Henry VIII was highly qualified, by education, interests and accomplishments.

Henry's education was based on the classics and was strong on grammar, poetry and rhetoric, both in English and, most importantly, in Latin. As was becoming increasingly common in European court circles, the King's education had been humanist in influence, designed not just to expand the mind intellectually, but to train it to absorb 'universal truths' and make it ready to apply them in government.[11]

Henry was just a child when he first met Erasmus; or, that is to say, when Thomas More ceremonially introduced Erasmus to Henry and his two sisters at Edward IV's magnificent palace of Eltham. Erasmus, the greatest scholar of the northern Renaissance, was impressed. Writing later he recalled that 'in the midst stood Henry, aged nine, already with a certain royal demeanour; I mean a dignity of mind combined with a remarkable courtesy'.[12] Erasmus was to exchange letters and compliments with the teenage Henry and was to hear much else that was laudatory about him both from More and from William Lord Mountjoy, a former pupil of his who was to have a marked educational influence on young Henry. Mountjoy brought Erasmus to England, where he stayed for the first five years of Henry's reign.

Henry may have preferred to spend his late teenage years away from business, indulging in the vigorous outdoor pursuits at which he excelled, but he had softer skills from the first. Against the lavish background of his court, he could create an extraordinary impression. Here, from Ambassador Giustinian, is an account from 1515 of how completely the promise of the boy at Eltham, then only second in line to the throne, had come to bloom in the man. He describes a visit to Richmond on St George's Day and his audience with the King:

> We were conducted to the presence, through sundry chambers all hung with most beautiful tapestry, figured in gold and silver, and in silk,

passing down the ranks of the body-guard, which consists of three hundred halberdiers in silver breast-plates and pikes in their hands; and, by God, they were all as big as giants, so that the display was very grand.

We at length reached the King, who was under a canopy of cloth of gold, embroidered at Florence, the most costly thing I ever witnessed: he was leaning against his gilt throne, on which was a large brocade cushion, where the long gold sword of state lay.

After around 250 words on the king's magnificent dress and jewellery and a mere 65 devoted to his nobles, prelates and heralds, Giustinian leads the reader to High Mass and to dinner. Then, resuming his narrative:

After dinner, we were taken to the King, who embraced us without ceremony, and conversed for a very long time while very familiarly, on various topics, in good Latin and in French, which he speaks very well indeed.

As with Ayala's description of the twenty-five-year-old James IV in 1498, the Ambassador's brief was to describe exactly what he saw, so that, in this case, Venice's Doge and Council of Ten could gauge the nature and power of the King. Giustinian gives his impression of King Henry:

His Majesty is the handsomest potentate I ever set eyes on; above the usual height, with an extremely fine calf to his leg, his complexion very fair and bright, with auburn hair combed straight and short, in the French fashion, and a round face so very beautiful, that it would become a pretty woman, his throat being rather long and thick.... He speaks French, English, and Latin, and a little Italian, plays well on the lute and harpsichord, sings from [a] book at sight, draws the bow with greater strength than any man in England, and jousts marvellously. Believe me, he is in every respect a most accomplished Prince; and I, who have now seen all the sovereigns in Christendom, and last of all these two of France [Francis I] and England in such great state, might well rest content.

Giustinian was no youthful novice on his first posting but a fifty-five-year-old with many years of ambassadorial experience. The fact that he was so seriously impressed is significant. Display was an extraordinarily important weapon in the diplomatic power game of international politics and as the experienced Giustinian hammered home to his masters, though Venice had lost badly in the recent war she must keep up appearances:

> She [Venice] is held in as great an account as of yore by these two Kings, who are the first in the world, so her ambassadors must bear patiently the cost of their outfit and that of their attendants, and of so many preparatives, for it all redounds most immensely to your glory and repute.[13]

By 1515 Henry had proved himself a master at presenting himself to ambassadors. This was a very different man to the one who referred the Spanish Ambassador Caroz to Fox in 1510.

Even as early as 1513, Henry had become more assured, reminiscent of how his brother-in-law James IV had appeared with Ambassador Ayala at a similar age. The two Kings had much in common.

There was for instance the connection with Erasmus, who had complimented James, when describing the King's son Alexander Stewart in these terms: 'No one was more talented in the highest pursuits aside from the King his father.'[14]

James was both highly intelligent and well educated. As Ayala reported to Ferdinand and Isabella:

> He [King James] speaks the following foreign languages: Latin, very well; French, German, Flemish, Italian and Spanish.... His own Scottish language is as different from English as Aragonese from Castilian. The King speaks, besides, the language of the savages who live in some parts of Scotland and on the islands. It is as different from Scottish as Biscayan is from Castilian. His knowledge of languages is wonderful. He is well read in the Bible and in some other devout books. He is a good historian. He has read many Latin and French histories, and has profited by them as he has a very good memory.[15]

James sought to encourage education and culture more widely. He backed to the hilt Bishop Elphinstone's educational initiatives – such as the first education act and the founding of Aberdeen University.

Much closer to home, he also made the very best education available
for Alexander Stewart, his son by Marion Boyd. There could surely
have been nothing better for the teenage Alexander than the company of the most accomplished scholar of the northern Renaissance
in some of the most brilliant cities of its Southern counterpart: in
1508–9 Alexander was tutored in Italy by Erasmus, spending time
in Padua, having a lengthy spell in Siena and then going to Rome.
It was a rewarding experience for all concerned, for Alexander was
Erasmus's star pupil, making the great man's compliment to James all
the better. Erasmus wrote about Alexander many years later and the
memories were still fresh:

> I once lived with the King's son in the city of Siena and I there taught
> him Rhetoric and Greek. Heavens! How quick, how attentive, how eager
> he was; and how many things could he undertake together! At that time
> he studied law – a subject not very pleasing because of its barbarous
> admixture and the insufferable verbosity of its expounders. He attended
> lectures on Rhetoric, and followed out a prescribed theme, using alike
> his pen and his tongue. He learned Greek, and each day construed his
> stated task in a given time. He gave his afternoons to music, to the mono-
> chord,[16] flute or lute; and he sometimes sang while playing on a stringed
> instrument. Even at mealtimes he was not forgetful of his studies. The
> chaplain always read some good book, such as the Pontifical Decrees,
> St Jerome or St Ambrose; nor was the reader interrupted, except when
> some of the doctors among whom he sat made a suggestion, or when
> he [Alexander] made inquiry about something which he did not clearly
> understand. On the other hand, he liked tales, when they were brief, and
> when they treated of literary matters. Hence no portion of his life was
> spent without study, except the hours given to religion and to sleep. If he
> had any spare time … he spent it in reading history, for in that he took
> extreme delight. Thus it was that, though he was a youth scarcely fifteen
> years old, he excelled as much in every kind of learning as in all those
> qualities which we admire in a man.[17]

Like that of Henry VIII, King James's interest in religion was sincere.
His faith and his affection for his Queen were shown in March 1507
by his 120-mile, eight-day journey on foot from Edinburgh to the

tomb of St Ninian at Whithorn to pray for the lives of Margaret and their newborn son.[18] It was faith rewarded because she recovered, as did their son, for the time being at least.

James's retreat to the Observantine Friary within Stirling Castle during Holy Week was an annual occurrence,[19] as were pilgrimages to Whithorn and St Duthac at Tain – supplemented by more occasional visits to St Mary at Whitekirk and St Adrian on the Isle of May. There is no reason to doubt James's piety at the shrines themselves, but the pilgrimage events – and it is right to call them events – were in effect fast-moving royal progresses that served a number of different purposes. Firstly James could be seen as a man of faith and piety, underlining his own sanctity as a king granted divine authority through anointing at his coronation, and he undoubtedly impressed his own clergy and the papal curia. Secondly, James could present himself to his subjects. A king, and particularly one as charismatic as James, generated awe among the mass of his people as soon as he came into view.[20] The effect was magnified when James was accompanied by his black Moorish drummers and his Italian minstrels.[21] He could very happily personally engage with his subjects, but the mere sight of the royal party riding past would have been impressive enough, with the general reaction being noted by those riding with him, be they courtiers or foreign diplomats.

For James, these trips would, as Dr Macdougall entertainingly notes, have been particularly appreciated as an alternative 'to staying in Edinburgh and enduring homilies from Bishop Elphinstone on the need to overhaul the entire fabric of civil and criminal law'.[22] James knew the importance of using brilliant display and entertainment to win the hearts as well as the minds of those around him, but it must have been fun for him too. The details are recorded in an unlikely sounding source of joy: the Treasurer's Accounts. These are, however, accounts with full disclosure. We know from them that the journeying of James and his companions to St Duthac at Tain in the 1500s included time at Darnaway Castle with Janet Kennedy and large amounts of food, wine and music.[23] We suspect that James may have played cards more for relaxation than for profit, when considering the debts paid to the likes of the Earl of Angus; though it is possible that his losses went through the books but his winnings were mostly paid to him direct. There are some startling inclusions, such as royal gifts in the period from 1508 to 1512 to a 'Janet bair ars',[24] whose role would seem obvious. More soberly, there is also an entry for 'the King's iron belt', which James wore as a penance for being unable to prevent the death of his father. [25]

The Treasurer's Accounts are a fantastic source of information about James himself and his reign. They show his interest in scientific matters, in medicine and in dentistry – though in James's case he actually paid his 'patients' for the privilege of pulling teeth – and in softer domestic-sounding skills, as there are entries describing the needles and thimbles, threads (of gold naturally), and silks and linen cloth for 'the king to broider with'.[26] The Treasurer's Accounts are an excellent companion – and often counterpoint and correction – to the work of William Dunbar, one of the celebrated poets at James's court, along with Gavin Douglas and Robert Henryson.

Dunbar is an entertaining, if eccentric and self-serving witness. For instance he tells us of the 'flyting' competition, before the King, between himself (in Scots) and Walter Kennedy (in Gaelic) to see who could win a verbal combat of competitive insult. According to Dunbar, it was him. He also gives his views of his bête noire (or 'French leech'), John Damian, Abbot of Tongland, whom he mocks in two poems.

Firstly, Damian is satirized for his birdman attempt to fly from the high walls of Stirling Castle to France, which ended all too quickly but with just a broken thigh bone, because though he dropped like a stone he managed to land in the castle cess pit. Damian blamed a rogue contractor for including some earthbound hen feathers with the far more expensive and more naturally soaring eagle feathers he had ordered.[27]

Secondly, Damian is disparaged for conducting alchemic experiments involving vast amounts of whisky; though, in his defence, he could counter with the alchemist's belief that the creation of high-strength alcohol through distillation and its fusion of the two normally opposing elements of fire and water, was the way to Aqua Vitae or the very elixir of life.[28]

It is obvious that Damian's greatest crime in Dunbar's eyes was that he was on better terms with the King, playing cards with him and competing in shooting contests. To the modern mind, Damian might seem 'the mad scientist', but it should be remembered that alchemy was also to have an important place in the scientific theory of those later titans, Robert Boyle and Isaac Newton. Indeed, James's support of Damian was just one part of a Renaissance kingship that married together classical scholarship; medieval chivalry; Christian belief and practice; cultural and sporting pursuits; and technological innovation and scientific experiment. James's open-minded approach to the latter was to place Scotland in the forefront of military technology. It was also to provide the final *coup de théâtre* of one of the most thrilling entertainments of the age: the Edinburgh Tournament of May–June 1508.

This was held at Holyrood, where the works to celebrate James's and Margaret's marriage, with features reminiscent of Henry VII's Palace at Richmond and of his remodelling at Windsor and the Tower of London, were to all intents and purposes complete.[29] The honoured guest who enjoyed them was, in spite of having the Scottish name of Bernard Stewart, actually French, as designated by his title: Seigneur d'Aubigny. The grandson of a very distant relative of the Scottish royal house who had gone to France to fight the English in 1419, d'Aubigny was a distinguished diplomat, military commander and strategist, being particularly admired for the importance he gave to reconnoitring terrain.[30] Though d'Aubigny was ostensibly travelling to Scotland for a pilgrimage to St Ninian, he was tasked by Louis XII to gain James's renewal of the 'Auld Alliance' between France and Scotland. For James, with his passion for all things military, d'Aubigny would have been a welcome companion, just as Surrey had been in 1503. Dunbar's ballad marking the occasion compared d'Aubigny to famous commanders of old: Achilles, Hector, Hannibal and most appropriately Arthur, as James IV himself had brought Arthur closer to Holyrood, by calling the nearby volcanic rock 'Arthur's seat'.[31]

James himself represented the very flower of Arthurian chivalry and in three days of appearing thinly 'disguised' as the 'Wild Knight', he defeated all comers from France, Denmark, and England to win the Black Lady of Moorish origin, who entered the event borne on a triumphal chair by two squires.[32] Dunbar, in his bawdy poem 'On a Blackamoor', describes how the winners got to kiss the 'meikle lipps' of her mouth and the losers her hips.[33] The festivities included rich banquets, plays, music, dancing, conjuring and magic,[34] with the most applauded trick being the disappearance of the Black Lady into a cloud suspended from beneath the roof of the Great Hall. It was 'magic' made possible by the clever application of the latest technology.[35]

For those in attendance, the tournament was designed to be a festival of fun. But behind the entertainment there were very serious purposes indeed. It successfully projected James as the potent leader of a united nobility. As it was held in honour of a famous French ambassador, it was affirmation, to any who might need it, that peace with England did not mean that Scotland would desert its historic links with the French. James was determined to govern independently, to have the same sort of freedom of action in foreign affairs as he did at home.

James IV of Scotland and his brother-in-law Henry VIII were in many ways very similar men. They were both highly intelligent, educated, forward-thinking humanist intellectuals, with a keen interest in theology and a deep religious faith. They were both cultured and cultivated. They had both elevated the majesty of their position to a level far above their predecessors. They were both late in deciding to exercise power and then distanced themselves from their fathers' policies and united their nobility through waging war against their traditional major national enemy: England and France respectively.

But when Henry VIII took up active kingship in 1511 there was one fundamental difference between them. Henry VIII was a new ruler, whereas James had been an active king for the better part of two decades. The approaches of the respective Kings of England and Scotland were reversed from what they had been a decade and a half before. So while they were both masters of majestic display, it was now James who viewed it as a substitute for war; whereas Henry saw it as means of preparing for it.

13

Seapower

European politics had been profoundly affected by two events which occurred at opposite ends of the Continent in 1453; and James IV's subsequent ambitions to enhance Scotland's international standing were influenced by both. The first was the fall of Constantinople to the Turks, which had major economic and political consequences as well as cultural ones. The second was the expulsion of the English from France, leaving them with just Calais as their continental foothold.

Charles VII's victory at Castillon in July 1453 finally won the Hundred Years War and made permanently French the vast territories of Normandy to the north and Aquitaine and Gascony to the south. The removal of English power enabled further acquisitions such as French Burgundy, Franche Comté and Provence by Louis XI, so that France under his son and successor, Charles VIII, bore a far closer resemblance to the nation of today than it had done a mere fifty years before.

The Anglo-French Treaty of Étaples in November 1492 suited both parties. For Henry VII it ended French support for Warbeck and gave him a large payoff. For Charles it meant he could concentrate his energies elsewhere: in September 1494, with a force stiffened by the inclusion of Swiss mercenaries, he invaded Italy.

So began a series of wars stretching over six decades of sometimes bewildering changes of alliances between France, Spain, the Papacy, the Hapsburg Empire, Venice and a kaleidoscope of Italian states. In military terms, England and Scotland were able to stand broadly aloof from the continental conflict for the best part of the first two decades. But they could not do so diplomatically, particularly as the specific conflict between France and the Papacy was normally central to the whole.

In this context and bearing in mind Scotland's traditional French alliance, James's achievement in maintaining an iron grip on appointments within the Scottish Church and the diversion of so much of its revenue into his own coffers is all the more impressive. In 1507, not long before a multi-party alliance against Venice briefly ranged the Papacy with France rather than against it, James received a particular mark of papal favour from Pope Julius II. This was the gift, brought by a special emissary, of the blessed Sword and Hat. It was awarded to James 'as a defender of the rights and liberties of the Church and of the Apostolic See'[1] and he was the first Scottish king in more than three centuries to receive it.

The 1453 fall of Constantinople had led to calls for a crusade against the Turks to regain it. Some were genuine, such as that planned by Pius II, but most of the others – from popes and kings alike – were not. Besides which, trading peoples such as the Portuguese and the Genoese sought to remedy the disruption of the Mediterranean trade to the Near and Far East through new oceanic routes. A new type of ship, better able to withstand the pounding of waves and to ride the winds and swell of the oceans was created: the Portuguese carrack, which was a vessel far more stable than anything that had gone before. This was the ship design of Christopher Columbus's *Santa Maria* in 1492 and of the major ships of James's navy, including the *Great Michael*, which James offered Pope Julius II as the potential flagship for a crusade. But before that, James had another more immediate use for this type of ship.

The stability of the carrack enabled it to be used as a platform for heavy guns. In 1504 James and his Admiral, Andrew Wood, planned and unleashed a new type of campaign against the rebels in the Isles. They used ships that acted as gun platforms to attack the shoreline fortresses of the enemy. The bases for the seapower of the Lords of the Isles were now vulnerable and began to be bombarded into defeat. It was the seaborne equivalent of James II's use of his dominant artillery to batter the castles and shatter the power of the Earls of Douglas in the 1450s. This approach to naval firepower, never seen before

– at least in northern waters – was revolutionary.[2] And what was suitable for land-based targets was equally applicable to those at sea. The traditional sea fight, which involved closing with enemy ships and either ramming them or taking them by use of grappling hooks and boarding parties, was now supplemented by the ability to disable them by firepower from a distance. Henry VIII might be known as the 'Father of the English Navy', but when it came to naval tactics his Scottish counterpart had got there before him.

In the *Michael*, James combined firepower with magnificence. This was a vessel so large that the existing shipyard at Leith was too shallow to accommodate it. A new yard, and an accompanying town for the workforce, was constructed at Newhaven further along the Forth; and another, for refitting the *Michael* and James's other warships such as the *Margaret*, at Airth.[3] The *Michael* was referred to as the *Great Michael* from the first, for the most obvious of reasons: it was enormous, the biggest European ship afloat. It was large enough to take three hundred sailors, a thousand troops and most importantly twelve cannon on each side. In addition there were three large basilisks, two aft and one forward[4] and a huge array of guns of smaller calibre.

James's new ships were not only designed to fire large shot but to deflect and withstand it. The *Great Michael* had walls said to be ten feet thick that were highly effective, as James ensured by having his own cannon fired at the ship's hull before he paid for it.[5] The *Michael* was launched in 1511 and after De La Mothe, the French Ambassador, saw it in 1512, he wrote to King Louis XII that 'It is so powerful, there is nothing else like it in Christendom'.[6] And that was the *Great Michael*'s entire point. It was one of just thirty-eight ships that James used in his reign,[7] for 'daunting the Isles', for his nation's defence or, in the case of ships such as the *Michael* and the *Margaret*, for projecting his power. With the *Michael*, size was everything.

In 1514 when priorities had changed and the *Great Michael* was sold to the French for £18,000 Scots – less than two-thirds of its building cost of £30,000 Scots – the ship was considered a white elephant. But it most certainly was not in the years before. James viewed his navy and his big ships in particular as a means of cutting an independent figure in Europe. In one sense the *Margaret* and the *Michael* were prestige projects, as much objects of display as any of his palaces on land, and James used them to entertain – there are records of tapestries and silver plate being brought to the *Margaret* in the same way as such things of value were transferred between palaces;[8] and De La Mothe's observation is testimony to the powerful impression made by the *Michael*.

Just as in the Borders, it had long been difficult for Scottish and English kings to ensure peaceful conditions at sea, whatever the prevailing relations between them. In the early years of James's reign, there is no sign that they tried, with hostilities continuing in spite of truces on land. English ships in particular attacked and captured Scottish merchantmen, even sailing unopposed into the Firth of Forth as far as Leith.[9] There was a greater will for cooperation from 1498 onwards; but James, with his construction of a powerful Scottish royal navy, aimed to prevent a recurrence of such a humiliation, as well as to project Scottish power and prestige abroad. After 1502, at least in James's eyes, sporadic Anglo-Scottish disputes in the seas around the British coast could, like infractions in the Borders, be subject to justice through the Warden Courts.

But sensitivity to the possibility of conflict at sea actually allowed for full-scale naval warfare *within* the terms of the Treaty of Perpetual Peace. An important clause of the Treaty stated that 'either king may give aid to his ally, but not by an invasion of the other's territories'.[10] For James, as Dr Macdougall observes, 'the treaty gave him a loophole to the effect that, as long as he did not invade England, the Scottish king might help to defend the territories of any princes who were at war with England without breaking the alliance'.[11] This would probably mean France, with the likelihood that the French would pay for the navy if it was brought to their aid.

The French king was not the only possible candidate to provide the subsidy that was necessary, certainly in the medium term. And the idea of James putting his great ships out to hire was not that extraordinary. It was the maritime equivalent of the use made of the finest troops in Europe: the Swiss. For not only did Swiss mercenaries fight for the French, but Julius II contracted ten thousand of them for the

Papacy, thus starting a tradition of protecting the Pope, which has its continuation today in the Vatican's Swiss Guard.

The clue to James's thinking is in the name of the *Michael*. As James had called his second ship the *Margaret*, it might be anticipated that he would call his first ship the *James* – rather in the manner of his young brother-in-law, who, not to be outdone, commissioned a fractionally larger copycat version of the *Great Michael* and called it the *Henri, Grace à Dieu*, known as the *Great Harry*. Henry VIII, as would become his common practice, thus brought both himself and God into the equation. James was more subtle. His ship was called the *Michael* after the crusading archangel and he wrote to Julius II, putting the ship at his service for a crusade against the Turks, or rather offering it to Julius, should he wish to pay for it. Julius demurred, as he was more concerned with military matters in Italy.[12] However, the idea of James putting the *Michael* at the disposal of the Pope was far from outlandish. In one fell swoop he would gain prestige at home and abroad as an independent Christian monarch and defray the burdensome cost of his ship.

There was also a possibility, not to be completely discounted, that the English might want to hire the *Michael*. Certainly an interest was expressed. But could the English be trusted in this or, indeed, in any matter relating to Scotland?

⊰ ✝ ⊱

Henry VIII was bent on imitating his hero Henry V and invading France, but England needed firm and trustworthy allies before launching a fully fledged invasion. On the basis of general European fear of French power this might have been expected to be relatively straightforward. Diplomatic support was soon forthcoming, but gaining military backing proved difficult. Henry's fellow heads of state were older, experienced and rather more devious than both the gung-ho young King and, at this stage at least, his new chief minister, Almoner Wolsey. On the surface, the older rulers seemed to offer much; but it proved to be a mirage. The complex gavotte of continental diplomacy would continue for some time.

England's first hostile action – at sea – was, however, soon to arrive and it was not against a ship of France but one from Scotland.

The men responsible were Howards, the Earl of Surrey's two sons, knighted at Ayton: his heir Thomas and his second son Edward, who was a particular favourite of the young king.

Edward had been at the centre of court ceremonial from the start of the new reign. He had taken the symbolic role at Henry VII's funeral of wearing the dead king's armour. He was made the Royal Standard Bearer the month after Henry VIII's accession and this gave him an important function at the coronation.[13] He had continued in favour afterwards and, with his older brother Sir Thomas, was given the honour of leading a punitive operation against Andrew Barton, one of a seafaring family who combined operations for King James with activities on their own account. By June 1511, Andrew, it seems, had very much blurred the difference between acting as a pirate and being a privateer licensed by the Scottish king, when he began attacking English merchant shipping. At the end of the month, the Howards' hired ships, the *Barbara* and the *Mary Barking*, were lying in the Downs at the southern end of the North Sea, when they spotted Barton and his two ships, the *Lion* and the *Jennet of Purwyn*, heading north, presumably back towards Scotland. Thomas gave chase to the larger vessel, the *Lion*, and Edward the *Jennet*. Both ships were separately caught, grappled and boarded and there was fierce fighting on their decks. Barton, in the heat of battle, again mixed his official with his private capacity and blew long and hard on his admiral's whistle to inspire and encourage his men but it was to no avail. The ship was captured and the wounded Barton died on deck. The *Jennet* was also taken after a bitter struggle and the two ships sailed back to port as prizes.[14]

When Barton's captured ships were brought into Blackwall in the Port of London,[15] it wasn't just anybody who went to interview the crews. Richard Fox was the man sent and the deal he offered the Scottish sailors was simple: if they admitted they were pirates they could go home immediately to Scotland. Faced with the alternative of years rotting in an English gaol, they agreed en masse.[16] Thus when the later demand came from James that the Howards appear before a Warden's Court, Henry responded contemptuously that 'it did not become a prince to levy the breaking of a treaty against another prince for bringing a pirate or thief to justice.'[17]

The later sixteenth-century chroniclers, the English Edward Hall and Scottish Bishop Lesley, both claimed, from their opposing patriotic viewpoints, that James's initial response was one of fury and that he sought reparations.[18] In fact, that initial response was far more muted. For one thing, the ships were not his: the *Lion* was Barton's own, while the *Jennet*, belonging to James's cousin, King Hans of Denmark, had been commandeered by Andrew Barton. And that explained the other reason for James's more low-key reaction: Barton had become a freebooting embarrassment, far exceeding any royal orders he might have been given. So although James may have written to Henry protesting about Barton's death and seeking the speedy repatriation of the captured Scottish sailors, there was no talk of reparations, then.[19] But the whole affair was by no means forgotten.

In Henry's eyes, the Howards had passed their audition, though it was the younger of the two, Edward the court favourite, who was made Admiral of the Fleet on 7 April 1512.[20] And as far as Edward Howard was concerned, continuing belligerence was the order of the day. After all, he was the second son and a successful war offered him the opportunity to gain rank and wealth on his own account. As Wolsey noted in a letter to Fox of 30 September 1511, Howard was urging the King against the Scots, 'by whose wanton means his Grace spendeth much money, and is more disposed to war than peace. Your presence shall be very necessary to repress this appetite.'[21] Wolsey may have realized that the key to favour was to give Henry what he wanted, but he feared that Sir Edward's bull in a china shop approach was fraught with potential disaster.

Although Surrey's two eldest sons were being favoured by Henry VIII in the summer of 1511, the Earl himself most definitely was not. This was quite a reverse for Surrey, because at the time of Henry's accession, he had every expectation of emerging as the new king's First Minister. Surrey certainly had a powerful role initially and it was he, along with Fox and Ruthall, who signed the Anglo-French Truce of March 1510.[22] Yet though the old warrior's courage never failed him, in 1511 his skills as a courtier certainly did. Surrey did not take heed that Henry's earlier compliance was vanishing. He sought and gained an audience with Henry and argued for the continuation of the Anglo-French peace. As both an experienced military commander and Lord Treasurer, he had some insight into how expensive a French war would be. His entreaties were extremely ill received. As Wolsey reported in a letter to Fox, the Earl had 'such manner and countenance shown to him that on the morrow he departed home again and, as yet has not returned to Court', before adding conspiratorially, 'with a little help now he might be permanently excluded'.[23] It seemed that the fortunes of the Howard family would now rest wholly upon the shoulders of his sons, both mature men in their thirties, who were more than ready to take on the challenge.

⅏ ✝ ⅏

On the Continent, the diplomatic dance of changing alliances was continuing. In 1509 Pope Julius II sided with the Venetians against the French. This proved a major miscalculation as France won a succession of victories. But then Louis XII, in temporary alliance with the ever-shifting Emperor Maximilian, over-played his hand. He took it upon himself to call a Church Council at Pisa for the autumn of 1511 in a move to replace Julius. For the other European powers this was a move far too far. Challenging Julius's temporal aggrandizement was one thing, but for France to challenge his spiritual position was quite another. The other European rulers, with their memory of the schism in the Church and of France's annexation of the pontificate to Avignon, rallied to Julius's aid.

England joined the diplomatic flurry and sent an ambassador to Louis to remind the King of his duty to the Pontiff. Henry's representative received short shrift. But this was actually the result that Henry wanted, as he now had his 'casus belli'. Louis was excoriated for placing 'the Church in danger' and Henry's Council fell in behind their King. In November 1511, England joined a 'Holy League' consisting of the Papacy, Ferdinand and, shifting back again, Emperor Maximilian.[24] Henry had his powerful alliance against France.

Two months later, in January 1512, Parliament voted funds for an Anglo-Spanish assault against Guyenne, the southern part of Aquitaine, England's former possession lost in 1453 at the very end of the Hundred Years War. The English troops were commanded by

Henry's cousin Thomas Grey, 2nd Marquess of Dorset. Like Edward Howard, his contemporary, Dorset was a thirty-something jousting companion of the King; and again like Howard, his naval equivalent, he had no experience of commanding forces in war. He was not to gain it now.

The attack was planned for 1 April. With hindsight the date is ironic, because Henry's father-in-law King Ferdinand treated the English as fools, and for the second year running: in 1511 Ferdinand had asked for English volunteers for a crusading action against the Moors, then after they had arrived under the command of Thomas, Lord Darcy, said he no longer needed them.[25] In contrast, when the English eventually arrived in the summer of 1512, Ferdinand did want to use them, but not as part of an attack aimed at regaining an outpost of England's former empire, but rather to assist him in adding the small Pyrenean state of Navarre to the Kingdom of Spain. Dorset, very sensibly, refused to countenance this change of orders.

Regardless of the shouting matches that ensued, Dorset's decision actually made little difference to Ferdinand, because the English troops were so positioned that they were threatening the lines of communication of any French relieving force. Dorset had to wait for fresh instructions, but what happened next in the English camp at Fuenterrabia in Northern Spain was highly predictable. The greatest enemy of an army marooned in one place is disease. In this instance another was added: the fierce heat on the Spanish border meant the thirst of the troops had to be slaked with copious amounts of beer. Then the beer ran out and was replaced by wine. So to those, such as Dorset himself, laid low by sickness, were added others who were drunk, fighting drunk. And they started fighting the Spanish locals. At last when orders came through from England – surprisingly to join the Spanish forces in Navarre – the rabble became rebellious and refused. Dorset had no choice but to evacuate them home in disgrace.[26]

In tandem with the attack on Guyenne, it was intended that one be launched at sea. It was made clear to Edward Howard, as he received his instructions on his appointment in April, that he was expected to control the entire English Channel and the sea lanes between London and the Continent 'scouring the sea, to and fro, as the case shall require'.[27] For that task it was laid down that 'The said Admiral shall have … eighteen ships … in such manner rigged, equipped, tackled, decked, and furnished with ordnance and artillery as to such a voyage and service for the honour of our said Sovereign Lord'.[28] Included among the eighteen were both the *Jennet* and the *Lion*; but they were small fry at 70 and 100 tons respectively, with the *Jennet* the smallest of all. They were dwarfed by the *Mary Rose* at 500 tons[29] and the *Regent* at 1,000 tons.[30] The ships between them had 3,700 mariners, soldiers and gunners on board, with 700 on the *Regent* alone.

By the end of April, Howard's fleet, bar the *Regent*, was at sea and menacing all foreign shipping. Even citizens of England's allies of Spain and the Netherlandish Duchy of Burgundy were not excepted. One poor man, Jacques Berenghier of Lille (which at the time belonged to Emperor Maximilian and not to Louis XII of France), had all his goods seized, was tortured on the rack so badly that he lost a foot, and was then sent to Southampton and threatened with being hanged; and all because he spoke French,[31] which, if a crime, then every cultured person in Europe was guilty. In comparison to these actions, Andrew Barton's activities look pretty small beer.

In early June, Howard's fleet put soldiers ashore in Brittany and they conducted raids of destruction and pillaging as far as seven miles inland. Howard had no respect for the landed property of his fellow mariners, deliberately targeting and burning the house of the French naval captain Hervé de Porzmoguer (called Piersmogun by the chronicler Holinshed). From there, after raiding along the coast of Normandy, it was back to Portsmouth.

Ferdinand had promised the services of the Spanish fleet, but, naturally, it did not arrive. Even without it, the English had forced a reaction from the French. Louis had been caught out: he had assumed that a crushing victory over the joint papal and Spanish forces at Ravenna, together with English concern over the possible actions of Louis' putative ally the King of Scots, would hold Henry back. Not a bit of it.

Henry might have strategic objectives, in the manner of other contemporary rulers, but he also had more immediate ones. He wanted the destructive glory of war for its own sake that would set him on a par with his illustrious predecessors, Edward III and Henry V. His father's novel policies had placed a treasure chest at his disposal and he fully intended to use it for traditional warlike purposes. In any event, his involvement seemed to have a strategic impact too, at least for the rest of the Holy League. Louis was forced to order his Mediterranean fleet to leave Italy and sail into the Channel to oppose the English.

By the beginning of August, the English and French fleets were approximately the same size, with twenty-two French ships to twenty-five for the English. The two largest English ships were the *Regent* of around 1,000 tons and the *Trinity Sovereign* of at least 800 tons, while the biggest of the French, the *Louise* and the *Cordelière*, were 790 and 700 respectively.[32] Both fleets suffered from poor victualling, which caused ships to be unnecessarily delayed in port, though the French were not short of ordnance and there were sixty barrels of gunpowder on the *Cordelière* alone.[33] However, all the biggest vessels were involved on 10 August, when English ships surprised the French off the coast of Brest.[34]

The engagement began at around 11 a.m. with a cannonade from the English shooting away the main mast of the *Louise* and she had to break off the action immediately. But this was not to be a new kind of naval battle of ships standing off and firing broadsides at each other. For seven hours, five English ships manoeuvred around two of the French, before one of the latter extricated itself, leaving just the carrack *Cordelière*, commanded by Hervé de Porzmoguer. She fought on. The *Trinity Sovereign* seemed about to position herself to launch her grappling hooks, but either her master was unsighted by smoke or he bungled the manoeuvre. Instead it was the *Regent*, commanded by Howard's brother-in-law Sir Thomas Knyvet, who got alongside and with grappling hooks and ropes the two ships were secured together. Under a hail of crossbow bolts, Knyvet and his raiding party fought their way on board. What happened next is uncertain. Whether it was, as the otherwise impeccably impartial French naval historian Alfred Spont suggests, the action of a self-sacrificial French gunner determined the English should not take his ship;

or, as seems more likely, the spread of fire on board reached the gun-powder on its own, the result was the same. The *Cordelière* and the *Regent* were both blown apart. In the circumstances, it seems extraor-dinary that as many as six men from the *Cordelière* and 180 from the *Regent* survived. Knyvet was not among them.

This loss was a real blow to Henry and Katherine. Knyvet had been a court favourite. So much so that Wolsey wrote to Fox on 26 August that 'Sir Edward [Howard] has vowed "that he will never see the King in the face till he hath revenged the death of the noble and valiant knight, Sir Thomas Knyvet".[35] Perhaps Sir Edward need not have worried as Henry seemed satisfied enough and made him Lord Admiral on his return from the Battle of Brest. He succeeded Henry VII's stalwart warrior, the recently deceased Earl of Oxford.

14

King or Vassal

Henry had replaced James as the younger of the two British kings and from 1511 was the one acting without restraint. As James had acted aggressively against Henry VII in the 1490s in asserting Scottish independence, now Henry VIII proceeded aggressively to curtail it. In the matter of diplomacy and the preparations for war, France was his main focus and the manner of the treatment of Scotland was in the way of a sideswipe. All the same it was brutal, with the official statement of the English position made clearly and visibly public. In the preamble to the 1512 Subsidy Act put through Parliament, the King of Scots was declared 'the very homager and obediencer of right to your Highness'.[1] This was more than 'a shot across the bows', it was an assault on Scotland's essential status and a blunt reassertion of the overlordship last made by Henry's grandfather Edward IV in 1482, which had been implicitly revoked on a permanent basis by the Treaty of Perpetual Peace.

The English justification lay in the claim that James had broken the peace and was preparing for war. This was completely specious, as James had by then not even bowed to Louis' pressure and renewed the 'Auld Alliance'. The clumsiness of the claim also undercut the very point it was seeking to make. If James's 'breach' of the treaty was the cause of England's reassertion of overlordship, then, by the same token, an unbroken treaty denied it. Had an honest broker been available, it would have been recognized that, firstly, James had not broken the treaty and, secondly, that he had autonomy. In theory there was a 'court of appeal': the Papacy. But the Papacy was now an ally of England, and Christopher Bainbridge, the Cardinal Archbishop of York, was both England's Ambassador to the Holy See and a member of the Pope's advisory council. Furthermore, the Archdiocese of York had a traditional claim of overlordship regarding the Scottish Church, including the right to make appointments. Bainbridge was no friend to James.

Louis XII had been trying urgently to persuade James to renew the French alliance. From Louis' viewpoint that was the purpose of Bernard Stewart's mission in 1508. James may have put on a fabulous display and made all the right noises, but he had not renewed, as Louis was not offering a sufficient benefit in return. Henry's belligerent stance helped do Louis' work for him. If James needed any clarification of Henry's intentions, it would have come from Andrew Forman, Bishop of Moray, who stopped briefly at Henry's court in mid-February en route from France to Scotland and noted an even more fervent anti-Scottish sentiment than normal.[2]

James could not be seen to be cowed by the English. At the end of February he summoned a Scottish General Council and with their wholehearted support he submitted new terms to Louis. He did not intend, however, to become a mere client of the French, nor was he going to accept that he had been diplomatically frozen out within the papal curia. For the next year Andrew Forman would shuttle between Scotland, France and Rome – often indeed, just to and from France and Rome – in an attempt to settle the central dispute of Louis XII and Julius II. Venice and Maximilian might change sides, though principally so they could oppose each other; and Ferdinand certainly proved an unreliable ally for the English. But from 1510 to 1513 the defining conflict was between France and the Papacy.

In the aftermath of Flodden, Forman would be the target of a great deal of hostile criticism: he was denounced as a warmongering agent of France who had sacrificed the interests of his country to further his ambitions to become a cardinal and perhaps even more. Certainly Forman was ambitious and the French did make him the Archbishop of Bourges in July 1513; but he also had expectations of a cardinal's hat from Julius II,[3] from which one can at least deduce a balance of self-interest. Yet he was not a French stooge: he had been one of the main negotiators of the Treaty of Perpetual Peace and had opposed the renewal of the French alliance in 1508. Most importantly, he was the instrument of royal policy – changing tack as James required.[4] Though not in the most propitious circumstances, he was gaining diplomatic recognition for James by shuttling between the major European powers. It would have been far better, of course, if his efforts had been not as an attempted mediator but as a coordinator of the Christian rulers in defence of Christendom against the Ottoman Turks, supposedly their common enemy. And there was a pressing reason for action from 1512 onwards, as the new Sultan Selim I was urging the Ottomans towards further territorial expansion. The Knights Hospitaller were under threat at Rhodes and had written to the Pope for support.[5] Bearing that in mind, the plans for a crusade outlined by James do not appear to be quite so outlandish. Even if James recognized that Louis, the Papacy and the Venetians were only honouring the crusading idea in principle, discussion of principle helped continue the round of diplomatic activity as a means of winning time to strengthen Scotland's position. If Scotland was to be drawn into war, she needed time to prepare. But war might be averted if events in Italy took a defining turn during the intervening period.

On 11 April 1512, they very nearly did.

⊰ ✟ ⊱

Napoleon Bonaparte won lasting fame for his Italian campaigns while still in his twenties. He had an eminent predecessor who was even younger: Louis XII's nephew, Gaston de Foix, Duc de Nemours. In 1511 at the age of just twenty-one, he took charge of the French armies in Italy and led them to a string of brilliant victories in Lombardy and Emilia Romagna. In the spring of 1512 he moved southeast to Ravenna and on 11 April his forces faced the predominantly Spanish army of the Holy League outside the City. The Battle of Ravenna showed how lethal the new weapons of war could be in the hands of a superb tactician. Nemours' coordination of the devastating firepower of well-placed field artillery, disciplined infantry stiffened with German Landsknecht pikemen, and the tactical support of fast-moving cavalry, won a bloody victory after a hard-fought battle lasting between five and six hours.[6] It might well have decided the entire campaign, except that Nemours was killed at almost the end of the battle and his successors failed to maximize the potential gains of the victory. Thus the French lost Milan within a month and Louis withdrew his forces to France. Fortunately for Louis, his enemies squabbled over their spoils; but the value of his potential allies had still increased, as did the price he was prepared to pay to James for his support.

James continued to hold out. It was the view of one particular Englishman, Thomas, Baron Dacre, that James had no intention of invading England. And Dacre was in an excellent position to judge. As Warden of the English West March, Dacre had got to know James well in 1504, when the two men made a dual assault on the Reivers in Eskdale in the lawless Debatable Land. The action was designed to bring order in accordance with the spirit of the Treaty of Perpetual Peace, though with the actual border unclear it was also in James's interest to police any area that could be considered part of Scotland. All the signs are that the two men got on well, joining together in hanging bandits and playing cards. Dacre was a colourful character and a courageous one: in 1487, when denied access to his heart's desire, the local heiress Elizabeth Greystoke, he kidnapped her from Lord Clifford's castle of Brougham in Westmorland. This took some nerve, as she was a royal ward of the new king, Henry VII, and Dacre was an erstwhile supporter of Richard III.[7] But like Surrey, Dacre managed to convince Henry of his loyalty, though the wary King kept him under control through the threat of fines.

Dacre was less constrained under the new King, and in 1511 his remit was increased to take in all three Marches. Henry's view of the Scots was made clear in the indenture of 12 December 1511, extending Dacre's wardenship of the East and Middle Marches 'till Easter next and further, if the peace continue' and including the phrase 'if the Scots will not be contented with reason he shall make reprisals'.[8] Dacre and Dr Nicholas West, the Dean of St George's Windsor, went on a joint diplomatic mission to James in June 1512 and Wolsey wrote to Bainbridge on 1 July with their report that 'James IV wishes to keep the peace but the people are against it'.[9]

It was also noted that the Frenchman De La Mothe was there at the same time. He had used his accompanying warships on the journey across to sink three English merchantmen and capture seven more, deliberately inflaming the atmosphere by sailing his captured vessels into the port of Leith.[10]

James may have finally given formal agreement to the renewal of the Auld Alliance by July 1512,[11] but this was a gesture rather than a commitment. It was still possible for Scotland to remain neutral in an Anglo-French war and Louis could not count on James's active support against England – certainly not on land. De La Mothe would return again in November and stay until 14 February 1513, but even then he could not assure Louis that he had James's support. However the pace of events was quickening.

Henry would not offer James anything to counter the proffered, though undelivered, blandishments of the French. He ignored the information from Dacre, in a letter of 17 August 1512,[12] that the Treasurer of Scotland had told him that 'Henry might arrange matters by sending 4,000 or 5,000 angels[13] to the King his master'. That same letter noted James's fury that a legacy due to Queen Margaret from her father's will continued to be withheld and that James believed that Henry had done it deliberately 'in malice of him'. Dacre submitted that 'it would be honourable to pay it' and went on to point out 'the sum is so small'.[14] It was wise advice. This matter would continue to fester over the succeeding months.

Perhaps Dacre's opinion was considered to be compromised through his earlier association with James, just as pleas for peace on the Scottish side from Bishop Elphinstone and the Earl of Angus would be considered suspect because of previous 'Anglo' associations. However, the main reason Dacre was ignored was quite simple: Henry had no interest in appeasing James, because his focus was on France. He knew that James could disrupt his plans at sea or on land, but it was a problem that he would counter by threat and intimidation, not by conciliation. There seems to have been no insight that James was restraining his people's bellicosity towards England, that his chivalric and military displays of independence were just that and not a prelude to action.

Henry was convinced that James was himself bent on war, that he would behave as his medieval predecessors had behaved when given the opportunity: ally with France and attack England. Henry also believed that, whatever the implications of the Treaty of Perpetual Peace, the King of Scots owed him obedience. This was a 'certainty' he carried throughout his reign, perhaps best shown when towards the end of it he produced 'proof' that Kings of Scots had paid homage to their English counterparts on no fewer than seventeen occasions over a period of half a millennium.[15] Once Henry formed a conviction, it was extremely difficult to get him to change his mind, as Cardinal Wolsey advised a future Privy Councillor in later and very different circumstances:

> Rather than he [the King] will either miss or want any part of his will or appetite, he will put the loss of one half of his realm in danger. For I assure you I have often kneeled before him in his privy chamber on my knees, the space of an hour or two, to persuade him from his will and appetite: but I could never bring to pass to dissuade him therefrom. Therefore, Master Kingston, if it chance hereafter you to be one of his privy council, I warn you to be well advised and assured what matter you put in his head, for you shall never put it out again.[16]

Considering Wolsey's own unhappy embassy in 1508, one can only surmise what he might have said when Henry asked him for his view of the Scottish King. Whether Wolsey stoked the fire of this growing personal animosity is not known, but that there was increasing hostility between Henry and James cannot be in doubt. At core was James's position in relation to the English throne: through Margaret he was the heir. Over the months, as letters and ambassadors travelled between the two courts, this fact became an increasingly unpleasant running sore. It was all the more contentious because both Kings, having sired baby heirs, lost them soon afterwards. That is until 1512.

James was none too subtle in using his babies for propaganda purposes. In October 1509 Margaret bore him a son who was to live for eight months. The baby was christened Arthur: not after Margaret's and Henry's elder brother, but to advertise the Scottish claim to the Arthurian legend and, as Dr Katie Stevenson persuasively argues, as a British name for a potential British king.[17] Then on 10 April 1512, Margaret gave birth to another boy, to be called James. This boy, the future James V, was still alive and well a year later. Margaret had previously upstaged Henry in her time at the English court as the betrothed Queen of Scots and thus of higher rank than her young brother. Now she was upstaging him by outbreeding him, for during the entire period of growing tension, up to and beyond the Battle of Flodden itself, Henry was without a child heir. As the exchanges became increasingly bitter, James was not above hinting that not only did he have right of inheritance through Margaret as a Tudor, but he had a claim to the English throne of far longer descent, from St Margaret, Malcolm III's Anglo-Saxon Queen.[18] For his part, Henry told James that if he broke the peace, he would be disinherited and that if he hoped that Louis would help him on to the English throne then he would be disappointed because Louis was going to support Richard de la Pole, Suffolk's younger brother, who was now in France.[19]

Henry had an even stronger card to play. James had anticipated its use by writing to Pope Julius on 5 December 1511, at the time of the increase in tension following the death of Andrew Barton. Both claim and request were concise, stating that: 'The present King of England – though he has ratified the treaty – pursues, slays, and imprisons the Scotch by land and sea, and takes no notice when [King James] demands redress' and continuing that he [James] 'presumes, therefore, that both are absolved from their oaths'.[20] James did not intend to sunder the peace, but he feared that, if war did break out, then he and not Henry would be excommunicated for breaking his oath. His appeal was ignored. He was not absolved and he was right in his anticipation, because Julius was persuaded in February 1513, even as he lay on his death bed, to impose an interdict. The instigator, naturally, was Cardinal Bainbridge and the interdict was a general censure against the Scottish people.[21] It simultaneously supported the Cardinal's claim, as Archbishop of York, to have authority over the Scottish Church and attacked James's own position. But more than that, Julius gave Bainbridge an additional power and one that he could exercise even after the Pope's own death: that of excommunicating James himself.[22]

15

1513 – Breakdown

In late March 1513 Dr Nicholas West set off on another embassy to Scotland. As was the case with Wolsey five years before, West was unable to see James immediately; not this time because James was occupied with guns and gunpowder, but because the visit coincided with Holy Week and the King was secluded with the Observantine friars at Stirling.

West busied himself in Edinburgh by exchanging fierce letters with Forman; with the latter irately claiming that he would have been made a Cardinal by the recently deceased Julius, but for Henry refusing him the required safe conduct and thus blocking his journey from Scotland.[1] West then travelled to Stirling and arrived on Thursday, 24 March. When he finally got to see the King, just before High Mass on Easter Sunday, 27 March, he was told that he would have a formal interview the next day. That night West dined with the Queen. He informed her that Henry intended to invade France and begged her to keep James from entering the war. She asked about her legacy and was told quite bluntly that she would only receive it if her husband kept the peace.

The next day West saw James properly for the first time. The King informed him that he was sending Forman to France and then to Rome to get the new Pope, the Medici Leo X, to withhold confirmation of Julius's sentence. When West asked James to whom the King would appeal should the Pope condemn him, James 'answered him laughing,[2] 'to the French Admiral Prester John (Prégent) of course'. West did not share the joke. After dinner, he offered James a small sum of 1,000 marks (£666 13s. 4d) to settle the outstanding claims of infractions on the border, so long as he agreed to keep the peace with Henry. James told him angrily that he did not need the money, but he became far angrier when he asked about his wife's legacy and learned that it would be paid on condition he kept the peace and that, if he did not, then not only would he lose the legacy but his finest towns.[3] That provoked a tirade from James. No one could accuse West of not faithfully representing his master, but perhaps it was fortunate that at this point the Dean of the Chapel Royal arrived to tell James that the Friar was ready to begin his sermon.[4]

So began two weeks of short, missed and unscheduled meetings combined with West arriving to see James unannounced because he believed that the King's councillors and his secretary, Patrick Panter,[5] had begun to 'trifle him forth'.[6] There were promised letters that did not arrive and others that did which were full of complaint from James. The court moved from Stirling to Holyrood and West with it, but there was still no progress. West's instructions had been clear: he was not to leave until he received, preferably in writing, a statement from James of what he planned to do. It was not forthcoming. The best he could get, on Friday, 1 April, was a statement from the King's Councillor, Archibald Campbell, Earl of Argyll in front of Alexander Stewart, Archbishop of St Andrews, and James Beaton, Archbishop of Glasgow, and 'many other lords', that 'they would keep the peace if England would do the same'.[7] The meeting then descended into farce. West asked if he might write it down and repeat it before the King 'as he would not trust his own memory in so weighty a matter'. To which 'they said he might write it with pleasure, but not read it before the King or them, for their King needed to make no new promise, being bound by the treaty'.

When James arrived, they went through the same rigmarole, except that when West repeated Argyll's earlier statement to him, James said 'that was his answer for that time'; and when West offered to write it down and read it back, the King said there was no need 'as he trusted him well enough'. When they were alone, James told West that 'he was obliged to speak sharply before his Council, as they would certify it to France, and he should lose the French King if he professed too much friendliness to England'.[8] In effect, that it was he who was sustaining the status quo and that West and the English should back off.

On Tuesday, 5 April, West received dispatches from Thomas Ruthall, Bishop of Durham, which contained a copy of a letter from Leo to Henry.[9] The next day he showed it to James, who remarked that Henry was lucky to have such a Pope. At that same meeting, West mentioned again a previous request to have the *Michael*, on terms unspecified, but James said that the French had asked for her. When West replied that he hoped the French would not have her, James said that 'he knew not'.[10] This time James waxed lyrical about his ship and added 'that he had more artillery than the French King ever had at any siege',[11] which West 'thought a great crack'.[12] But on this occasion James was not joking.

It is clear that West was neither a popular guest, nor a good one. As early as his letter to Henry of Friday, 1 April, West was remarking that he would have preferred that his King had asked him 'to tarry in Turkey, because this country is so miserable and the people so ungracious'.[13] He then goes on to criticize the Scots for being upset at his plain speaking. At that stage, West still had more than ten days to go.

On 9 April, after a final, inconclusive meeting with James in the chapel at Holyrood – again interrupted, perhaps by design, by the Chapel Dean – West asked for leave to depart. It was granted readily, but with the instruction that he go and see the Queen and Prince James at Linlithgow the following day. There Margaret gave him tokens for Henry, for their younger sister Princess Mary and for Queen Katherine. West was taken to see the young Prince and reported to Henry that he is 'truly a very fair child and large for his age', which Henry may or may not have been pleased to hear.[14] There was no mention of the legacy, but it was to be just one of many items of complaint from James in a follow-up letter to Henry which took them no further forward.

It is a letter to Henry from Margaret dated 11 April, the day after her final meeting with West, that is more striking. It is written with a smattering of words in her new native tongue of Scots, most notable of which is 'fremdly'. Wrongly printed as 'friendly' in an early nineteenth-century reproduction,[15] its use was taken to be ironic. Not so, as 'fremdly' is the exact opposite of 'friendly'. It means 'strangely, unkindly and unfriendly'.[16] The letter may focus on the matter of the legacy, but more importantly it captures Margaret's rejection of Henry's attitude. After the usual niceties it comes to the point, here broadly rendered in modern English:

> I cannot believe that you conceived or commanded that I be so fremdly treated in relation to our father's legacy. I would not have spoken or written about it if the Doctor [West] had not raised it. My husband knows from what West said that it is withheld because of him and he will recompense me accordingly. I am ashamed about it and I wish to God it had never been raised. It is you in your letters about it who are treating it as a thing of importance. I lack nothing.

It is a straightforward repudiation of Henry's 'force of nature' approach to negotiation, his inability to separate the public and the private, his readiness to use anything, even such a thing of personal value as this, in order to get his way. The relationship between the two courts had broken down.

⇜ ✝ ⇝

In 1512 Edward Howard had not encountered France's best admiral. In 1513 he did. In the intervening period, Prégent de Bidoux, known as Prester John to the English and Scots, had worked his navy north around the Spanish coast. He did so in defiance of the Spanish fleet, which notionally at least was still supporting the English, and he found shelter in Portuguese ports before safely negotiating the final leg of the journey. He arrived in Brittany in the autumn.

Both the English and the French spent the winter of 1512–13 preparing for war. They did so without aid of allies. Ambassadors shuttled between France and Scotland. As for Henry's father-in-law, Ferdinand let down Henry once more and signed a truce with Louis on 1 April.

Both the English and French fleets were much stronger than they had been the year before. By the middle of March 1513 Howard had at his disposal twenty-four ships of a tonnage of 8,460 with 6,480 soldiers, gunners and sailors.[17] This compared very favourably with the eighteen ships of 4,750 tons and 3,700 men of spring 1512.[18] And so it should have done, because this was not a fleet designed 'to scour the sea', but to command it. Its pre-eminent purpose was to ensure the safe passage of Henry's invasion force from the English port of Dover to the English enclave of Calais. The navy was also needed to blockade its French counterpart and to protect against the real possibility of a French counter-invasion.

France had not had much of a navy when it successfully supported Henry Tudor's landing in 1485. But after the marriage of Anne of Brittany to first Charles VIII and then his cousin Louis XII, the addition of Breton vessels made France a major maritime power.[19] With the support of Scottish and possibly Danish ships it could secure control of the Channel for long enough to land an invading army. Louis even had a candidate for the English throne who in many eyes was far more plausible than Henry Tudor had been.

An effective blockade by the English required organization, including the efficient and timely provision of ordnance and of food and drink for the men. As Admiral, Sir Edward Howard was as responsible for this as he was for the fighting itself; but it proved to be beyond him. If the victualling of the year before was inadequate, then in 1513 it was a shambles. On 19 March, the fleet reached the end of the Thames Estuary en route to the Downs off the Kent coast. A mere three days later, Howard was writing to Henry from his flagship, the *Mary Rose* – a ship for which the King had a particular regard, as he may have helped design it.[20] In among the due obeisance, there was an intemperate, even desperate plea: 'Sir, for God's sake, have your Council send us our victuals.'[21] Howard could not hold position for long but had to beat back to port. On 5 April he wrote from Plymouth to Wolsey, who in contrast, was proving himself to be a brilliant planner and organizer: 'I pray to God that we linger no longer, for I assure you was never army [sic] so falsely vittalled.'[22] There then followed a litany of complaint and finger-pointing.

Well supplied or not, Sir Edward had to react to the potential movement of the French fleet out of Brest. On the 10th he left Plymouth, arriving near Brest the next day. The bulk of the French fleet was in harbour but well protected by natural defences and by manmade ones installed by Prégent. The French admiral also had the advantage that his Mediterranean fleet of galleys could lie in much shallower water. There was no way that Howard could sail into Brest and attack; he had no alternative but to blockade and hope for regular supply ships. These were only sporadic and the situation became acutely difficult. So much so that by 24 April he had a stark choice: either lift the blockade and return to England in shame and dishonour or find some means of attack. He chose the latter.

It was the foolhardy plan of a desperate man. It would have been difficult, even if undertaken at night and with the training of one of today's crack units such as the British Special Boat Squadron or the US Navy Seals. But there was no sense of stealth, as Howard launched an attack by rowbarges and smaller boats in the broad daylight of four o'clock in the afternoon of Monday, 25 April. With him in the leading barge were eighty men and perhaps a similar number in a second as, with the smaller boats in support, they rowed towards Prégent's galleys.[23] These lay in rock-protected shallow water and were defended, in Prégent's own words, by 'bulwarks full of ordinances[sic], the which were so thick with guns and crossbows that the quarrels and gunstones came together as thick as it had been hailstones'.[24] Miraculously, the leading rowbarge made it to Prégent's own vessel. Well armed and armoured, Howard led the charge on board. But only seventeen men followed him. The rope securing his boat to the galley had been cut, either by the French or, very possibly, considering the seemingly suicidal nature of their position, by his own crew. Howard got as far as the main deck, but once there, the French made short work of him and his men. Prégent's pikemen pushed Sir Edward against the ship's rails and then thrust him overboard. He sank like a stone. The rest of the assault craft made some impotent gestures of attack and then withdrew.

Three days later, French divers brought the English Admiral to the surface. To prevent the body's utter corruption while Prégent awaited Louis' instructions for its committal, it was at first salted and then properly embalmed. Sir Edward was buried somewhere in Brittany,[25] but possibly without his heart, as Prégent had asked for that himself. And there were further trophies for the French. Sir Edward Howard may have denied them one of his admiral's whistles because he had thrown it into the sea, but the other was sent to Anne of Brittany; and his clothes and, presumably, his armour, were sent to Louis' daughter Madame Claude.[26]

The English fleet quit their station and returned to Plymouth on 30 April. Their King was beside himself with rage. This was not because he was distraught at the loss of a friend; far from it. He was appalled at Howard's foolhardiness, at the breaking of the blockade, at the renewed threat of French invasion and the now near-mutinous state of the fleet. He turned to Edward's steadier elder brother Sir Thomas to sort out the mess as a matter of Howard family honour, and made him Lord Admiral in his turn. But this time Henry was less trusting and appointed that consummate administrative professional, Richard Fox, to assist him.

Time was now extraordinarily short to prepare for the invasion. The organization of the victuals improved but not the morale of the waiting men, who 'were in great fear of the galleys, and would rather go to Purgatory than the Trade [Brest],[27] as Sir Thomas wrote to Wolsey on 7 May from the *Mary Rose* in Plymouth. Desertion was a major concern, only partially allayed by Sir Thomas's erection of a gallows. There was a problem with the beer, not this time the lack of it, but, and this highlights the growing querulousness of the men, because they started being choosy and the blame was laid at the Lord Admiral's door. Four regional customs officers responsible for provisioning together wrote on 12 May to complain about it:

> Since the Admiral's coming, he has given orders, notwithstanding the King's and Council's commands, that no more beer is to be made in the West, as, being made of oaten malt, it will not keep so well as that made of barley malt. The soldiers are not as willing to drink it as the London beer brewed in March, which is the best month. Nevertheless, when in Brittany, they found no fault with it, but received it thankfully, and since they have been in Plymouth they have drank twenty-five tuns in twelve days; but now so much beer is come from London that they will not drink the country beer.[28]

The trouble was that these men, together with supplies for the invasion, were stuck in the Devonian and Cornish ports by contrary winds. The new Lord Admiral wrote to Wolsey and the King in detail. He even hurried up to London to explain in person, but tellingly, both Henry and Wolsey refused to see him. Henry had lost patience with Howard excuses and the Admiral, seeing which way the wind was blowing figuratively as well as literally, himself paid for the procurement and delivery of provisions for the troops massing at Southampton.[29]

Towards the end of June, everything finally came together for the invasion of France. It was achieved through the extraordinary hard work needed to please the impatient King, with the ultimate responsibility for coordinating operations falling to Wolsey. Fox offered him the true sympathy of someone who has endured a similar experience. He was writing specifically about the need, as ever, for new supplies of beer, 'which I pray God send us with speed' and he also had more general words of comfort, looking to the almighty to 'soon deliver you of your outrageous charge and labour'. However the old minister could not resist a bit of heavy teasing of his younger successor, by continuing with 'else ye shall have a cold stomach, little sleep, pale visage, and a thin belly, cum rara egestione [and hardly a bowel movement][30] all which, and as deaf as a stock, I had when I was in your case.'[31]

As for the Lord Admiral, he did not command the invasion fleet from Dover to Calais, but a diversionary one further south. He then hurried north to join the inner circle around the King, only to be told that his place was not there but back in England.[32]

⊰ ✝ ⊱

Following Dr West's return from Scotland, Henry's councillors were convinced that James would take some kind of action; but they were unsure about his specific plans.

On 4 June 1513, Fox wrote to Wolsey. The relationship between the two ministers was close enough for Fox to offer private criticism of the King's confrontational approach towards his Scottish counterpart. He commented drily, 'these recriminations do not tend towards amity'; it was still his opinion that 'James will make no actual war, but rob and spoil the King's subjects, especially by water'.[33] In short, that it would be a naval action that could, just, be accommodated within the Anglo-Scottish treaty. And that appeared to be what Louis wanted initially, though he vacillated between the idea of James assisting by land or sea. It was a long period of negotiation during which Louis' priorities fluctuated. In the end, it was a combination of three factors that decided matters.

Firstly, the lateness of the final agreement between James and Louis made it far more likely that the combined French and Scottish fleets would be able to counter Henry on his return from France, rather than on his outward voyage.

Secondly, James believed that Henry was now bent on subjugating him. Though he maintained that Henry had broken the peace, he knew that the judge and jury of the Pope with Bainbridge behind him would put the blame on him. With an Anglo-Scottish clash now almost certain, he would be advised to make a punitive raid against Henry's much weaker second-best army than against his best.

Finally, in terms of hard cash, Louis probably offered more for James to fight both by land and sea. With Henry seemingly determined to break the Perpetual Peace, any continuing advocacy by James for a purely naval war was no longer tenable. And with all-out war now inevitable, it made sense for James to negotiate the best possible price: certainly better than anything Henry was prepared to offer him. In short, he and Louis haggled. It may not have been the finally agreed amount, but in a letter of 8 May Louis was offering to stock Scottish ships with arms and armaments, including powder and guns, and to pay 50,000 francs – provided the ships arrived.[34] Louis even offered to throw Richard de la Pole into the deal, asking James whether he would like him sent over with the returning Scottish ships or 'kept till it is decided what is to be done with him'.[35] It seems the latter was chosen. Louis would not yet have known, but by 8 May, Richard de la Pole had become even more important: his elder brother Edmund, Earl of Suffolk, had been executed on Henry's orders four days before.

Louis wanted James to declare war immediately, but James was far too smart to do that. He was not going to risk Henry changing his target for attack – though that, of course, would have been fine for Louis. In any event, as soon as Henry had embarked his army for France, Louis expected James to invade 'in great force' so that 'he may more easily attain to the recovery of the crown of England', which he said 'belongs to the King of Scots as heir of St Margaret, Queen of Scotland, and also through his wife, elder daughter of the late King Henry'.[36] As the Papacy had sanctioned Henry's claim to the crown of France, Louis was quite happy to return the disfavour through supporting Henry's Scottish rival. As to James's own attitude, unless he had the added bonus of Henry being killed in France, the aim of his campaign was likely to be rather more limited. However he fully believed that he had justification for the action he would now take.

There would be just one further embassy between the two Kings, sent by James to Henry in France. It was the most important of all in clarifying the fundamental point of disagreement between England and Scotland. On 11 August, James's senior herald, Sir William Cumming of Inverallochy, Lyon King of Arms, arrived at Henry's camp at Thérouanne with the final letter from James, dated 26 July.[37] Henry read it immediately. There was no equivocation from James. He now believed that Henry had 'no intention of keeping good ways of justice, equity or kindness' as shown by the 'grievous injuries' that James had 'for long suffered', 'inflicted on himself and his subjects'. There followed a substantial list including: the failure to hand over, to face Scottish justice, the Bastard Heron and his accomplices for the murder of the Warden Sir Robert Ker; the imprisonment of Scottish subjects; the withholding of Margaret's legacy, just to spite him; 'the failure to redress the slaughter of Andrew Barton, carried out by Henry's own command; and the retention of Scottish ships and artillery'.[38] He also condemned Bainbridge's malign influence at Rome.

James then told Henry that he had completely lost faith in him. Most especially because Henry had refused to grant a safe conduct to his ambassadors – 'an action unheard of, even among infidels'.[39] Now, because justice had been denied to his subjects and because of Henry's unprovoked attack on Louis, to whom he was bound for mutual defence, James wrote that he 'will do what he trusts will make Henry abandon his attack on him'.[40] In short, it was war.

According to the near-contemporary chronicler, Edward Hall, the English King's response was extremely trenchant. Henry believed that James had revealed himself as the man he truly was: a coward, hypocrite and liar just like his Scottish forefathers.[41]

There was really only one defining point at issue, underlying everything else. It is captured in *Hall's Chronicle* in just a few words from the King of England and an even shorter riposte from the ambassador of the King of Scots. Henry's words were these:

> Say this to your master. I am the very owner of Scotland and he holds it through homage to me. Now contrary to his bounden duty as my vassal, he rebels against me. And tell him that with God's help I shall expel him from his kingdom on my return.

To which Sir William responded:

> Sir, I am his natural subject and he my natural lord … I may not say such words of reproach to him to whom *alone* I owe my allegiance and faith.[42]

The exchange represented the two positions exactly. They were irreconcilable. Either Scotland was an independent kingdom or it was not. The Treaty of Perpetual Peace was no more.

Sir William took a letter back from Henry, but by the time he arrived it was no longer relevant. Flodden had already been fought.

16

1513 – Katherine, Regent and
Governess of England

By Letters Patent of 6 June 1513, Henry made Katherine of Aragon's position clear before the invasion fleet left Dover for France on 30 June.[1] The Queen was declared: 'Katherine, Queen Consort. To be Regent and Governess of England, Wales, and Ireland, during the King's absence in his expedition against France.'[2] She was given complete military authority with the appropriate executive and monetary powers. She could 'issue commissions of muster and array'; 'appoint sheriffs'; employ the signet 'to warrant the Chancellor to use the Great Seal' and 'issue warrants under her sign manual to John Heron,[3] treasurer of the King's chamber, for payment of such sums as she may require'. In addition, in everything bar the appointment of bishops, Katherine was to have the same control over church appointments as Henry himself. She was to be aided by a small council led by the Lord Chancellor, Archbishop Warham, and by the Treasurer of the Household, Sir Thomas Lovell. They were there to advise her, but Henry made it clear that her word was to be taken as his own.

Katherine was the one whom Henry ultimately trusted to provide additional supplies for the war in France and – as guardian of the realm – to defend England against a Scottish invasion. It spoke of the closeness of their relationship and was a recognition that Katherine's loyalties were to Henry and to England. She may not yet have produced the male heir which she herself, her King and her country craved, but she was given an extraordinary amount of power for a Queen Consort. It would be Katherine, rather than Henry, who would be James's strategic rival in 1513.

The previous November, the well-connected Venetian merchant

Lorenzo Pasquaglio described Henry as a 'King bent on war', united with his Queen who 'wills it' against a Council 'averse to it'.[4] With her Regency, she was now an active partner as well as a supporter of her husband.

In April 1513, Ferdinand had signed his truce with France and thus let down Henry for a third time, sparking Katherine's comment in a letter of 26 July to Wolsey in France that she trusted to God that Henry, with Emperor Maximilian, would have 'as great a victory as any Prince in the world; and this I pray God send him without need of any other Prince'[5] – namely her father. Though now disappointed by Ferdinand's diplomatic vacillations and deceits, Katherine could take inspiration from the role that he and, more particularly, her mother had played during her childhood. Ferdinand and Isabella had been companions in arms as much as joint rulers of Spain and, when it came to their wars, Isabella had taken the leading part. Isabella's own kingdom of Castile was larger and historically more powerful than Ferdinand's Aragon, but she had needed to display military prowess as well as political cunning to inherit and then secure it. It was only after she had control of her own future that Isabella linked her kingdom to Ferdinand's.

She had proceeded to demonstrate her strategic mastery during the decade-long war against the Moorish kingdom of Granada. Astute in her campaign planning, she had organized the supply of men and materials. She had also shown a keen interest in military tactics and the weapons needed for their implementation. It was Isabella who ordered supplies of gunpowder from across Europe and set up new forges in Spain to produce the siege artillery required for battering the enemy's citadels into submission, bringing final victory in 1492.[6]

Isabella had moved continually to keep close to her advancing army and in control of it. Even when she was pregnant, as in 1485 with Katherine, she did not stint. Unusual for her time, she did not want to be considered unique within her own family and expected the same sort of application to be shown by her children, female as well as male. Through education and upbringing, Katherine was prepared for her role in 1513. She took to her task with zeal.

In matters of war, as in much else, Isabella had ensured that

Katherine would share her interests. Henry's Queen may have participated in the same cheerleading activities as earlier English consorts, writing to Wolsey that she was 'horrible busy with making standards, banners and badges,'[7] but these were for troops under her own command. Indeed, she had been fully involved with weightier matters for some time. It had been Katherine, rather than Henry, who the previous November had asked the Venetian Ambassador, Andrea Badoer, about the cost of galleys and shown herself to be 'very warm in favour of this expedition'[8] against France.

It would be she who wrote to the Mayor and Sheriffs of Gloucester on 4 August, expressing surprise that her 'former letters, for the Council's information as to men and harness in that town, are unanswered.'[9] There would be no need of a further reminder: the Mayor and Sheriffs gave her everything she required and within the strict time limits set down.

With Chancellor Warham managing routine administration, Katherine took charge of the defence of the realm. Warham proved to be more hindrance than help when he reignited a long-running diocesan turf war with the Bishop of Winchester, his fellow Councillor Richard Fox.[10] Far more useful, indeed indispensable, to the Queen was Lovell, a Privy Councillor of Henry VII who under his son had retained importance as a man of considerable financial acumen, administrative competence and reliability in matters of national security.[11] He deputized as Lord Steward for George Talbot Earl of Shrewsbury; as Earl Marshal, in place of the Earl of Surrey; and for the Queen herself, to discharge those military duties for which she deemed herself, as a woman, unsuited.[12]

As soon as the fleet set sail, bearing the young King on his French adventure, Katherine began the return journey to London. She was accompanied by the two Thomases upon whom she would now rely most closely: Sir Thomas Lovell and Thomas Howard, Earl of Surrey.[13]

Katherine was in need of consolation after the departure of Henry, her passionate belief in the rightness of his cause being tempered by the fears for his personal safety that would pour out in her letters to Henry himself and to Wolsey.

She was not alone in being disconsolate: Surrey, England's leading military man, with battle honours going back over forty years and with dedicated service to both Tudor Henrys, was not going to share in what promised to be the most glorious military undertaking of his life. He was to be left behind. Long returned from his temporary 'retirement', Surrey had given enormous service in recruiting troops and inspecting the country's defences in preparation for the 1513 invasion of France, a venture designed to bear comparison with the great enterprises of Henry V. But he himself was to have no role there.

Instead, he was asked to patrol the North. Before his departure from Dover, Henry had turned to Surrey and said: 'My lord, I trust not the Scots, therefore I pray you not be negligent.'[14] It had elicited the respectful reply: 'I shall do my duty and Your Grace shall find me diligent and to fulfil your will shall be my gladness.'[15] Surrey also had darker thoughts which he left unsaid to Henry. He knew that personal access to the King during Henry's expected campaign of glory would have helped to reinvigorate the Howards' fortunes. The traditional role of the nobility was to serve as a warrior class *with* their king and it was a dishonour not to be a part of 'the flower of all the nobility'[16] fighting on French soil. This was particularly so for Surrey, a man of unrivalled military experience forced to give way to novices at fighting real wars. Displaced by Wolsey from Henry's close political counsels, Surrey was now excluded from his military ones. In exchange, he was expected to return, with his sons, to the type of fighting he had undertaken so often before, that of unglamorous border warfare, with its raid and counter-raid; this time with the fear that a cross-border incursion by the Scots would not be a feint but the real thing, bringing devastation to the country and destruction to the Howard family in its wake.[17] He would also have noticed that Thomas Grey, Marquess of Dorset, the disgraced commander of the year before, was at Henry's side.

And that Lord Thomas Darcy, who had served under him in the 1497 campaign, was going to France with Henry, which was remarkable for two reasons: not only had Darcy been the leader of the aborted 1511 Moorish campaign, but he was also Captain of Berwick and had taken men from Northumberland to fight with him in France. At one and the same time it showed the Howards' fall from prominence and betokened a worrying lack of concern about the Scottish threat.[18]

Surrey could not utter any criticism of the English King for this setback, but he most certainly blamed the Scottish one, saying: 'Sorry may I see him ere I die, that is the cause of my abiding behind. If ever he and I meet, I shall do all that lies within me to make him as sorry, if I can.'[19] No longer James's boon companion of the 1503 wedding celebrations and the Perpetual Peace, Surrey began to prepare for war with efficiency and grim determination.

Most immediately, he began to recruit from his own household and tenants. The five hundred men gathered from this source were likely to be dependable on the battlefield, as their futures were interwoven with the Howards themselves. This number, raised from one noble's own resources, might have been of concern during the Wars of the Roses. But the spectre of bastard feudalism had now gone; these men were placed at the service of the King and of his Regent, the Queen. The parade of Surrey's troops in London on 21 July, formally mustered in front of Lovell, was the most likely occasion[20] for the oration by Katherine of Aragon, proudly reported later that year by Pietro Martire d' Anghiera, the Italian humanist who had been her teacher in Spain:

> Queen Katherine, in imitation of her mother Isabella, who had been left regent in the King's absence, made a splendid oration to the English captains, told them to be ready to defend their territory, that the Lord smiled upon those who stood in defence of their own, and they should remember that English courage excelled that of all other nations.[21]

The next day, Surrey's forces began the journey north, integrating new recruits en route and holding them to a strict discipline. The common soldiery were banned from playing cards and dice, to

Henry VII

As a measure to secure his throne and dynasty, he agreed the Treaty of Perpetual Peace with James IV of Scotland. By novel and arbitrary means he raised vast sums of money and spent lavishly on ceremony and display. His clothes in his later years may often have been sombre, but they were of the richest and most expensive fabrics.

James IV
Having succeeded his father in deeply suspicious circumstances, the youthful James matured to unite his country and assert Scotland's position as an independent European power.

Margaret Tudor
James IV's Queen. It was through her – and not through her brother Henry VIII – that future Kings of England, as well as Scotland, would ultimately descend.

The arms of Henry VII

VIVE LE NOBLE ROY HENRY

The arms of James IV

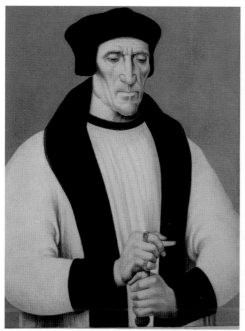

(top left)
Richard Fox, Bishop of Winchester (formerly Bishop of Durham)

(top right)
Thomas Howard, Earl of Surrey, the English Commander at Flodden

(right) **Thomas Wolsey**, whose service to Henry VIII was (as shown here) to bring him rich rewards.

A model of Richmond Palace on the River Thames – 'this earthly and second Paradise of our region of England'.

The Great Hall of Stirling Castle – James IV created brilliant settings for his exercise of power through heightened ceremony.

(top left)
Alexander VI (the Borgia Pope) by Pinturicchio

(top right)
Julius II (the Warrior Pope) by Raphael

(left)
Leo X (a Medici Pope) by Raphael

(top left)
Mazzoni's bust of a boy
(purported to be Henry VIII)

(top right)
Henry VIII as a youth

(right)
Erasmus, the great humanist
scholar who was impressed by
Prince Henry and who tutored
James IV's brilliant son, Alexander.
Portrait by Holbein.

Katherine of Aragon

Henry VIII's Queen and 'Regent and Governess of England, Wales, and Ireland, during the King's absence in his expedition against France'

Henry VIII

It was between the years 1509 and 1513 that Henry changed from a hesitant youth to the commanding figure shown here in c. 1520.

James IV in 1507 – the year the Pope awarded him the blessed Sword and Hat 'as a defender of the rights and liberties of the Church and of the Apostolic See'. He was the first King of Scots in more than three centuries to receive it.

Pattern for James IV's projected gold coin of 1513. The obverse shows the crusading archangel Michael slaying a dragon; the reverse depicts a ship and a Latin legend meaning 'Saviour in this sign hast thou conquered'. The coin echoes the intended use for James's navy in 1513.

A model of the *Michael* – James IV's great ship, the largest in Europe

The *Mary Rose* – it was the Howards' flagship in 1513

(top left)
Emperor Maximilian by Dürer

(top right)
Louis XII of France enters Genoa in 1507.

Maximilian's children: Philip the Fair of Burgundy (Henry VIII's childhood hero) and
Margaret of Austria

Admiral Howard in later life as the 3rd Duke of Norfolk. Portrait by Holbein.

Brian Tuke, who served as Henry VIII's and Wolsey's correspondence secretary during the 1513 campaign. Later portrait by Holbein.

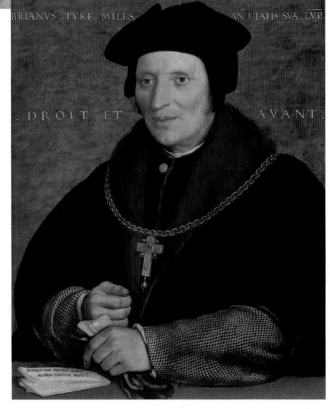

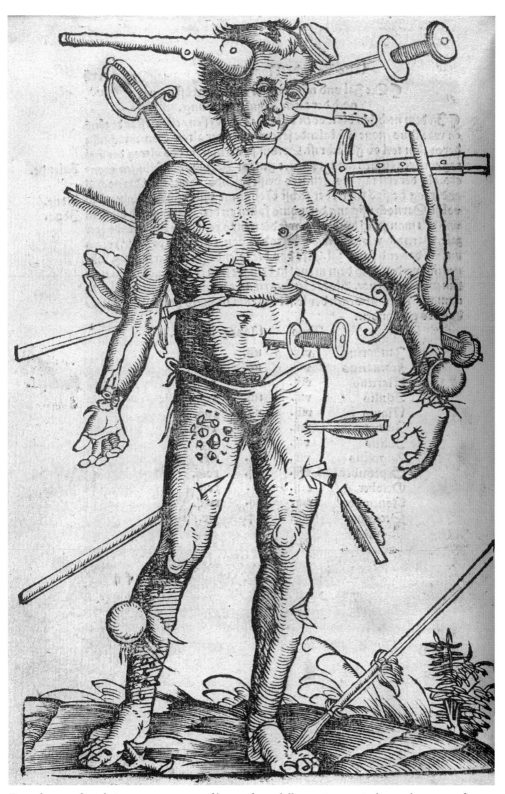

From late medieval times, surgeons used 'wound men' illustrations to indicate the types of battle injury they would need to treat. This 'Wound Man' was published in 1517.

The Flodden Monument on Piper's Hill looking towards Branxton Hill.

On the down slope of Branxton Hill, after heavy rain. On the ridge to the north-west (top left) is the Monument.

avoid the violent gambling disputes that went with them, though noblemen and captains were trusted to 'play at their pleasures within their own tents'.[22] At Doncaster, Surrey commanded Sir William Bulmer to advance with all speed northwards. Bulmer, a Yorkshire landowner who had distinguished himself at Norham in 1497 and been knighted for it,[23] was now to wait near the Border with two hundred mounted archers and look for any signs of Scottish troop movements.

❧ ✝ ❧

On 21 July, the same day that Surrey paraded his troops in London, Henry's army of 28,000 men began the march south-east out of the town of Calais and into the surrounding area known as the Pale. That afternoon and night, they marched in driving rain and mud, before making camp at Fréthun. Though they were still in English territory, they had to beware enemy movements and to post a strong watch guard, which gave Henry the opportunity to ride among them in the early hours of the morning, in imitation of Henry V before Agincourt, and to raise their morale by doing so.[24]

Because the Pale of Calais was an enclave eighteen miles long by eight to ten miles deep and because the pace of the march was dictated by the slowness of the all-important train of siege artillery, it was not until 25 July that the English army moved into enemy territory near Ardres. As if with precise synchronization, Katherine, from Richmond, wrote to Wolsey the next day, worrying about Henry's safety and asking for regular reports, 'for when you are so near our enemies I shall never be at rest unless I often see letters from you'.[25] It would be another week before Henry's forces, travelling at a rate of around three miles per day, reached Thérouanne. They arrived outside the town on 1 August and joined the advance guard, which, under the command of the Earl of Shrewsbury and Lord Herbert, had begun the siege operation just over a month before and were thus already well entrenched.[26]

Katherine's next letter is missing, though we know of her unease, because she wrote from Windsor on 1 August to Maximilian's daughter, Margaret of Austria, and asked whether she might send her physician to Henry, to be sure that he would have the best care. On the

13th, she was back at Richmond and her letter to Wolsey contained expressions of inadequately concealed apprehension:

> Until I saw your letter, I was troubled to hear that the King was so near to the siege at Thérouanne, because of the personal danger; but now I thank God you have assured me of the good care he is taking to avoid all manner of dangers. I pray that you, good Master Almoner, remind the King to always continue in the same way.[27]

Katherine understood the role Henry was playing. So inspired by the example of his illustrious predecessor Henry V, and now four years off the leash of his father's protection, Henry VIII could well turn out to be rash in leading his troops. It was far from unknown for an English king to be killed in battle – Richard III's death had established the Tudor dynasty – or to be mortally wounded in siege warfare like Richard I. Katherine's letters to the Continent relate her own actions and those of her Council, commending the latter and cleverly inciting Henry to do the same,[28] but they are also fraught with anxiety. For she knew her Henry well enough: that he wanted to be seen to be in the thick of the action, inspiring his men by showing no sign of fear of physical danger. After all, it was he, rather than Arthur, whom God had chosen to rule.

Katherine's concern went beyond that of a loving wife. She was alarmed for her own sake, as she had practical experience of being the widow of a Tudor prince. She was also anxious for her adopted country, as the death of Henry without an heir would mean the end of his dynasty and almost certain chaos. It was a point well put by perhaps the most hated of his father's ministers: Edmund Dudley. In *The Tree of Commonwealth*, which Dudley had time to write in the year between his arrest and his execution, he addressed the new King directly about hazarding his health in sport: 'And, in the reverence of God, somewhat beware of dangerous sports for casualties that might befall, and the more so because in your single person depends the whole wealth and honour of this your realm.'[29] Pertinent in 1510, it was even more applicable in 1513, because Henry was still without an heir and the danger was no longer sport but war.

With no clear male heir to succeed, Henry's death would

probably return the English nobility to civil war. Or, perhaps even more unthinkable in the summer of 1513, it could give England over to Henry's senior blood relative, Margaret Tudor, which would mean the effective control of her husband – James IV of Scotland.

17

1513 – War

All had been quiet on the Scottish Border in the days before the English invasion force sailed for Calais. Dacre for one was unalarmed about Scottish intentions. On 25 June, in response to Surrey's queries about potential Scottish incursions, he wrote back that he 'neither sees, hears nor knows of any such appearance or likelihood in the Scots'.[1] Indeed, he found the Scots officials 'so well disposed touching the good rule of the Borders' that he 'has no cause of complaint'.[2]

In Edinburgh, a little over forty miles north of England's border fortress of Norham, the scene was rather different. Preparations were being made in earnest, though of course, the Scots were hardly starting from scratch. James had artillery weapons from the time of his grandfather James II such as Mons Meg, even some from his great-grandfather James I. He was not, however, relying on old wrought-iron equipment. Entries in the Treasurer's Accounts from 1507 onwards show that James, like his European fellow rulers, was turning to bronze.[3] His absorption with guns at the time of Wolsey's visit was scarcely an isolated event. The newer pieces being produced by the Frenchmen who had been working since 1511 under the direction of the King's 'Master Melter' Robert Borthwick,[4] were state of the art. Additional guns had come from Louis: 'eight serpentines of brass for the field' were delivered by De La Mothe to James in December 1512, as the vigilant Dacre reported to Henry.[5] James also had others bought from a Dutch foundry.[6]

This time Mons Meg would be left behind. The Treasurer's Accounts reveal the full extent of royal expenditure on the casting and manufacture of new guns between March and August 1513,[7] for use both on land and at sea.

On 24 July the King issued proclamations to 'all Scotland, east and west, south and north – as much in the Isles as inland – that they should be in readiness within twenty days warning to pass with him where he pleased with forty days provision'.[8]

The very next day, the Scottish fleet set sail along the Firth of Forth, with King James himself on board as far as the Isle of May. It may have been smaller than the English fleet, but it contained the King's great ships: the *Michael*, the *Margaret* and the *James*. In all, there were probably twenty-two vessels.[9] Commanding the fleet was the King's cousin, James Hamilton, 1st Earl of Arran, who had presided over an unsuccessful Danish expedition in 1502. Its failure being ascribed to the ships themselves rather than their commander, and with Arran in any case being an intimate of James, further preferment had followed, vindicated by a successful assault against the Isles in 1504.

The ships did not steer south when they reached the open sea, as might have been expected. Instead they turned north. As ordered by James, and presumably agreed by Louis, they were to arrive at the English Channel by the longer route, through the Pentland Firth and down the West Coast of Britain. This gave them the opportunity to combine with the Irish chieftain O'Donnell and stir up trouble for the Anglo-Irish in Ulster, the principle being that any action that might divert English forces from France would be beneficial. Arran bombarded Carrickfergus, the chief English stronghold there, but there was no sign that it leeched away any of Henry's resources in men and munitions from the war on the Continent. In fact, with a delay in Ayr taking on supplies and another through storms, the ships did not reach France until September.[10] It was a month later than Louis had originally expected and the pride of the Scottish navy, including the *Great Michael*, instead of coordinating with the French fleet, lay idle at Brest.[11]

This could not have gone according to King James's plan. His intentions are indicated by the special coin in preparation in 1513. On the obverse of the surviving pattern is the crusading archangel Michael slaying a dragon and on the reverse a ship with the Scottish arms and a telling phrase. In Latin it says '*Salvator in hoc signo vicisti*' – 'Saviour in this sign hast thou conquered'.[12] The coin was intended to be part of James's propaganda to indicate to Europe's other rulers that he was sincere in his advocacy of a crusade and to illustrate his original intention that the Scottish action in the impending European conflict would be naval.

This sense of priorities was also reflected in James's allocation of his best gunners. These were highly valuable technicians, some of whom had been with James since before the 1496 campaign. Their importance is highlighted by their being mentioned individually by name in the Treasurer's Accounts. There they are still: the Flemish Hans, the Frenchman Guyane and the Scotsman Robert Herwort – men who had shown their skill in royal service in the 1490s against England and in the campaigns against the Isles. For 1513 there are star names such as the Fleming Henrik 'Cutlug' and his compatriot Jacob 'the Maister gunnar'.[13] Having your best gunners on board your ships made sound sense if you were anticipating a naval battle. For one thing, firing at a moving target from a moving platform required greater skill than firing on land; for another, with the advent of naval firepower, there was the opportunity, at the very least, to disable your enemy from afar. If the Scots and the French were denied the chance to intercept Henry's invasion fleet en route to France, then there was certainly the potential to do so on the return voyage.

As luck would have it, the Franco-Scottish ships were scattered by hostile winds and the English had no trouble in making it safely home. It was certainly not James's expectation that his fleet would play such an insignificant part in the events of 1513. The allocation of James's master gunners is proof enough of that, with the vast majority being sent to sea.[14] It would be up to the likes of Patrick Panter, former tutor to Alexander Stewart and then the King's Secretary, to fire James's artillery at Flodden.

⊰ ✝ ⊱

In the event, James's actual war was to be on land. At around the time that his final letter reached Henry, English and Scottish troops had clashed.[15] Alexander Lord Hume and a large force of Borderers had crossed the Tweed in early August and embarked on a hard-riding spree of theft and destruction in North Northumberland. They largely did so with impunity until they were just a few miles from re-crossing the river on 13 August.[16] Surrey's strategic good sense in sending Sir William Bulmer north with his mounted archers was now made manifest; so was Bulmer's tactical nous. The archers, hidden among thick bushes of broom on Milfield Plain, ambushed the Scots. Many of Hume's men were killed and the rest, to save their lives, left their plunder behind. For good reason, it became known as the 'Ill Raid'.[17] The action was in no way significant in deciding the outcome of the main encounter; though it might have had an influence on James's later decision to avoid fighting on Milfield Plain.

❧ ✚ ☙

Two days before, in France, Henry had been joined by his ally Emperor Maximilian[18] and together they planned an ambush of their own. Spies had discovered a French scheme to break through the siege lines and relieve Thérouanne, but not its exact timing. Thus, though in place by midnight on 15 August, the Anglo-German troops spent most of the next day waiting with the mixed emotions of soldiers faced with possible but not certain action. The feelings of its exhilarated young commander were, as later letters testify,[19] rather different. He had at his side and in an advisory role, the Holy Roman Emperor Maximilian, the grandest ruler in Europe and the father of his late hero, Philip of Burgundy. Furthermore, Maximilian was more than willing to make tactful suggestions, such as giving Henry the idea of placing some light artillery on a small but strategic hill.[20] So he should have been, as Henry was not only paying him a fat mercenary fee, but also conducting the campaign just over Maximilian's own frontier, making the Emperor the better placed to benefit. Even Maximilian's wearing the cross of St George was not a selfless compliment to the English King, because it was also the badge of his own Order of Chivalry. None of this mattered to Henry: he had money to burn and he was burning it. As Steven Gunn has so pithily put it: 'for Henry VIII and those around him, war was something great kings did.'[21]

After the pacific approach of Henry VII's later years, waging war was a popular policy with the warrior nobility. It gave many of them a sense of place and purpose in the Tudor monarchy; for although they had a new King and, from 1511, a different foreign policy, that did not mean that the growing grip of the central administration and the threat to the more slow-witted of the noble class had abated. Turning to Gunn again:

> Many noblemen felt rather uneasy in Henry's England. At court they were edged from power by monopolistic ministers, rakehell favourites and low-born lawyers. In the country their influence was undermined by centralizing law courts, royal dependence on the gentry in local government and restraints on their recruitment of retinues of political and military followers.[22] War made noblemen feel at home. They could follow in the footsteps of the ancestors who had won their titles on the fields of France. They could recruit men with the King's blessing, dress them in their livery colours and family badges and bond with them on campaign. If all went well, they could win the King's confidence, gratitude and reward.[23]

This would best be done at close quarters, of course; hence Surrey's cry of anguish at being excluded from the main event. But as Gunn has noted, only one of the thirty-four English peers of fighting age was not engaged in some way with the 1513 campaign, either in France, at sea, or against the Scots.[24] In the late afternoon of 16 August, outside the village of Guinegatte, south of Thérouanne, those with Henry and Maximilian were given their opportunity.

France's elite cavalry, the gendarmerie, came into the ambushers' view. The French, unaware of the cannon, archers and cavalry of the Anglo-Imperial forces, sped on. They were met with a combination of artillery fire and an arrow storm, coming from the front and to the side of them. To escape the trap, the leading horsemen tried to pull up and those behind crashed into them. The pride of the French crumpled into chaos. For any riders still able, there was no alternative but to turn and attempt to race away at full gallop, with their enemy's cavalry in hot pursuit. At this suitably named Battle of the Spurs, Henry's army captured nine standards and two hundred and fifty men, including five high-ranking nobles. In terms of size it was not a major engagement but all the same it was an extremely important one. Henry, after so many false starts, had his victory at last; it was the French and in particular the gendarmerie, who had to cope with the humiliation of being called 'hares in armour'.[25]

No doubt Henry would have enjoyed fighting personally, but he had to take on the more important role of kingly generalship. After the shambles at Fuenterrabia, the humiliation against Prégent's galleys and, further back, the disastrous end of the Hundred Years War, he had restored the dignity of the English as a fighting force. The invasion of 1513 was far more spectacular than the sorties into France of Henry's grandfather Edward IV in 1475 and his father in 1492. These had brought material rewards, through the respective treaties of Picquigny and Étaples. But where was the prestige when there was no real fighting? Where was the honour in being paid to go away? Henry had thirsted for glory and he had won it. He had taken illustrious French prisoners and been able, ever so gallantly, to patronize them over dinner.[26] This brash young upstart King had won himself a place at the top table of European affairs.

England's success was amplified by France's failure. Through the very presence of Henry's army – and of the Sforza-funded Swiss invasion of French Burgundy following their crushing victory at the Battle of Novara – Louis had to remove his forces from Italy. It was a reverse for the French plan to dominate the Italian peninsula, the core of French foreign policy, overtly from 1494 and more covertly for many years before.

Katherine received the news from Wolsey. She replied, telling him that she was reassured now that Henry had the benefit of Maximilian's 'good counsel' because 'his Grace shall not adventure himself so much as I was afraid of before'.[27] Her sense of relief intermixed with joy is palpable. Perhaps Wolsey over-egged the report, or perhaps it is an indication of her anxiety, but Katherine went completely over the top in declaring 'the victory so great that I think none has been seen before'.[28] She was under strain and also possibly pregnant. She was certainly not pleased to hear a few days later that Henry was sending her home a trophy in the form of King Louis' cousin, François, Duc de Longueville. Henry was harking back to the Battle of Agincourt: King Louis was the son of Charles, Duc d'Orléans, captured at Agincourt and held in captivity in England for almost a quarter of a century. Henry relished the symbolic power of placing another Orléanais duke in honourable English confinement. But as Katherine wrote to Wolsey on 2 September, Lord Mountjoy, the last potential host, was about to depart for Calais. There was no one suitable to look after Longueville, so he would have to be lodged in the Tower. She herself was fully occupied, 'specially the Scots being so busy as they now be, and I looking for my departing every hour'.[29]

The Scots were indeed 'busy'. They were in the north of Henry's kingdom, with James's siege artillery blasting England's remaining border fortresses into submission. Moreover, the size of James's army indicated the seriousness of his intent. Katherine and Lovell were preparing to leave for the Midlands to raise more troops.

Katherine was composed in her reply to Henry, apparently describing the duke as a great gift, but hoped in her turn to send Henry a king.[30]

⇛ ✝ ⇚

In France, Henry took possession of Thérouanne. With the rout of its relieving troops, the town faced starvation and surrendered in a week. Henry gave it as a gift to Maximilian, who, with the exception of the cathedral, razed the town to the ground.[31] The season was now too late for a further push towards Paris. There was no disgrace in that; even Henry V had needed rather more than one campaign to take the French capital with his Burgundian allies. There was still time, however, to move north-east, in order to besiege Tournai, which was on the very frontier of France and the Burgundian Netherlands.

But first Henry went to Lille to see Margaret of Austria, Duchess of Savoy. In addition to being Maximilian's daughter and Regent of the Netherlands, she was also the sister of Henry's friend Philip and guardian of Philip's son, the future Charles V. In true Burgundian fashion, Margaret kept a glittering court. Henry and his gallants delighted in the opportunity for rest and recreation. The Milanese Ambassador, Paulo da Laude, described Henry as 'wonderfully merry' and getting on famously with Margaret: 'the king danced with her from the time the banquet finished until nearly day, in his shirt and without shoes.' Da Laude even commends Henry's dancing style: 'in this he does wonders and leaps like a stag'.[32]

Soon, however, it was back to the war. Brian Tuke, personal secretary to the King and Wolsey,[33] wrote to Richard Pace, Bainbridge's secretary in Rome and summed up Tournai's importance, stressing, perhaps inadvertently, its value to Maximilian. He described it as 'the largest city in all Flanders, and the most populous of any on that side of Paris'. He also explained that Henry was placing himself in danger once again: 'the besiegers walk close to the walls daily, and the king himself does so occasionally, for three hours and a half at a time'.[34] Katherine was preoccupied with events in the North, but had she known, she would have been horrified. Not for long though, as Tournai surrendered after just eight days.

The prestige of capturing Tournai was undeniable, but the strategic advantage of retaining it was far less obvious.

18

Invasion

The final muster of King James's Scottish army was to be at Ellem, north of Duns. Some of his forces, brought together by his nobles and by his compliant clergy from the length and breadth of his kingdom, went directly there. Other troops assembled on Edinburgh's Burghmuir, the common moor south of the city walls, then an expanse of five square miles. It was from Edinburgh that James's guns were transported, his five cannons starting two days before the rest, hauled by teams of thirty-six oxen yoked fore and aft to act as motor and brake for their journey up hill and down dale to the Border.[1] Later came the lighter guns and the stone and metal balls, together with the vast quantities of powder needed to fire them.[2] On the morning of Friday, 19 August, James's leading troops marched out of the city and James left Edinburgh the same evening.[3]

The experience of James's campaigns of 1496 and 1497 prepared the way for the transport of his ordnance in 1513. Its conveyance was much easier this time, as he felt able to leave Mons Meg behind. The giant bombard's days were over; James's new guns were lighter, readily transportable and more effective. Made of bronze, they were manufactured using the same techniques employed to make church bells – a neat reversal of the biblical homily of turning swords into ploughshares. They were cast in one piece rather than the wrought-iron guns' two layers bound with hoops. This made them less likely to explode and thus safer than their predecessors. They were also extremely potent: they could be fired more often and carry a much heavier charge of powder which, combusting with far greater force, propelled their iron balls a vast distance.

The bronze of the guns lent itself to rich decoration and made these weapons objects of conspicuous display akin to a royal tapestry

or a painted window. They were much more expensive than their predecessors and highly valued by the rulers who commissioned them.
In fact, as Professor Thomas Arnold notes: 'Princes thought of their
cannon as pets, like great metal horses or dogs.'[4] Henry VIII, James
IV, Maximilian, Louis XII – indeed, all the militarily active rulers
of Renaissance Europe – took a keen personal interest in their artillery. In peacetime, cannon salutes were made at every ceremonial
opportunity; in warfare they were most often used for destroying the
redoubts of recalcitrant noble subjects or the town walls or castles of
foreign rulers and their peoples.

We know that in 1513 James's artillery at the very least consisted of five cannon, two culverins, four sakers and six serpentines
as well as other smaller pieces.[5] The first seven larger guns were
called the 'Seven Sisters' by Robert Lindsay of Pitscottie, a historian writing a half-century or so later.[6] They had a greater range
than Mons Meg, particularly the longer-barrelled culverin,[7] and
though they had a much smaller ball of perhaps 22.75 kg (50 lbs)
as against Meg's 330 lbs, they caused more damage. The iron (as
opposed to stone) balls crashed against a fortification wall with
vastly greater velocity – particularly at close range from the shorter-
barrelled cannon. This added firepower was due to the guns themselves and an improved understanding of gunpowder. Not only could
the bronze guns take a larger quantity of powder, the chemical com-
position was far more explosive. By experimentation, or even trial and
error, the right grades and mixtures of sulphur, charcoal and potas-
sium nitrate (saltpetre) had been discovered. No doubt James was
enjoying himself, but he was also engaged on serious business when
he and Abbot Damian were experimenting in 1508 and keeping
Ambassador Wolsey waiting. The smaller guns, the sakers and the
serpentines, had a smaller ball but a range comparable to the larger
guns.

James's entire force came together at Ellem on 22 August and the
bulk of it crossed the Tweed near Coldstream.[8] At 42,000 it was the
largest ever Scottish army to invade England. This shows the commitment behind the campaign: for unlike their English opponents,
the Scottish army was unpaid. It was raised on a feudal basis through

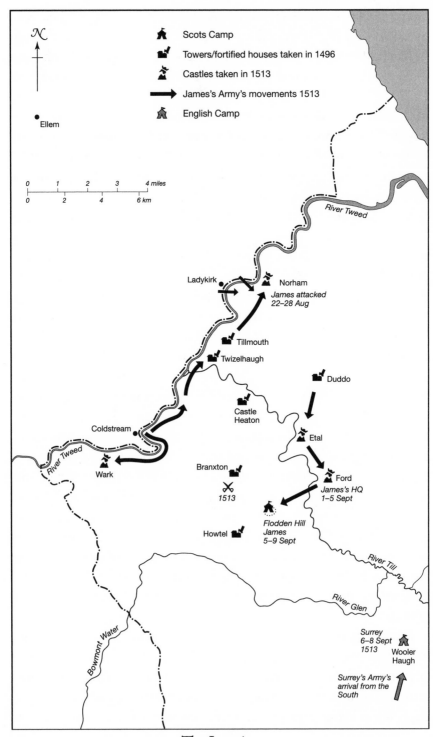

N

Scots Camp	
Towers/fortified houses taken in 1496	
Castles taken in 1513	
James's Army's movements 1513	
English Camp	

• Ellem

0   1   2   3   4 miles
0   2   4   6 km

River Tweed

Ladykirk •

Norham
*James attacked
22–28 Aug*

Tillmouth

Twizelhaugh

Duddo

Castle
Heaton

Etal

Coldstream •

River Tweed

Wark

Branxton

✗
1513

Ford
*James's HQ
1–5 Sept*

Flodden Hill
*James
5–9 Sept*

Howtel

River Till

River Glen

Bowmont Water

Surrey
*6–8 Sept
1513*
Wooler
Haugh

*Surrey's Army's
arrival from the
South*

The Invasion

personal obligation of lesser rank to higher. This operated through the well-named bonds of 'manrent', formal contracts of mutual assistance and protection – a system that could break down into a form of bastard feudalism under a weak ruler; and through a national levy. Under James, there was greater reliance on the levy. In Scotland, as in England, every man between the ages of sixteen and sixty was considered to be of fighting age. In both countries, musters or wappinshaws were held on a regular basis, either semi-annually or quarterly, to check that the potential recruits owned the proper equipment.[9]

Theoretically, all Scots in that age band could be called to serve at their own expense – and to carry their own food – for a maximum of forty days per year.[10] It meant that Scottish campaigns had to be short and focused. Though men owed loyalty in a network of obligation, firstly to their immediate superior and beyond that to the King himself, a close watch had to be kept for potential deserters. However, for the brave and the enterprising there was the prospect of booty; for everyone there was the incentive of fighting the English.

From Coldstream, one part of the Scottish force moved a mile and a half south-west to Wark, while the rest proceeded eight miles to the north-east and Norham. It is likely that most of James's guns, in the manner of 1497, opened up against Norham Castle from the Scottish side of the border. Then, when the south bank of the Tweed had been secured, the King's prized artillery was taken across the fords on either side of Ladykirk, in order, in the words of Edward Hall, to 'sore abate the walls' of the castle from close range.

James had not gained Norham's surrender in 1497 and its defences were even stronger in 1513. Bishop Ruthall had added a wall that included gun casements.[11] The Bishop had also returned rapidly to England from Henry's invasion force in France and, as one of the King's leading administrators, had no difficulty in arranging food and munitions for John Anislow, his captain at Norham.[12]

On 24 August James called a Council at Twizelhaugh, midway between Coldstream and Norham. It was bound to be considered a more formal General Council[13] because the bulk of his politically active nobility and many of his senior clergy were there and came from all parts of James's newly unified country. James's key commanders knew each other well; they had worked together in administration and on James's Council. For example, it is not strange that Alexander, Lord Hume, from the Borders and George Gordon, 2nd Lord Huntly, whose power base was in the Highlands, should fight together at Flodden with the men from their very different areas, because they had been allies in Council.

As well as Huntly, there were at least nine other earls on the campaign, and aside from Hume there were at least thirteen other lords of Parliament. In spite of later claims,[14] Archibald Douglas, Earl of Angus ('Bell the Cat'), was almost certainly not there – he was in dispute with William Bunch Abbot of Kilwinning who used the Council to settle it in his favour.[15] Angus was sixty-four, with known pro-English sympathies, and though he was no longer imprisoned he was not restored to full royal favour. Two of his sons, however, including his heir, George, Master of Angus, were with James, as was David Kennedy, the brother of Janet and since 1509 1st Earl of Cassillis.

There were great numbers of knights and gentry and, from the clergy, abbots such as Bunch and church leaders such as George Hepburn, Bishop of the Isles, and the most senior churchman of all, young Alexander Stewart, Archbishop of St Andrews and Chancellor of Scotland (though no one could be sure of his prowess in battle, not due to any unwillingness to fight for his father but because of his short-sightedness).[16]

At Twizelhaugh, James granted exemption from payment of wardship and other feudal dues to the heirs of anyone who was killed, mortally wounded or died from disease while with the army. Bearing in mind the monies that James had raised through such dues, it was a reasonable recompense for lords who could expect preferment but not payment for fighting for him. This was by no means a unique concession; it had happened before 1513 and would happen again.[17] So while the 'Act of Twizelhaugh' does not provide proof that James's mind was definitely fixed on a major battle with the English, it is a strong indicator that he was expecting one, as were his nobles. Most probably it would come as Bannockburn had done and many battles in the contemporary Italian Wars, when a large relieving army, this time Surrey's, would attempt to raise a siege. A larger army would be needed to resist it.

But there is another reason for the size of James's force: his entire campaign, though provoked by Henry's intransigence, was intended to underline to James's magnates, almost entirely now the sons of the men who had held titles at his accession, the entirety and integration of Scotland as a kingdom. The long years of peace had helped James to create his nation and, echoing Henry VIII, he was now forging a united Scottish noble esprit de corps through success in war. First, though, there was Norham.

Norham should have been a major test for James's artillery but its outer walls were smashed and the castle captured on 28 August after a siege of just six days. Hall suggests that Anislow was at fault for wasting his ordnance, that he ran out of the means of defence and had to surrender.[18] This sounds fanciful, though not as much as Henry VIII's description of Norham in a letter to Maximilian as a 'weak and ruinous little town'[19] in an attempt to diminish James's success in taking it.

Norham was certainly ruined when James had finished with it and Ruthall did not take the loss of his fortress so lightly. He was distraught. He wrote to Wolsey 'that the King of Scots had sieged, assaulted and in a great stormy night scaled and won the castle of Norham; which news touched me so near with inward sorrow that I had rather have been out of the world than in it, especially as I had been assured of its security'.[20]

Wark Castle also fell in short order. James now had complete control of a winding seven-and-a-half-mile stretch of the Tweed, together with its crossing points. Norham had been James's number one target, not only for its strategic importance but also for its symbolic significance: Norham was where Edward I had sought to decide the fate of Scotland and where Scottish subjects had been killed by the garrison in 1498. Retribution had now been taken.

James had surpassed the successes of his previous campaigns and with Norham falling on 28 August he still had forces at his disposal for another month. The towers he had destroyed in 1496 – Twizel, Tillmouth, Duddo, Branxton and Howtel – had not been repaired.

Nor had the castle of Heaton. Why should they have been if the intended permanent state between England and Scotland was perpetual peace? James could now advance along the Till valley and destroy the remaining fortresses in the English East March. In terms of exacting retribution for perceived English crimes, his actions had symbolic as well as strategic importance.

A glance at the map just hints at an intriguing possibility. The English East March was a pocket of territory that was framed to the north and west by the Scottish border, to the east by the North Sea and to the south by the rest of England. Borders, certainly in Europe, do not necessarily run along straight lines, but an Anglo-Scottish national border running along the southern line of the East March would have been considerably straighter than the one we have today, leaving Berwick around fifteen miles from the border. In 1513, had the Scots and French commanded the sea, the town could have been isolated and, eventually, forced to surrender. By that same logic, the English army in France could either have been intercepted at sea or left isolated on the Continent. In the latter case, Henry would have been forced to do a deal to be allowed home and, just conceivably, James could have asked for the English East March. That said, should Henry have been killed in France, then James would have been well placed to treat the position of the Border as a minor matter. Henry may have disavowed James as his heir by right of Margaret,[21] but that could easily be reversed by a King with an army at his back. Such an army need not necessarily have been one made up purely of Scotsmen; it could have included Surrey's troops as well. Thomas Howard, Earl of Surrey, had a record of loyalty to successive adult wearers of the crown, to Henry VIII and to his predecessors, Henry VII, Richard III and Edward IV, all three of whom were usurpers. James had got on brilliantly with Surrey in 1503 and it is by no means out of the question that, had Henry VIII died, Surrey would have turned from opponent to supporter. Certainly, a remarkable series of events would have been necessary for such a situation to arise, but no less remarkable than the twice-fold elevation of Edward IV and those of Richard III and Henry VII.

If securing the East March as a whole was merely a contingent possibility, James's prime targets in the Till Valley were more imme-diate. By taking the castles of Etal and Ford, James captured and neutralized all the English fortresses within striking distance of the Tweed below Wark and Norham. James was particularly focused on Ford. Having captured it, he made it his headquarters from 1 to 5 September and then made an example of it. Puritanical Scottish historians of the later sixteenth century, who disapproved of James's 'licentious' ways, claimed that he had been ensnared by the chat-elaine of the castle and that his son, Alexander the Archbishop, was entranced by her daughter. James, so they said, had thus been delayed from his proper military tasks.

The castle was strategically important for the Scottish King, but there was also another reason for its significance: Ford was the seat of the Heron family, whose illegitimate progeny had killed James's Warden, Sir Robert Ker. For years James had asked first Henry VII and then Henry VIII to send the Bastard Heron to him for punish-ment. They had failed to do so.[22] The crime of Ker's murder remained unpunished, but now James had the opportunity to exact punish-ment himself: he burned Ford Castle to the ground and then joined his army, who were steadily preparing an impregnable position on Flodden Hill and its steep surrounding ground.

꒰ ✝ ꒱

James's campaign, using the most modern type of available artillery in Renaissance Europe, was proving extremely successful. He now had the time to create an extraordinarily strong battlefield position where he could wait for Surrey's army of northern levies with its old-style weaponry.

One cannot pinpoint the precise and final details of the agree-ment between James and Louis, bearing in mind that at least some of them would have been agreed verbally between the two kings via their ambassadors, principally Forman and De La Mothe – though the exchange of correspondence in the Flodden Papers collected by Marguerite Wood seems to show that James struck a good bargain with Louis once he knew that Henry VIII was set on curbing his independence.[23] To suggest that James tarried in England for Louis' benefit rather than his own, is wide of the mark. He had done enough

by the beginning of September to detain Surrey's army in Britain and
prevent it from reinforcing Henry in France; he could keep his side
of the bargain without bringing Surrey to battle and, as in 1496, he
could have retreated over the border. That James did not do so was
a result of his own kingship, his determination to be compared with
his Renaissance contemporaries and to rank with the greatest of his
Scottish predecessors.

James, in a manner unknown to his predecessors, had united the
nobility under his leadership and his country territorially. He was able
to maintain an unpopular policy of peace with England for a decade
and a half. Then, when he was forced to abandon it, he inspired his
secular and church leaders, with only a couple of loyal exceptions, to
give him full support for his policy of war. Now that the campaign had
gone so well, he was offered a glittering opportunity which he may or
may not have anticipated back in Edinburgh. The card-playing and
dice-playing King believed that he had set the odds overwhelmingly
in his favour to win a battle of strengths – one that he was bound
to win. He would not have known Surrey's numbers, but from the
strength of his own army, he had anticipated a large force. Like Bannockburn, it would be a remarkable Scottish victory, but even bigger
in terms of the troops involved, and it would take place on the 'English' side of the Tweed.

In Renaissance Europe, kings and generals had followed their medieval predecessors in turning again to the writings of the Roman military theorist Vegetius, who in his general maxims cautioned against
hazarding all in battle.[24] Of course, there are exceptions to almost any
rule and the greatest glory for a king and his nobility, as Henry VIII
was then seeking in France, came through success in war.[25] The only
question that seemed to remain was when Surrey would be able to
come to the field.

⇜ ✝ ⇝

Surrey had left London on 22 July and reached Pontefract by 1
August.[26] There he waited to gauge what James's movements would
be. Having sent Sir William Bulmer to the Border and put him in
a position to counter Hume's 'Ill Raid', the next point to consider
was when and where James would cross into England. The northern

counties of Cumberland, Westmorland, Lancashire, Cheshire and Northumberland had been put on alert, as had Durham under the auspices of its Prince Bishop, Thomas Ruthall; but they had not been mustered for war.

Surrey's forces were not organized for an invasion of Scotland but for a defensive role. Whether this was to fight off raiding parties or a fully fledged Scottish invasion could not have been known in August. He certainly did not want the financial burden of paying an army to stand idle, or the waste of manpower through desertion (a constant threat, in spite of the draconian punishments for those who were caught), or through sickness and disease. There was the danger of a repeat of 1497, of James manoeuvring close, but not too close, to Surrey's army, keeping it in the field at vast expense but with little result. Henry VII had been furious about the cost of that campaign and his son had already shown a talent for volcanic rage.[27] James might even have waited until Surrey's army had dispersed before making his move. With the Howards' current lack of favour made all too clear by their being in England and not in France, Surrey could not afford mistakes.

When Surrey called the 'Gentlemen of the Counties' for a meeting at Pontefract, Dacre urged a policy of 'wait and see'.[28] Surrey and Dacre had both spent time with James, although in truth a few years previously, but it gave them some insight into the workings of his mind. Surrey concurred. Though they could claim that the 'Ill Raid' had been an open breach of the perpetual peace,[29] that did not mean that they had to show their hand. They could wait. It probably helped that Norham, the likeliest point of attack, belonged to the Bishop of Durham and not to King Henry.

James had made his move across the border on 22 August, but Surrey's spies would have given their master a strong indication of enemy intentions some days before. Surrey was in Pontefract on the 25th and had ordered the northern counties and the Bishop's forces to assemble at Newcastle on 1 September. In addition, landowners such as Bulmer and Sir Marmaduke Constable in Yorkshire, Lord Dacre on the borders and Sir Edward Stanley in Cheshire and Lancashire were to bring their own men as well as mustering those of others.

Surrey's own initial 500 provided a core with the 1,000 veteran soldiers and sailors shipped by the Admiral along with the artillery to Newcastle. However, these men probably comprised just a little over 5 per cent of the whole. In contrast to Henry's troops in France, who were mainly from the English south and midlands and commanded by younger bloods, this was to be an Army of the North led, by and large, by men of an older vintage.

֍ ✝ ֍

Katherine, meanwhile, was continuing her actions in support of the war effort. One in particular would have a life-saving consequence for a member of the Howard family, but it was also an act of contempt towards King James and his claims against the English. On 18 August, Katherine signed a pardon for the Bastard Heron – or, as he was described in the document, 'gentleman or bastard'.[30] This was for a misdemeanour in England. It meant that the man whom James wanted to punish for the murder of his Warden, Sir Robert Ker, would be with the English army at Flodden.

Katherine and her Council were also acting against potential fifth columnists. On 27 August the following was drafted:

> An article to be added to the instructions of commissioners for inquiring after aliens, enjoining that, in consequence of the war between England, France, and Scotland, all Scotchmen living in England should be deemed enemies; but that all Scotchmen that have married English women and have children may remain, on forfeiture of half their goods and security for the other half; the same to be estimated by the sheriff and the King's commissioners. All others to have their goods seized and their persons banished, under penalty of their lives. All Frenchmen to have their goods forfeited and be committed to prison if they dwell near the sea coast; or else, if they dwell inland, to find sureties.[31]

With the addition of Bishop Ruthall's phrase 'except ecclesiastics' for the Scots and a few small amendments, this was what Katherine signed.

She and Sir Thomas Lovell were raising additional troops. At such a distance from their army on the Border, they had to be prepared for all eventualities. James's assertion that he would be in York by

Michaelmas (29 September),[32] might have been merely a jibe at its Archbishop, Christopher Bainbridge, the man behind his excommunication and his enemy at Rome. Katherine, however, had to take the threat seriously. Between 3 and 7 September Lovell was raising troops in the Midlands under martial law conditions, by command of the Queen. Katherine herself was putting together a third force, which, by the time Flodden was fought, was under her command at Buckingham, almost exactly fifty miles away from the twin cities of Westminster and London.[33]

19

Preparing the Ground

On Sunday, 28 August, the Earl of Surrey was at Durham attending Mass in its Cathedral. It was known that Norham, seventy miles away, was under attack and Surrey probably heard the news of its fall while still in the city. The Prior gave him his blessing and something more powerful, the Banner of St Cuthbert, the patron saint of the North of England, whose cult centred on his burial place of Durham.[1] The Anglo-Scottish war had taken on the element of a crusade, but it was not one that James could achieve his ambition and lead. There was no chance of that, because this one was against him.

From Durham, Surrey moved north, reaching Newcastle on the 30th. Over the next few days, other forces joined him under the command of Lord Dacre, Sir William Bulmer, Sir Marmaduke Constable and, in the words of the chronicler Edward Hall, 'many other substantial gentlemen, whom he retained as counsellors'.[2] They planned to camp at Bolton in Glendale, six miles west of Alnwick on the following Sunday, 4 September.[3] With the muster continuing at Newcastle, Surrey took an advance guard to Alnwick on the 3rd, where he was forced to stay until the 4th. There he waited for the arrival of troops delayed by appalling weather, not least those commanded by his son Thomas the Admiral, whose fleet, including his flagship the *Mary Rose*, had been battered by storms.

It was at Alnwick that Surrey 'ordered his battles', deciding which troops would fight where, and thus it was on Monday, 5 September, that his force arrived at Bolton in Glendale, around twenty miles away from Ford and slightly further from Flodden Hill, which James's army was now fortifying.

Thomas Hawley, Rouge Croix Pursuivant, the herald sent by Surrey to deliver a message to James, was probably en route to Ford when he was intercepted some way from the Scottish army's position. Having fulfilled his mission, he was honourably detained. The military intelligence the herald could have gained with even the most cursory inspection of James's camp was not going to be made available to the English commanders. Hawley had brought two letters with him. The first was from Surrey, the same Surrey for whom James had expressed commiseration in a letter to Henry written just months before. It followed the death of Surrey's second son, Admiral Sir Edward Howard, and James had risen above his general recrimination against his brother-in-law to say 'We are truly sorry ... through acquaintance we had of his father, that noble knight who conveyed our dearest companion the Queen to us.'[4] However, there could be no personal considerations now. Hawley brought a letter of challenge from Surrey, which declared James's guilt in breaking the peace and was designed to bring the Scottish King to battle on a day (Friday, 9 September) of Surrey's choosing. Written according to a chivalric formula, so much might have been expected.

The second letter was from Surrey's son Thomas, Lord Admiral, and was extraordinary for its bile. It was as expressive of the English approach to James's assertion of independent kingship as Henry's 'I am the very owner of Scotland' statement to Sir William Cumming, the Scottish ruler's Lyon King of Arms. There was no hint of deference from the Earl's son to the anointed King. It was from someone who was behaving as a lord on an equal footing, in effect from one British noble to another. Just as James was furious about the Howard treatment of his Admiral, Andrew Barton, so was Thomas Howard, Lord Admiral, at James's calls for retribution.

As reported in *Grafton's Chronicle*, this was the substance of it:

He [Thomas Howard] had sought the Scottish navy at sea, but could not engage them because they had fled to France by the roundabout route of the coast of Ireland. And because King James had many times and often been the cause of him being called at Days of Truce to make redress for Andrew Barton, who had been a Pirate for a long time before he had vanquished him, he had come personally to be in the vanguard of the coming action. He would justify the death of this Andrew in action against King James and all his people and on that day would lay the charge to rest. Furthermore, neither he nor any of his company would take any Scot prisoner, even if they were a noble, and they would die if they put themselves at his mercy; because he did not expect anything else from the Scots. The only exception to this being the King himself.[5]

The implication of this was that only the King himself was an equal. Unless one accepts the version repeated by Brian Tuke in his letter of 22 September to Richard Pace in Rome.[6] In that case, even the King of Scots himself was not excepted.

This was extreme stuff; but it was deliberately so. The Howards needed a battle because they needed a victory. It was the most likely and perhaps the only way to put them back in favour with their young King.

❧ ✝ ☙

In place of Thomas Hawley, Rouge Croix, James sent his own Islay Herald to Surrey that evening. That Islay had become the title of a Royal Herald, rather than the name of a representative of the Lord of the Isles, was a symbolic demonstration of James's grip over the territories that made up Scotland.

Like James, Surrey was wary of the spying potential of a herald, though his solution was different: Islay was kept well away from the camp and escorted to a village nearby by Thomas Tonge, York Herald.

Early in the morning of the following day, Tuesday, 6 September, Surrey and his leading commanders rode to the village and heard James's reply to his letter: if James deigned to offer a response to the Admiral, the chroniclers make no mention of it. As for his words to Surrey, via the Herald, they were extremely courteous – with James saying that if he had been at home in Edinburgh then he would have gladly come to meet Surrey.

However, James most certainly did not agree that it was he who had broken the peace. James gave his answer in a letter dictated to Secretary Panter and presented by Islay Herald. He recalled the 'oath' given to Dr West in front of the Scottish Councillors, that he would keep the peace providing Henry did so.[7] West himself,

Wolsey and Henry had not treated James's oath-taking seriously and had disregarded it. Not so James, who returned to it now. Once more he reiterated his accusations that it had been Henry who had broken the peace and that Henry had been asked many times for remedy. As to the crux of the matter, he said, 'this we take for our quarrel and with God's grace shall defend the same at your affixed time, which with God's grace we shall abide.'[8] It gave Surrey the very thing he wanted. James had agreed to fight. Surrey was 'joyous of the King's answer'.[9] He then rode back to his camp. As for the heralds, they had much in common and rather a lot to talk about. Islay sent a servant back to the Scottish camp letting James know that he was safe and well, which was a signal for James to release the English herald. As for Islay and York Herald, now joined by Sir Humphrey Lisle of Felton, they made 'good cheer'.[10]

Later on that Tuesday,[11] Surrey moved his army six miles further north to Wooler Haugh, next to an inviting place for a battle – a large open cornfield.[12] One can only assume that the corn had long been cut, because victuals were becoming a problem. In fact, everything was starting to go wrong for Surrey. For there was another issue that was even more immediate, news of which was brought by the returning Thomas Hawley, Rouge Croix. Two days earlier, before the issuing of challenge and acceptance, James had not wanted to reveal his position: now he certainly did. It was impregnable. To the naturally strong defensive mound of Flodden Hill had been added field fortifications. Already sited within these and sighted for action was James's artillery – as any group of Englishmen spotted in range would find out. James's flanks were completely protected: by a marsh on one side and steep slopes on the other. That seemed to leave just one direction of potential attack, a frontal assault across narrowing open ground, with the advancing Englishmen being blasted by the Scottish guns and then, when in disarray, the target of a coordinated counter-charge by close-packed Scottish troops carrying the proven infantry weapon of the Italian Wars – the pike. Whether it was James himself or the advising D'Aussi and his French captains who had planned and executed the position on Flodden Hill, they had done their job very well indeed.[13] Not surprisingly, the Scots were showing no signs of wanting to move towards their English opponents.

One of James's closest advisers and his Chancellor was now his brilliant young son Alexander Stewart, Archbishop of St Andrews. Perhaps it was Alexander's legal training, so decried by Erasmus, that had been brought to bear in the dealings with Surrey. There certainly was agreement over the date. But what about the place? Surrey was caught in a double bind: to advance on James's position was suicidal, but not to fight, now he had offered a challenge and it had been accepted, would be a humiliation. Surrey saw no alternative but to return Rouge Croix to 'reiterate' what had been agreed. So that there was no chance of further confusion, Hawley was given a letter. It was composed during the afternoon of Wednesday, 7 September, and delivered early the next day.[14] Here is the letter in modern English:

> Right high and mighty Prince, lately I sent you Rouge Croix Pursuivant of Arms and through him told your Grace that I and my Sovereign Lord's other subjects had come to press back and resist your invasions of this realm of my Sovereign Lord King. And to that intent I offered to give you battle on this behalf, next Friday coming, which message your Grace was pleased to hear, so I am informed.
>
> And by your Herald Islay, you answered that you were delighted at my request and would not fail to accomplish the same and would wait for me at the place where you were at the time my message was shown to your Grace.
>
> And although it has pleased you to change your spoken promise and to put yourself on ground that is more like a fortress, rather than being neutral ground suitable for trial by battle, I request, because the appointed day is now so close, that your Grace does the following: that to carry out your honourable promise, you will deploy yourself for your part, as I shall do for mine, with your host on your side of Milfield Plain. In like manner, I shall do the same with the subjects of my Sovereign Lord on my side of Milfield Plain and ready to give you battle between noon and three o'clock in the afternoon, provided that you give me sufficient warning by eight or nine in the morning by Rouge Croix.
>
> And just as I and the other noblemen of my company bind ourselves with our signatures to keep the aforementioned time for the stated

purpose above, may it please your Grace to write and sign with your own hand a letter binding your Grace in the same way. I trust that you will send our Pursuivant immediately, for we believe that any long delay to such an honourable journey would be dishonourable. Written in the field at Wooler Haugh on the 7th day of September at five o'clock in the afternoon.[15]

In order to lend his argument force, Surrey ensured that his own signature on the letter was countersigned by eighteen of his senior commanders.

⊰ ✠ ⊱

James received the letter the next morning and reacted with fury. When he had challenged Surrey to single combat in 1497, he had met with a polite refusal citing the English commander's inferior social position;[16] now, sixteen years later and over a decade after English recognition of James's royal status through the Treaty of Perpetual Peace, the King of Scots was being denied the expected respect from the English Earl. James refused to see Thomas Hawley, Rouge Croix. Instead, a servant appeared with a verbal message: 'That it was not fitting for an Earl to seek to command a King. His Grace will take and hold his ground at his own pleasure and not at the direction of the Earl of Surrey.'[17] As far as James was concerned, the time and place for the battle had been decided.

As to Hawley being returned to Surrey immediately, it did not happen for an unlikely reason. As if the unfolding events of the Flodden campaign were written in a tragedy by Shakespeare, the dark denouement was preceded by a scene of comedy – not one that Rouge Croix would have enjoyed at the time, in fear of what might happen next. Islay had not returned. As *Hall's Chronicle* tells it, Islay's servant caused Hawley and his servant to be forcibly detained, because he suspected that the English had done away with his master who should have returned the day before; indeed he was so sure of foul play that he swore, if Islay had not come back by noon, the two Englishmen would have their heads chopped off. However, 'as luck would have it', as Hall reports 'Islay did return before noon and showed of his genteel entertaining'.[18] Or to put it another way, he staggered in as drunk as the Porter in *Macbeth*, having got stuck into a major drinking session with York Herald and Sir Humphrey Lisle. Perhaps this was an aberration, maybe Islay's servant did not know his master very well or possibly he could not comprehend that a Scotsman might want to spend many hours in the company of a couple of Englishmen.

The drinkers probably had a reasonable quantity of fine wine. In contrast, Surrey's army had not had any ale or beer for several days,[19] and rations were scarce. This was not due to a failure of planning and organization akin to that of Surrey's dead son Sir Edward; the supply wagons had set out from Newcastle as expected, only to be attacked en route and looted in their entirety by English Border Reivers.[20] For the soldiery, the lack of alcohol was much more than a minor inconvenience, it was life-threatening. Unpurified water, particularly the sort available to an army in camp, was dangerous – a host to all sorts of diseases, such as the dysentery which had killed Henry V. A seemingly clear and clean hillside stream would soon become polluted by an encamped army; and, in any case, there was no knowing whether there would be a dead animal or two rotting away in the water around the next bend. Water needed to be boiled, cleansed and purified, and the best way of doing this was by turning it into ale or beer. The difference between the two being that hops were added as a preservative in the beer-making process. Though initially favoured by brewers, alehouse keepers and quartermasters for its keeping properties, beer was now preferred by many drinkers for its taste – particularly in Kent and the south-east where it was originally introduced.[21] From choice as well as familiarity, Surrey's mainly northern army might have had a preference for ale, in the same way many preferred rye to wheat for their bread – though for an army in the field, flour baked as biscuit rather than bread was a better bet, as it kept for much longer.

Surrey's army was around 26,000 strong and there was no chance that it could be supplied through living off the land, because the poor Border region had trouble feeding itself. The English soldier in the field was a hungry beast, as shown by the surviving figures for provisioning Henry VIII's armies in France. If all went well, the soldier could hope for a weekly diet along the following lines: 7 lbs biscuit; 4 lbs beef; 2 lbs pork; three-quarters of a salt fish; 12 oz. cheese; 2 pints of peas; 6 oz. butter; and 7 gallons of beer.[22]

The meat would be salted; thus salt beef and pork cured as bacon. The joints would be boiled. This had a double purpose. The meat was heated and some of the salt removed, but the resulting liquor could be used to cook up as potage, using dried peas, beans or oatmeal. Cheeses were made of skimmed milk and thus harder and with better keeping properties.[23] There had to be an accommodation of the fish days of church observance – all of Lent and every Wednesday, Friday and Saturday. The staple provision for this was dried cod (stockfish). Life would be much easier for English and Scottish quartermasters after the Reformation, when there was less of an onus on fish days; the standard fare of both sides during the English Civil War was cheese and biscuit.[24] It will be noted here that there was an absence of fresh fruit and vegetables. The fear would have been of anything that needed to be washed.

Good food and drink meant more than having basic sustenance. They were hugely important for morale. The Scots had no such problem: their army was well supplied, even though it was larger and on foreign soil, if only just; Coldstream over the border was less than five miles away and the crossing over the Tweed and the area between it and the camp seemed securely under Scottish control.

⊰ ✝ ⊱

Surrey was in a real predicament. He either had to fight or get resupplied, but whichever choice he made was fraught with difficulty. If he attacked James's position on Flodden Hill he would lose the battle and do so bloodily. If he opted for a tactical retreat, either back the way he had come or wide of James's left flank and north to Berwick, he would face the dishonour of having offered the challenge and flunked it, no doubt bringing permanent disgrace for himself and his family at the hands of King Henry. By the same token, James having accepted the challenge without any qualification, at least in Scottish eyes, could then march back over the Border with honour intact.

After the return of Rouge Croix, the English army struck camp. If they went north from Wooler Haugh, they would be advancing towards James's position on Flodden Hill. If instead they headed east across the River Till and then north, they would be moving in the direction of Berwick. The latter was chosen. The army probably crossed the Till just north of Clavering, where there is still a bridge at Weetwood. From there, a few hundred yards to the north-east is Horton and, just to the north of that, there is a junction with the Devil's Causeway, the old Roman road that was designed to take the legions from Hadrian's Wall at Corbridge to their fort and settlement at Tweedmouth. After five and a half miles of straight road, Surrey's forces reached the village of Lowick and camped just to the west of it on Barmoor, around eight and a half miles from Berwick. This march, with artillery and baggage in tow, would have covered the best part of ten miles. Quite a feat, as it was conducted in driving rain and all the more so if it began after midday. It could not have done much for the seventy-year-old Earl's arthritis and he had to undertake the journey in a chariot.

The unknown writer of the contemporary chronicle the *Trewe Encountre or Batayle Lately Don Betwene Englande and Scotlande* was thought to be a local Northumbrian when it was later republished in Edinburgh in 1866–67. If so he was probably not a native of the immediate area, because although he tells us that the English army camped that night at Barmoor, he also says that they were never more than two miles away from the Scottish army. The latter statement cannot be right because, even as the crow flies, Barmoor is more than six miles from Flodden Hill. He also says that the 'whole army in array' were 'in the sight of the King of Scots'.[25] Similarly that cannot be true, unless the chronicler meant that it was in the sight of the *scouts* of the King of Scots. If so, when they reported the position of the new English camp to James (particularly if they had been in a position to pass on any intimation of the lack of provisions of the English army), James would have judged that Surrey was bound for Berwick in order, at the very least, to take on fresh supplies. However, if James remained ignorant of the parlous provisioning state, then he might have concluded that Surrey would march into Scotland as he had in 1497, but would have felt that he could cut off the English route home with his better-equipped, more modern army.

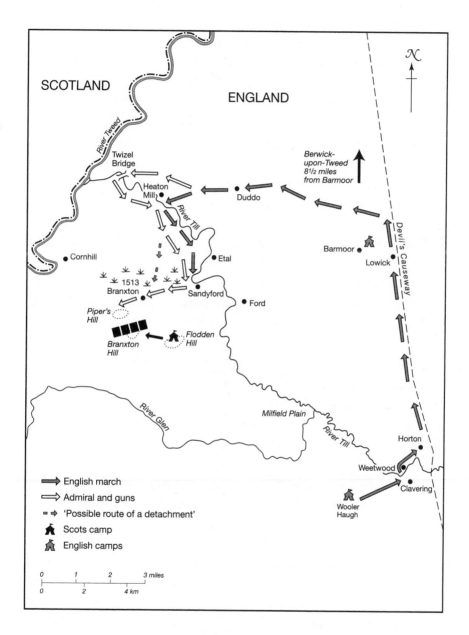

SCOTLAND

ENGLAND

River Tweed

Twizel
Bridge

Heaton
Mill

River Till

Duddo

*Berwick-
upon-Tweed
8½ miles
from Barmoor*

Barmoor

Lowick

Devil's Causeway

Cornhill

Etal

⚔ 1513
Branxton

Sandyford

Ford

*Piper's
Hill*

*Branxton
Hill*

*Flodden
Hill*

River Glen

Milfield Plain

River Till

Horton

Weetwood

Clavering

Wooler
Haugh

➡ English march

⇨ Admiral and guns

⇢ 'Possible route of a detachment'

♟ Scots camp

⛺ English camps

0   1   2   3 miles

0   2   4 km

Manoeuvring

Taking into account the parlaying of the previous days, Surrey's chosen course of action the following morning might have seemed dishonourable to a dispassionate contemporary. Certainly, it is of interest that the epitaph originally attached to Surrey's tomb mentions the 'broken promises' of the King of Scots not once but thrice. It talks more specifically about James acting 'contrary to his promise made to Rouge Croix',[26] though of course any promise was made through Islay Herald. It is pertinent that Surrey treated it as a matter of some weight: perhaps he actually believed James had broken a solemn oath and promise. Or maybe Surrey, given the choice between near-certain defeat and any possible alternative, chose the latter, believing the record of who said what to whom could be set straight later.

Thus, before dawn on 9 September, after a meagre breakfast of final rations washed down with water, Surrey's army was on the move again. But it did not set off north, but rather due west and southwest. The Earl of Surrey and King James were not to be denied their battle.

⊰ ✝ ⊱

The main weaponry of the two armies was different, reflecting the difference in their status in the eyes of the two Kings. James's army contained his leading nobles and the best Scottish troops, with the mass of his ordinary soldiers being better equipped than the English northern levies not taken to fight with Henry's principal army in France.

James embraced the idea of the Scots fighting with the pike. One can see why, for not only had it been successful on the battlefields of Italy, but it could be seen as an adaptation of the weapon the Scots had used so effectively for Wallace and Bruce against England. That had been the spear, which in vast numbers ranked together in a defensive schiltron – literally a 'bush step'[27] or figuratively a 'moving thicket'[28] – created a dense 'hedgehog' that proved impenetrable and deadly for the heavily armoured English knights at Stirling Bridge and Bannockburn.

The eight- to twelve-foot-long spear of the early fourteenth century[29] was, however, a rather different weapon to the Swiss/German pike of the early sixteenth. The latter was eighteen feet long, with a steel head of over a foot, making it far more unwieldy.[30] Nevertheless highly skilled, well-trained, properly coordinated and trusting and trusted groups of men could devastate opposing armies. That was the case even when the pike was used as virtually the sole weapon and in forcing attack, not defence, as it was during the devastating victory of the Milanese Sforza-hired Swiss at Novara on 6 June 1513. They surprised the French with a rapid advance just after dawn, with one section circling round to the French rear. A second, using the cover of crops, assaulted the French guns placed in the most forward advanced position. A third got even closer to the enemy and went undetected thanks to its men crawling along the ground. All these manoeuvres were made by men carrying heavy pikes. Although the Swiss took casualties from the French guns, they still managed to storm them, overwhelming the German Landsknecht mercenaries hired as guards. The Swiss neutralized the artillery and then turned some of the guns round and fired them against their previous owners. The French were routed.[31] The Swiss invaded French Burgundy and had to be paid off, very expensively, by King Louis XII.

Certainly the Swiss had been assisted by the French cavalry's poor positioning and their inability to support their own infantry. But at Novara, they had once again shown how irresistible the pike could be in the right hands, and particularly theirs.[32] What the Swiss had long mastered was the ability to move as a disciplined body and to hold firm when attacked by artillery or cavalry. Their cohesion was based on the intense loyalty they had to each other as a group.

Novara was just the latest example of the pike's triumphs. Almost forty years previously, the Swiss had shattered the military might of the Duchy of Burgundy at two successive battles in 1476.[33] Pikes proved a major nuisance to the Holy Roman Emperor for many years; so much so that Emperor Maximilian realized that the best way of countering them was through the adoption of the pike by his own mercenary forces, the Landsknechts. So successful were they, that by 1500 the pike was the main infantry weapon of the armies contesting the Italian Wars, and the Landsknechts or 'servants of the country' were being referred to as 'Lanzknechts'.[34]

The pike's adoption was also underwritten by the intellectual climate of the age. It was the perfect Renaissance weapon because it paralleled the fifteen-foot *sarissa* spear of Alexander the Great; and, held in forward-projecting overlapping ranks, it was recognizably comparable to the Greek phalanx and to the disciplined ranks of Roman troops.[35] The effective deployment of these weapons in antiquity called for ordered formations and precise movements; this was also true for their acclaimed descendant. Texts on warfare more than a thousand years old were studied once more by scholars. Warfare was becoming more complicated and, though Erasmus himself did not agree, intellectually respectable.[36] Military theory was very much the province of Renaissance kings.

James would certainly have been interested in the pike as the outstanding infantry weapon. In terms of its disciplined use by reliable infantry, he could rely on the Scottish soldier's strong loyalty to his noble commander and through him to the King himself. James could also expect his troops to hold their ranks under fire, certainly in any battle against the English. But would the pike-bearing Scots be sufficiently skilled? D'Aussi's French captains could quickly teach the basic techniques and manoeuvres, but the question remained as to whether the Scottish troops could cope with something unexpected and be able to innovate in a way that only comes from practice and years of experience.

As long as the connectedness and coherence of the serried ranks of pikemen could be maintained, the pike had a massive advantage over the bill, the traditional weapon of the Northern English common soldier: one of reach. In any case, surely the bill was nothing more than an adapted agricultural hedging and trimming tool?

Looking forward, the pike continued to be used by the Scottish long after Flodden, and to be feared. Ten years later, when Thomas Howard the 'Admiral' was back on the Scottish border and anxious about the manoeuvres of a pike-bearing Scottish army, he wrote to Henry, Wolsey and the Council asking for at least 4,000 German Landsknecht troops who would not only carry pikes themselves but would teach men in the 22,000-strong English force how to use them, as 'the English are not accustomed, but will easily learn when they see the order of the Almaynes [Germans]'.[37] It is striking that, a decade after Flodden, he thought pike should be fought with pike.

One weapon that the Sheriffs of Scotland were instructed to ban in 1515, because it was ineffective at Flodden, was the Jedburgh Staff. Consisting of a four-foot blade mounted on the end of an oak shaft, it lacked sufficient weight when landed on an opponent.[38] There was absolutely no thought of the Scots banning the pike.

In Italy, groups of pikemen were often flanked by handgunners with arquebuses. The Scots were promised a thousand handguns by their French allies, but although they landed with D'Aussi, his forty captains and his fifty men-at-arms, these weapons remained at the port.[39] This may have been an important oversight, or perhaps it was thought that the guns needed specialists to use them. In any event, it is open to question how influential they might have been at Flodden. Certainly the arquebus had proved useful, as the crossbow had been, as a defensive weapon in sieges during the Italian Wars. They had proved their worth at the battle of Cerignola in 1503 and again at Ravenna in 1512, when fired from behind a protective trench and earth parapet.[40] In contrast, without such protection, they could be ineffective and vulnerable, as at Novara, fought just two months before Flodden. They were not yet fully developed as support weapons in attack and certainly not within Britain.

As for the order of importance of the other types of weaponry, it was not yet clear. The Battle of Ravenna of 1512, in the view of Professor Jeremy Black, had 'represented a remarkable competition of different weapons systems. This reflected the state of flux in weaponry and the process of improvisation in adoption and adaptation of weapons and tactics.'[41] As well as the arquebus, all of the following were used at Ravenna: the crossbow; powerful and highly accurate artillery; infantry bearing pikes; infantry bearing swords; and cavalry. Ravenna had ultimately been a test of generalship of the opposing commanders. Gaston de Foix had won through his ability to deploy his varied forces more skilfully than his Spanish opponents.[42]

There was also a mix of weaponry at Flodden, with the older equipment having a very English stamp. The English gentry and nobility, like their fathers, favoured long hand-and-a-half swords and there was also the poleaxe, the knightly classes' staff weapon of choice during the Wars of the Roses. The poleaxe had a sharpened point at each end, with the one at the head forming a trinity with an axe on one side and a hammerhead like a sledge hammer on the other. The head might also have three spikes of different shapes, with one on each side of the pole at right-angles to the axe, and a third beak-like recurved spike mounted on the hammer itself. Specifically weighted in order to maximize impact, in powerful hands with a full swing, the poleaxe delivered a blow that could decapitate an unprotected neck with ease. Armour had been refined with ridges designed to deflect blows from hand weapons as well as from arrow heads, but pole weapons were still effective against it.

Some of the household troops of the nobles and gentry were equipped with the halberd, which combined as a spear and as a long-bladed axe with a recurved beak. Like various other developed staff weapons, it was a more sophisticated version of the bill, that adapted agricultural implement for hedging and chopping brushwood. The bill gave its wielder the ability to stab with the point or, if he swung the weapon down sideways, to hook behind an opponent's legs and either cut through tendons or pull him to the ground. It might also have a spike mounted on the side which could be swung to punch through the victim's protective layers. In the same vein, both sides also had maces[43] and some Scots, particularly Highlanders, had long-handled axes, known as the Lochaber axe.[44] But the main infantry weapon was Scottish pike against English bill.

Scottish weaponry and generalship, combined with English fool-ishness, had been decisive at Stirling Bridge and Bannockburn. The tables had been turned decisively at Halidon Hill in 1333 due to the extraordinary effectiveness of the Anglo-Welsh longbow that was to bring English arms such success at Crécy, Poitiers, Agincourt and Verneuil in the Hundred Years War. The archers would turn out once again at Flodden to fight with bow and arrow and – at close quarters – with sword, buckler and dagger.

The men of both armies were equipped with side weapons: swords, daggers and, among the Scots in particular, short-handled battleaxes

– some of the Highlanders carrying both the axe and an early version of the targe, a round shield.

As for protection, for his head the English common soldier had a sallet, though some archers preferred not to wear them when shooting their bows, as the edge of the helmet prevented them from bringing the hand that drew the bowstring close enough to the eye, impairing their accuracy. The Scottish lowland troops favoured the burgonet (or Burgundian sallet), with the better protected adding a visor for the forehead and a 'buffe' protecting the neck and jaw.[45] Their highland counterparts had long bassinets, with the more elevated wearing a protective nosepiece, similar to that of the Normans.

On their bodies, the ordinary English and lowland Scottish troops wore sleeveless jacks which were stuffed with tow – rough flax – and with layer upon layer of wool or linen material packed together. These could be surprisingly effective against a spent arrow or a glancing blow, but the more fortunate and better-connected men wore brigandines, where iron plates took the place of much of the packing material. Mail and assorted, often random pieces of armour would be used to protect their arms. The highland soldiers again were different, wearing patchwork linen daubed with wax or pitch and with a deerskin over the top; in their normal area of operation, the whole assemblage would then be dyed the colour of heather as camouflage for potential ambush.[46] Their nobles and key retainers were also different to their lowland equivalents, wearing mail rather than armour and wielding powerful two-handed swords.

Protection for the English and Scottish lowland professional soldier was better. A new form of matching breastplate and backplate (called the 'almain rivet' after their German origin) was produced in mass quantities. James and Henry had ordered these and their nobles followed their example, though in 1513 most of Henry's almain rivets were for his army in France.[47] For the top professionals, the men at arms, and for the nobles and richer gentry whom they served, full armour was worn, weighing between 50 and 70 lbs. This not only gave the wearer protection but could make him physically the hub of a fighting unit, rather like a Second World War tank with its supporting infantry exploiting the gaps it made in enemy defences. This was the way armed men had fought on foot during the recent Wars of the Roses. James and Surrey had cavalry, for potential use as scouts and for skirmishing, including the ponies of the Borderers. Flodden however was principally to be an encounter of foot soldiers.

Though the day of field artillery had dawned, that of the mass use of handgunners was not yet nigh, not for the British at least. As for the English army, in its bladed weaponry, its bowmen and its protective equipment, everything harked back to the Wars of the Roses. In British military history this would be a transitional battle: the opening exchange of fire from the artillery would be completely new, as would be the use of Scottish pike tactics, but most elements of the battle would follow traditional lines. Thus Flodden would be both the last medieval and the first early modern British battle.

20

Flodden – 9 September 1513

At 5 a.m. on Friday, 9 September, the English army prepared to strike their camp on Barmoor. They had spent an uncomfortable night in harsh conditions with little food. Even the dregs of beer were gone. Instead they had to rely on dangerous, potentially diseased water. The weather of the day before had worsened and the soldiers had to contend with teeming rain and strong winds. At councils of war, Surrey had prepared his commanders for the considerable risk they were to take: he was going to advance his forces towards James and in order to do so he was going to divide them.

Their objective was Branxton Hill, around a mile and a half from James's position on Flodden Hill. With that held, Surrey would have two alternatives. The first would be to advance against the northern rear of James's position on Flodden Hill. The second would be to mount a siege,[1] assuming, of course, that the English could establish a resupply from Berwick, otherwise Surrey's army might disintegrate through failing supplies and mounting sickness – as almost happened in 1497.

From Branxton Hill, the Earl could block Scottish retreat to the Tweed. With the use of Sir Edward Stanley's cavalry and Dacre's border ponies, he could harry any enemy troops who might try the far more arduous western escape route at the point where the Border runs from just west of Carham down to the south/south-east for around fourteen miles before continuing on its south-west axis. He could also pound the Scottish position with his artillery and force James to do battle on, for the English, more favourable terms.

The English army would need to divide before re-crossing the River Till. From then on communication between Surrey and his son the Admiral was certain to be difficult and would hinder their ability to adjust their plans. Furthermore, it was uncertain how long the vanguard and the rearguard would take to re-cross the rain-swollen river – at places a mile and a half apart – and arrive at Branxton Hill together. If one element arrived first, it might have to hold the hill against a Scottish counter-attack until support from the rest of the army could get there. That might take some time, particularly if that reinforcement was from the slowest-moving element escorting the guns and taking the longer route via the solid stone structure of Twizel Bridge, built just two years before. From the bridge, the guns would still have the best part of half a dozen miles to go before they would be pulled to the top of Branxton Hill, most likely from the gentler slopes to the east.

But of course the English commanders could not know when their movements would be noted by the Scots and what resistance they would meet.

Surrey's gamble had to stem from a judgment that the King of Scots, in his seemingly impregnable position, would be bluffed into believing that the English commander had moved his troops northwards to avoid battle. Though it was also possible that James may have become aware of the English army's lack of supplies and been convinced that they intended to make for Berwick and re-supply. Informed that Surrey's army was at Barmoor, just off the Devil's Causeway, James might well have come to the conclusion that Surrey had backed out of his solemn agreement to fight on 9 September and that the Scots merely needed to hold their position on the field to win the honour of the day and inflict dishonour on their English opponents: not only the Earl of Surrey but, through him, King Henry. It is even conceivable that James might, very incautiously, have recalled his scouts. Certainly on the 'surely he doth protest too much' principle, the triple mention on Surrey's epitaph of the 'dishonourable' behaviour of the King of Scots hints that the Earl feared he might be accused of discreditable actions himself. From Barmoor it would have been pretty nigh impossible for Surrey to have been ready for battle between twelve noon and three in the afternoon – if it were assumed that the time and not the place of battle were agreed.

In terms of outguessing their opponent, all those hours spent in each other's company ten years before might have given each commander some clue. On the other hand, James's 1503 delight in talking with Surrey the courteous courtier may have over-written his memory of the Earl as his 1497 enemy. He may also have failed to grasp how precarious was the Howard position within the new Henrician regime, dismissing the threats of the younger Thomas Howard as mere bluster and failing to appreciate the determined resolve of the elder.

⊰ ✝ ⊱

The division of Surrey's forces at 5 a.m. that Friday morning was clear-cut – their basic intended dispositions having been arranged well before Barmoor.[2] Surrey himself would lead the rearguard while the Admiral would command the vanguard.

With the Admiral in the vanguard's centre would be 9,000 men, including the troops who had sailed with him to Newcastle, Sir William Bulmer's victors of the 'Ill Raid', Ruthall's soldiers fighting under the banner of St Cuthbert, and men commanded by Lord Clifford and other lords, gentlemen and esquires of Yorkshire and Northumberland. The Admiral's right wing would have 3,000 men, mainly from Cheshire and Lancashire and be commanded by his younger brother Edmund Howard; and the left, under Sir Marmaduke Constable and his son-in law William Percy would also have 3,000 from Yorkshire and Northumberland.[3]

The centre of Surrey's rearguard, numbering 5,000 under his direct command, would be strongly Yorkshire-based. Dacre would captain the right wing with 1,500 of his mounted Borderers from Cumberland and Westmorland and 1,500 men raised by James Stanley, Bishop of Ely, the sixth son of Henry VIII's late step-grandfather, Thomas Stanley, Earl of Derby. This last group were Lancashire and Cheshire men with strong Stanley loyalties, as were all 3,000 under the command of the Bishop's older brother, Sir Edward Stanley, who commanded the left wing.

Whereas the Admiral's vanguard and the guns crossed the Till at Twizel Bridge, Surrey's rearguard used the shallows beside Heaton Mill, a mile and a half further upstream. There is no record of opposition, though it is likely there would have been some Scottish presence on Twizel Bridge. If so, it must have been light for the English army to have travelled from Barmoor to the battlefield in less than eleven hours. James would presumably have had scouts to alert him to the English troop movements. Other sources claim that the Admiral reached Twizel Bridge at 11 a.m. and that the Scottish camp had sight of the English at the same time. That would have been physically impossible, but the sighting could have been communicated quickly by Scottish mounted scouts.[4]

James reacted decisively to the news. He saw that Surrey's move would block his retreat north to Scotland. He also surmised that Surrey's target was not Flodden Hill but Branxton Hill, from where the Earl could put him under siege and might force him into fighting up a steep slope into cannon – a very similar trap to the one he himself had planned. If, however, he got to Branxton Hill ahead of Surrey, then he would still have a dominant battlefield position, even if it was not the totally commanding one of Flodden Hill. Provided he got there first he could pummel the English with his artillery while they manoeuvred. The artillery assault alone might break their ranks, but if not, then the follow-up advance he envisaged down the steep slopes of Branxton Hill across generally open treeless scrubland and directly into the English lines would certainly do so. The only risk would be that any advance would be on ground he had not planned to cross, but, if the plan worked, the English would be sent into headlong retreat and they could go in only one direction, northeast towards Berwick. Along the way, they would encounter rivers and burns. As the defeated Lancastrian troops had found in their Wars of the Roses routs, first at Northampton[5] and even more catastrophically at Towton,[6] a beaten army with a river at its back was between the Scylla of pursuing enemy troops and the Charybdis of deep, fast-flowing water, where the jacks or metal-lined brigandines of the common soldier would become saturated and pull them down, and where the weight of the armour of the nobles, gentry and men-at-arms would make them sink in a manner reminiscent of Edward Howard at Brest.

James gave the order to strike camp. This would not have been a simple matter; the guns built into emplacements would need to be unsecured, mounted on their carriages and moved over rough ground saturated by the continuous rain. There would be no time to take the baggage and supply trains. Just as the English had done at Barmoor, the Scots had to leave these behind. Now both armies were on the move.

Though James had lost some of his troops from his original tally of 42,000 – some having gone down with sickness while others, risking the summary punishment for desertion, had made their way home with any booty they might have plundered – he still had an estimated 34,000[7] and outnumbered the English by 8,000. Even before today's penchant for packaging, such a large number of people would generate a phenomenal amount of rubbish. After the army's departure, this was stacked and then fired. The wind direction can be gauged as south-easterly, for the armies approached each other still unseen, because, in Edward Hall's words, they did so:

> always under the cover of so much smoke that both the hosts were very near to each other, within the space of a quarter of a mile, before one of them could perceive the other through the smoke.[8]

The Admiral and the vanguard were close to Branxton Hill, when they reached the Pallinsburn near Crookham. To their right this stream flowed into the treacherous marshland stretching behind Branxton, but here, at a 'sandyford', they crossed it without difficulty. It was when the vanguard was moving on to the ground beyond that the Admiral received a shock as enormous as it was unexpected. The smoke suddenly cleared to reveal that the Scots had already reached Branxton Hill, that they were there in full force and with sufficient artillery in place to fire on the English. The Admiral's reaction was to 'stay in a little valley until the rear joined one of the wings'.[9] Edward Hall reports matters less calmly:

> Then the Lord Admiral perceived four great battles [divisions] of the Scots, all on foot with long spears like Moorish pikes: which the Scots had made ready for war ... [and he] sent his Agnus Dei medallion to his father, the Earl of Surrey.[10]

The Agnus Dei was something very personal to the Admiral and in sending it with a messenger he was stressing the urgency of the situation. It was essential for Surrey to provide reinforcements immediately, because if the Scottish pike divisions moved forward against an English vanguard of less than half the size of the Scottish army, given the chaos of their deployment, then the outcome seemed certain. The vanguard would be routed and the rearguard, as a consequence, would break in flight. Many Englishmen would die and so would the collective future of the Howard family.

But James did not attack. Certainly it would have taken some time to get all the guns in condition to fire, the likely precursor to any infantry charge, and the Admiral's 'little valley' was large enough to serve its purpose. But even if James had known that the valley sheltered half the English army, it would have been a risky manoeuvre to unleash his pike divisions against an unseen enemy. Why take such a risk for a small victory, when patience would be rewarded with a far greater one? The defeat of half the English army would have been significant; but a rout of its entirety would be historic. A King crowned on the anniversary of Bannockburn would have been all too aware how such a victory would echo down the ages. James did not attack and in this case Pitscottie gets it right, giving James the words: 'I am determined to have them all in front of me on one plain field and see what all of them can do against me.'[11]

Surrey had time to come to his son's aid. Seeing the four battles of the Scots, he rearranged his own forces facing them into four. The Earl advanced his army on to a ridge on the long down-slope of Piper's Hill, on the summit of which the Flodden Memorial now stands. Edmund Howard commanded the right, the Admiral was in the centre, Surrey himself to the left and Dacre in reserve. These manoeuvres did not involve Sir Edward Stanley, who had been given a different plan of attack. It was four o'clock in the afternoon.[12]

The dispositions of the two armies placed Edmund Howard against Hume and Huntly. Opposite the Admiral was the division commanded by the heads of families with land in the north-east of Scotland, so there was cohesion in terms of the regional identity of their troops, if less in the coherence of their leaders. These were William Hay, 4th Earl of Erroll; John Lindsay, 6th Earl of Crawford;

and William Graham, 1st Earl of Montrose. Montrose was the older man, around fifty at the time of Flodden, who had skilfully proved his worth to James IV early in his reign, having previously been a steadfast loyalist of James III.[13] Erroll and Crawford were younger men. John Crawford was a younger son who had become heir to the earldom after the suspicious death of his elder brother Alexander, murdered it is said by Alexander's own wife Janet Gordon and by John himself.

King James has come under criticism for imposing such a multiple and potentially divisive leadership on his separate battles. However, if all went to plan, his would be the only direction that would be needed. Whatever disputes about lands and titles there may have been among the different families, their loyalty to the King and their hatred of the English brought coherence.

The second central battle and the third across from west to east was commanded by the King himself. Those with him included his son Alexander. Also there, with their retainers and affinity were three of his earls: David Kennedy, 1st Earl of Cassillis; William Leslie, 3rd Earl of Rothes; and William Sinclair, 2nd Earl of Caithness; as were Lords Herries, Maxwell, Borthwick, Sempill and the Stewart Lords of Avandale and Innermeath.[14]

The fourth battle contained Highlanders and Islanders, commanded by Archibald Campbell, 2nd Earl of Argyll, and Matthew Stewart, 2nd Earl of Lennox. They were the sons of the men who had been on opposite sides during the rebellion of 1489 and both had played an active part in supporting their fathers, but those events were long gone and the two men now had the family connection of being brothers-in-law.

Some sources mention a fifth reserve battle commanded by the Earl of Bothwell. He was definitely at Flodden, but not as commander of a reserve.

The Admiral may have seen the Scots with pikes prepared for battle, but they were not yet ready to use them. For the very first time on British soil a battle was to begin with an artillery duel between the field guns of two armies.

There were longbows on both sides at Flodden, but they were

not effective in the opening exchanges. Improvements in defences against them – including ever more effectively ridged armour which the arrowheads slid off on impact and the use of pavisse shields,[15] held above a soldier's head during the opening 'arrow storm' – had reduced the longbow's killing capacity. The conditions of swirling wind and a long period of rain and damp meant that bowstrings became stretched and less taut, reducing the power of the bows. But there was a more fundamental reason as to why they played no part at the beginning of the battle: the two sides were well out of range of each other's longbows.

In contrast, the guns, firing over distances of around 600 yards were well within range to inflict death from afar.[16] The problem facing the Scots, however, was one of nearness rather than of distance. The large heavy cannons and culverins that had been so successful at Norham were being used as field guns firing downhill. It proved extraordinarily difficult to get the elevation right, with cannon-balls flying over English heads or, if short, plugging in the mud. Moreover firing guns in the field necessitated a much faster speed of loading than was required during sieges. Yet with no time to build a stable platform cut into the hill, and with a recoil taking the guns back several feet, reloading took longer than it would have done from their former prepared positions. Re-sighting and re-siting was also more difficult. Had the English made their expected suicidal advance towards the guns based on Flodden Hill and in line with those to the side on Flodden Edge, the Scottish gun crews would have known the optimum elevation of the barrel for firing; but now it was far from certain. The very best gunners, identified by name in the Treasurer's Accounts, who had experience in adjusting their aim and firing from a rolling ship could perhaps have coped; but that was exactly where most of them were – on board ship with the Earl of Arran, unused. In their stead were mainly second-rate men, or worse, men like James's own secretary, Patrick Panter, a man whose experience was confined to keeping an English Ambassador at bay, not an English army.[17]

The English were having much greater success with falcons designed as proper field guns, and teams of gunners experienced in their use. Smaller, lighter, mounted on wheels, they could more easily cope with the recoil and be moved back into position. Their longer barrels dealt better with the heat of firing, and the shot, only two inches in diameter, was highly effective. Aimed to hit the ground just in front of the Scottish columns and to skim like a stone off the surface of a calm pond, it had the power and penetration to kill or maim four or five men in line.[18]

English chroniclers claimed that their gunners had such accuracy that they were able to knock out the Scottish guns and to kill their crews including Robert Borthwick, the 'Maister Gunnar' and Secretary Panter. Robert Borthwick, however, was not at the battle and Panter survived it. As for the Scottish guns, including the Seven Sisters, they were found to be undamaged the next day. Though some Scottish gunners were killed, causing disruption among the crews, it is far more likely that because the Scottish guns were so slow in being repositioned, reloaded, re-aimed and then fired at a rate of far less than once a minute, it may just have seemed that they had been silenced. In response, the English guns unleashed at three shots per minute. The English commanders were also astute enough to realize that, with the Scottish guns proving less of a threat, greater advantage would be gained by firing into the mass of the assembled Scottish pikemen.

The first part of James's plan had gone awry and his prized artillery had grossly underperformed. In theory his powerful guns with their vast cannonballs should have gouged gaping holes in the English ranks, skittling the soldiers like ninepins, breaking their morale as well as their formation and setting up James's decisive tactical move.

However, James had not expected the artillery barrage to be the critical element; it had been designed merely as the preliminary for what came next – the pike charge. The plan had always been for the Scots to charge the enemy, though they had hoped to do so when the English were in disarray. But with their own men being cut down by English fire, there was no point in delaying any further. James picked up a pike and stood in the front rank as the signal to move.

The King was criticized by later sixteenth-century Scottish historians such as Pitscottie and Buchanan for leading from the front, echoing the words that Dudley had written for Henry VIII and the view of medieval military writers[19] that a king should not risk himself in the forefront of battle. They also said that James's involvement in the thick of the action prevented him from making tactical adjustments once he had committed himself to the fray. But they failed to understand the nature of James's kingship and of infantry tactics, as understood by James, D'Aussi and the French captains they had brought to the battlefield. James was a 'participatory' king,[20] the active leader of all around him in all he did, in war as in peace. The whole success of his reign lay in his personal connection and direction. This type of active leadership was expected by his people, it was in his nature and it worked. It is relevant to return to Ambassador Ayala's character description of James of 1496: 'He does not think it right to begin any warlike undertaking without being himself the first in danger ... For this reason and because he is a humane prince, he is very much loved.'[21] That description is as relevant to the forty-year-old James of 1513 as it was to his younger self of 1496, with one difference: by 1513 he was not so reckless.

No fine adjustment of tactic was needed for a successful pike charge when three or four massed groups of pikemen, arranged diagonally in echelon formation around two hundred yards apart,[22] smashed against opposing infantry in separate but successive and coordinated waves. Once in motion, the advance was not designed to be finessed, but set up to deliver one devastating assault and to sweep the enemy from the field. The English opposition at Flodden did not possess mercenaries with arquebuses to punch holes in the pike columns, nor did they have the heavy cavalry to exploit the gaps. Pikes had shown complete battlefield supremacy against smaller staff weapons in European wars. Just as the Bruce had been at Bannockburn, James was in the forefront to inspire his men by his example and to lead them personally to certain victory.

The English artillery may have outgunned its Scottish counterpart and disturbed the ranks, but the authoritative *Articles of the Battle* describes the pike divisions as advancing 'in good order, after the Almayns [or Swiss/German] manner, without speaking a word'. This matches the words of Wolsey's Secretary Brian Tuke in his 22 September letter to Richard Pace in Rome: 'the Scots came down the hill in very good order after the German fashion, with iron spears in masses'; and he also says 'in this battle the bows and ordnance were of little use'.[23] The pike charge was a completely new form of warfare to English troops and the sight of their foes advancing silently across the rain-swept field was extremely intimidating. They had no choice but to ready themselves to counter them.

The most forward part of the pike echelon was that of Hume and Huntly. The mix of Borderer and Highlander, far from confusing the attack actually assisted it, because the Border pikemen were flanked by archers with bows shooting at close range and by heavy swordsmen equipped to slash the breaking ranks of billmen. In contrast, Surrey's arrangement of troops worked against his son Edmund. As the two divisions clashed, many of Edmund's force of men from Cheshire and Lancashire mixed with those from Yorkshire, feeling themselves under alien and, to them, unproven leadership, lost their nerve as the Scots smashed into their lines.[24] They broke and ran.

Edmund Howard, isolated with just a few men, was soon fighting for his life. As those protecting him were cut down, he was knocked to the ground three times. But the Scots did not move in for the kill for good reason: they could see he was valuable and wanted to capture him for ransom. It was an important delay, because Surrey, seeing the desperate position of his younger son, also realized the potential for the disintegration of his entire force through panic. He committed Dacre's mounted reserve. Even heavier fighting ensued and the position stabilized with heavy losses to both sides. Edmund Howard, badly wounded, was rescued by the man James was so keen to apprehend: John Heron, 'bastard and gentleman', was able to fight his way to Howard and, with assistance, move him to the rear.

The rallying English troops would have been heartened by seeing that the second part of the Scottish echelon under Erroll, Crawford and Montrose had been making much slower progress. The rain-soaked ground might be expected to turn to mud under the weight of thousands of troops, with some at the front in their fifty-pound armour churning it up more than most, but Hume and Huntly had been able to cross it without any problem or loss of momentum. That was something that seemed to be lost to the three earls when their pikemen reached the bottom of Branxton Hill, even before they attempted what from afar had appeared a much gentler slope, but now presented a considerable challenge. As the Scots struggled to maintain formation and to move towards the English forces, the latter with a starting position of a hundred yards away would have narrowed the distance in order to engage with their clearly struggling adversaries.[25]

The nature of the landscape, with its dips and ridges, makes it entirely possible that James could have seen the initial success of Hume and Huntly, but not the movement of Dacre's reinforcements. And though he may have noted the slow going of the second part of the echelon, James was unlikely to have seen the precise nature of its difficulties before he ordered his best troops forward. Even if he had possessed full sight of the battlefield and known that Hume and Huntly's division, far from pushing the English off the field, were standing off their English opponents, would that have changed his thinking? Would that have made James decide to leave Erroll, Crawford and Montrose to their fate? There is no way that James could have done so. The nature of his kingship and his personality were proof of that. He believed in taking full personal responsibility for all things, in war as in peace – the earls may have lost the crucial momentum needed to make the pike tactics work, but that need not be the fate of James and his troops. Even at the distance between them he could see from the banners arrayed that his forces faced Surrey's. One decisive advance by his own men that succeeded in killing or capturing the English commander was all that was needed for victory.

Yet as his men reached the bottom of the valley, James would have seen the increasing difficulty of the ground. This was more than a question of it being soaked by the continuing rain and then turned to mud by the heavy tread of thousands of feet. Lowland pikemen followed the example of their highland compatriots; they removed their boots and advanced barefooted so they could get a better grip in the slippery earth.[26] It would be wrong to talk of a surface, because the legs of the men were sinking deep into the ground before gaining some sort of purchase in what had become a quagmire. James's men

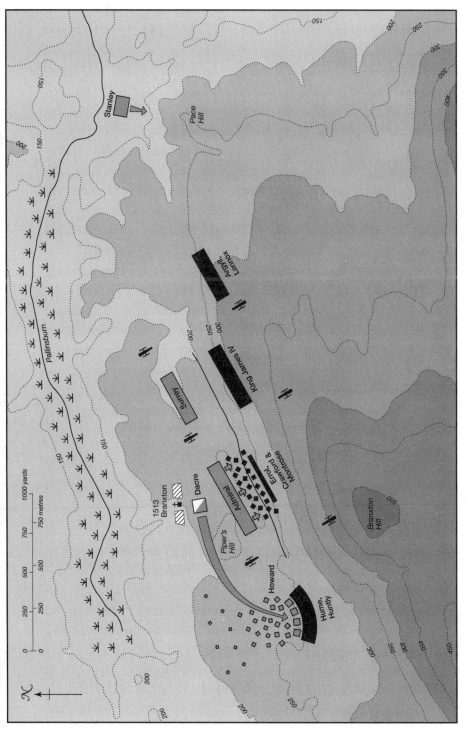

Engagement

struggled through it and up the slope the other side. In spite of their difficulty they still had sufficient momentum to push Surrey's troops back towards likely oblivion in the marshy ground of the Pallinsburn at their back, until the force of that momentum was lost and Surrey regrouped.

James's artillery had failed, but now so had the pike charge. The Scottish infantry, exhausted from their initial advance and disordered from their close-packed ranks, found their eighteen-foot pikes singularly unwieldy as the English darted in with their eight-foot bills. The pikes were abandoned: 'so many weapons lowered that it seemed as if a wood were falling down'.[27] The Scots turned to their side arms, their swords and axes. Yet they were still at a disadvantage; they may have had weapons that were more manageable, but a four-and-a-half-foot sword was outreached by the bills. And the bills were in the hands of men who used them in their daily work.

The Scots were numerous and they were brave. As the *Trewe Encountre* describes it, 'the Scots fought manfully and were determined either to win the field or die'.[28] For the Scottish nobles and gentry, to fight just a few minutes in full armour was exhausting, but this fight continued for more than two hours. Remorselessly the English gained the upper hand. The Admiral was true to his pre-battle message to James via Rouge Croix that:

> Furthermore, neither he nor any of his company would take any Scot prisoner, even if they were a noble, and they would die if they put themselves at his mercy; because he did not expect anything else from the Scots.[29]

James and his closest warriors tried to fight their way through to Surrey. They got to within a spear's length.[30] Meanwhile the Admiral's vanguard were grinding through the Erroll contingent and turning their attention to James's, tearing into its left flank. The Admiral had the assurance that Hume and Huntly, who continued standing off the action, were shadowed by Dacre.

James's right flank remained unsupported because Argyll and Lennox had not advanced with their Highlanders.

In the unequal struggle between Scottish side arms and English staff weapons, the jacks and brigandines would have given little protection against slash upon slash of the English bills. Full armour did not ensure survival either. The nobles, gentry and men-at-arms benefitted from wonderful craftsmanship, with armour made to distribute their weight evenly and to allow free movement of limbs. However carrying a weight of more than three and a half stone when exerting oneself to the fullest degree and over a prolonged period of time, was exhausting for the fully armoured man; and particularly so for those fighting at a disadvantage and for whom the battle was going awry. Some must have weakened from fatigue and been pulled to the ground by bills. By that stage even those wearing a German armet, a close-fitting closed helmet,[31] would not be protected, as the narrow slit above the rim of the fixed visor that would normally give them visibility was wide enough for a dagger thrust into the eye and through to the brain. Some with visored sallets may have pulled the visor up, desperate for the extra vision to counter threats from more than one direction, rendering their faces vulnerable as a consequence. Bishop Ruthall later described the armoured Scots as 'such large and strong men, they would not fall when four or five bills struck one of them.'[32]

The Scots may have started the engagement with a numerical advantage, but the English were able to bring more men to bear in the very press of battle. The Scots were under attack from two sides. To these was added a third.

The longbow had been signally ineffective against the Scots at the beginning of the battle. In Ruthall's words: 'They were so cased in armour the arrows did them no harm.'[33] The ghastly weather of wind and rain[34] and the long range also told against them. It was a different matter when the bows were shot from close quarters into the Scots' unprotected right flank. For Argyll and Lennox did not move forward. Perhaps, seeing the difficulties below them, they were waiting for the command or some notification of a 'Plan B'. But there would have been no provision for a 'Plan B', because the pike charge had previously been thought to be irresistible; after all, it had never been known to fail in an open battle such as Flodden.

More likely they were not given the opportunity to advance. Sir

Edward Stanley's men, wearing the badge of the eagle's claw, had made an undetected flanking manoeuvre up the eastern face of Branxton Hill. His archers were shooting their quivers of arrows into the poorly protected Highland troops with devastating effect.

As a counterpoint to the opening artillery exchange that marked a 'first' on a British battlefield, this was the last time that the longbow would prove its worth. In addition to its impact on Branxton Hill, it was added to the slaughter below. One of the men wounded was the most important of all: an arrow had embedded itself in the lower jaw of James IV, King of Scots. It didn't kill him, but it is likely that it disabled him sufficiently for the attacking billmen to move in and slash him with their weapons, virtually severing his left hand and finally, mercifully, slicing him across the throat.

Those of his nobles who were still alive fought on, as surrender was not an option. It seemed that their only chance, as the sun sank lower in the sky, was to continue fighting until nightfall and try to get off the battlefield under cover of darkness. Those who made that move beforehand were easy meat. Exhausted in their heavy armour, they had no chance of getting away from the billmen or the packs of swift-footed archers who, dropping their bows, used their secondary weapons of short swords, buckler shields and daggers. In previous battles, nobles could have reckoned on capture, their value to their opponents coming from them being taken alive and ransomed. Such, after all, had been the Scottish approach that had saved Edmund Howard's life. There was no such attitude from the English. If a Scottish noble or gentleman offered them a purse to establish his value and as a down payment for his life, the purse was taken and he was killed anyway. His residual value consisted of his weapons and armour, and he was stripped of them all.[35]

The Howards had made it clear that calls for mercy should be ignored and there should be no quarter. Only this can explain the extraordinary death rate among the Scottish nobility. Of the commanders, only Lord Hume and the Earl of Huntly, from their disengaged position standing off Dacre's Englishmen, managed to get away. Earls Erroll, Crawford, Montrose, Bothwell, Caithness, Cassillis, Rothes, Argyll and Lennox were killed. Lord Patrick Lindsay

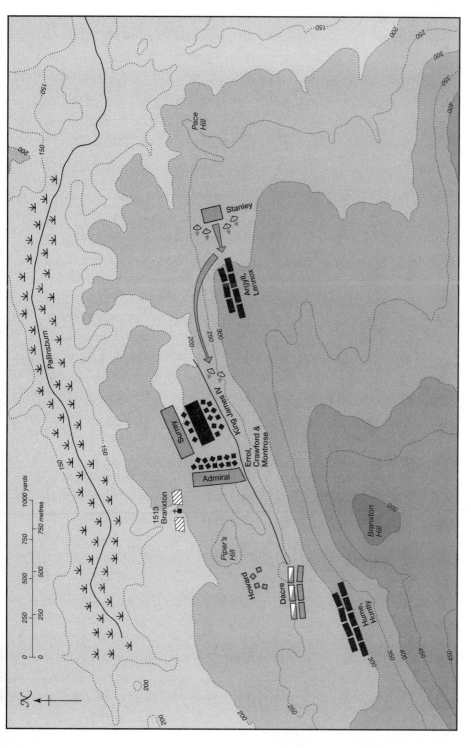

The Killing Fields

of the Byres escaped – though the latter's third son did not; but the list of lords who died is long. Lords Avandale, Borthwick, Elphinstone, Erskine, Hay of Yester, Herries, Innermeath, Maxwell, Ross, Sempill, Seton and Sinclair all fell, as did Sir John Ramsay, the disgraced former Lord Bothwell who had been reconciled to his King. Angus was not at the battle, but his two eldest sons were: both died. So did the heir and two other sons of the Earl of Cathcart, so did the heir to Lord Ruthven. Death did not come singly: two brothers of Lord Glamis were killed, as were two brothers of Lord Herries and two uncles of the Earl of Bothwell. There were disastrous losses among the gentry and their sons. Wider family groups fought and died together: possibly as many as eighty-eight Hays perished at Flodden.[36]

Members of the clergy were slain too: William Bunch, Abbot of Kilwinning; Lawrence Oliphant, Abbot of Inchaffary; George Hepburn, Bishop of the Isles; and, in the eyes of Erasmus, most appalling of all, his star pupil, the short-sighted Alexander Stewart, Archbishop of St Andrews and Chancellor of Scotland. Erasmus's sense of loss and anger at what he believed to be the futility of young Alexander's death was still apparent over twenty years later, when he wrote: 'What hadst thou to do with Mars, of all the gods of the poets the most infatuate, thou, who wert the disciple of the Muses and of Christ.'[37]

As for the army as a whole, it is estimated that 10,000 or just under a third of the Scots were killed.[38] This was a calamitous number and in certain communities the proportion of combatants killed was close to that of their leaders.[39] Those who were closer to the rear, free of armour and swifter-footed found it easier to get away.

In contrast, English losses numbered 4,000.[40] Of lords there were none and of gentry a mere dozen or so. The extent of the victory became clear the next day with the sight of the thousands of corpses strewn across the battlefield. But as night fell, matters looked less clear-cut and Surrey could not be entirely sure that he had achieved final victory. He still feared the Scots might mount a counter-attack.

English troops harried the retreating Scots, intent on capture and plunder. In the confusion of pursuit, as soldiers stumbled into fleeing groups, including those of non-combatants used but not nec-essarily protected by armies, some of the Scottish troops turned and made a stand. One English contingent overreached themselves and the would-be captors became captives. Yet in truth there were few prisoners.

Surrey made sure he captured and secured the Scottish guns. Dacre took them to Etal Castle,[41] where they were placed in the care of Sur-rey's brother-in-law, Sir Philip Tilney. Some of the more fortunate troops made for the Scottish camp, which they found well supplied with food and with those most precious of commodities, beer and ale. So well stocked was it that some Englishmen, though wracked with hunger and thirst, could not believe their luck; they presumed the bounty to be poisoned and began destroying it.[42] Men from the Bishop of Durham's detachment had no such doubts: they tucked in with a vengeance to 'their abundance of victuals, wines of all sorts, bread, beer and ale ... to their great refreshing'.[43]

Those who made it back to secure the English camp at Barmoor had no expectation of victuals, but if they had hoped to find it intact they were disappointed. While their fellow countrymen had been risking their lives for King Henry, the English Border Reivers had killed the sentries, stolen the horses and stripped the camp bare.[44]

Surrey, though aged around seventy, was an energetic man and still vital enough to have sired a child the previous year, but he must have been exhausted. It is thus no surprise that it was his son the Admiral who is credited with writing the *Articles of the Battle between the King of Scots and the Earl of Surrey on Branxton Field, on the 9th day of September*.[45] He wrote the next day to Queen Katherine, stating, almost accurately, that 'there is no great man of Scotland returned home, but the Chamberlain (Lord Hume)'.[46] Hume had not gone home with-out a further fight, trying manfully to recapture the Scottish guns with his Border horsemen and only being thwarted by stout English resistance.

By this time James's body had been found. It might have been any one of a number of English commanders who recognized it. Surrey himself was certainly one of these, but there were other men who had known James well and might be expected to identify his corpse.

There was Stanley, who had been with Margaret's procession in southern Scotland in 1503 and had sung ballads on the evening of music-making when James had played the clavichord and lute. Then there was Dacre, who had joined James on the 1504 hanging expedition in the Debatable Land.

In the event, it was Dacre who recognized him.[47] James was without the iron belt, but then that is hardly surprising for a man who had been wearing a fifty-pound suit of armour and carrying a pike.

⊰ ✝ ⊱

The Scottish force that crossed the Tweed with James IV was the largest army to invade England. It was over twenty times that of Henry VII's landing in 1485. The beginning of the campaign had been supremely successful in taking Wark and, most importantly for its symbolic significance, the capturing and dismantling of Norham Castle. Crossing the border and forcing England to deploy troops to counter him would certainly have fulfilled James's obligations on land to Louis XII of France. James's prime military interest to Louis was his navy, and there could even have been a solely naval war between England and Scotland *within* the terms of the Treaty of Perpetual Peace. Henry VIII's belligerence had made that response impossible.

Taking Norham and then re-crossing the border would, as in 1497 against Surrey, have been enough to celebrate as a victory in the eyes of James's subjects. But James, by adding Etal and Ford and preparing an impregnable battlefield position on Flodden Hill, had set up a far better position for himself. He had even outwitted Surrey diplomatically, by making the Earl seem to be the one rejecting the agreed terms of engagement. Had he known the state of Surrey's army, he could have stayed on Flodden Hill with plentiful supplies of food and safe, drinkable water from what is now known as Sybil Grey's Well, only a few yards from the summit.[48] Surrey, lacking food and water, unless resupplied, would have found himself in a desperate position; because it seems that even an assault against the northern face of Flodden Hill would have been hazardous, given the recent findings by archaeologist Chris Burgess and his team which indicated that this too was fortified.[49]

But there seemed no need for James to wait for that, provided he reach the summit of Branxton Hill first — which he did. Having done so, in the words of the military historian Niall Barr, 'James IV and his army still held all the cards'.[50] This was a battle he seemed almost certain to win.

True, his artillery had malfunctioned, but the guns were not expected to be the decisive weaponry — that role fell to the echelon advance of massed pikes, which, far from being rushed together and broken up by English artillery fire, proceeded 'in good order'.[51] The first part of the advance under Hume and Huntly had gone outstandingly well. Their attack had, with difficulty, been held up through Surrey's deploying Dacre's reserve to reinforce Edmund Howard; nevertheless, had the rest of the Scottish attack possessed the same fluency and momentum, the English would have been swept off the battlefield and into the obviously treacherous marshy ground of the Pallinsburn beyond. The Scots would have replicated the manoeuvre that had triumphed in open battle in continental Europe.

Instead they met with disaster. Perhaps the best, most experienced Swiss troops would have been able to rearrange and reorganize themselves after being stopped in the quagmire, but it is unlikely, because the problem was not a failure of discipline but one of momentum, which once lost would have been almost impossible to regain. James has been criticized for putting himself at the front of his troops and thus being unable to redirect them once things began to go wrong. But given his personal style of kingship and his personality, he could have done nothing else: once a pike attack began, it was a case of all or nothing. Its effectiveness lay in the power of the initial assault. He judged that he would be most influential in ensuring the success of that opening move through inspiring his troops, lifting their spirits with the sight of his banner advancing towards the English.

The fact remains that James had led Scotland to its worst ever military defeat. He had taken the risk of fighting on ground that was unsurveyed for battle. Yet seeing the initial success of Hume and Huntly, from his position high on Branxton Hill, it would then have seemed scarcely a risk at all.

James certainly knew the importance of 'ground' — normally 'high ground'. The works of the Roman military theorist Vegetius were well-known, thanks to the writings of the remarkable fifteenth-century French noblewoman, Christine de Pisan.[52] 'Ground' was one of the three key factors for securing 'the advantage of the field', together with 'wind' and (less important in cooler climes) 'sun'. James had also spent time with Bernard Stewart, Seigneur d'Aubigny, master of terrain reconnaissance.[53]

However, the area at the foot of Branxton Hill and the slope to the ridge beyond it were particularly difficult to survey from James's lofty position. The slope appears a gentle incline from high above, but close to it is far more challenging. Crucially, the true nature of the ground towards the base of Branxton Hill was completely disguised. It may have appeared wet, but the battle was fought in wet conditions. Even with twenty-first century drainage, water runs across the foot of the hill – but not in a fixed enough way to give it a name as a rivulet or a stream. This is groundwater discharge, intermittent and governed by rises and falls in the water table. In 1513 surface water from the seepage zones would have been dispersed over a large area and, not very deep at under six inches, would have been disguised by grass (true wetland plants require greater depths). It would have been extremely difficult to realize this from a distance, particularly in rainy conditions, with the firm ground used by Hume and Huntly indistinguishable from that to be marched over by the troops of Erroll, Crawford and Montrose and of King James himself. Perhaps, and this we cannot know, James waited to be sure that the ground under Hume's and Huntly's men was firm before ordering a general advance.

We now know far more about the treacherous nature of the ground than James did, as we have access to the work of Professor Paul Younger, one the world's leading hydrogeologists, who has surveyed the ground at Flodden and made available his conclusions in works such as the article 'Crouching enemy, hidden ally: the decisive role of groundwater discharge features in two major British battles, Flodden 1513 and Prestonpans 1745'.[54]

The death of James IV and, with him, so many of his countrymen was not down to the sort of vainglory described by Ayala in 1498. The forty-year-old King James was a mature and experienced ruler, a very different individual to the more impetuous man in his mid-twenties whom Ayala knew. In 1513, it was James's young brother-in-law, Henry VIII, who was vainglorious, the more likely to submit himself to personal risk, as reflected in Queen Katherine's letters of concern.

There were many factors that caused the Battle of Flodden to be fought and to unfold in the way it did. At every stage in the days leading up to the battle, James seemed to have outmanoeuvred Surrey.[55] At the outset of the battle he seemed set to deploy pike formations in Britain for the same sort of crushing victory they had achieved in continental Europe. It seemed likely that this great Scottish Renaissance king with a passionate interest, among many others, in science and technology, would triumph with the wonder weapons of early sixteenth-century warfare. He was undone by his ignorance of a science that has only gained widespread recognition since the mid-twentieth century: that of hydrogeology.[56]

James IV had sought to remain independent, but had been unable to escape the centuries-old rivalry between the kings of England and France. Once drawn in, he had enjoyed a run of military successes that led him to 'risk all in battle',[57] in quest of the victory that would resound down the ages. The human element that undid him was a rivalry that he could not acknowledge, one between a crowned and anointed Scottish king and a mere English earl. But it was made real enough on the battlefield by the Howards, a family desperate to regain their own King's favour and secure their future existence.

21

——

Aftermath

The military historian Gervase Phillips writes in his Introduction to *The Anglo-Scots Wars 1513–1550* that 'most historical events and battles in particular can hinge on the tiniest of chances'.[1] Such was the case with Flodden. Though in the days, months and decades that followed, there were many, Scots and English alike, who were ready to ascribe a variety of different reasons as to why the English won and the Scottish lost at Flodden.

Bishop Ruthall wrote to Wolsey on 20 September with some observations based on military analysis, saying that the Scots had possessed the advantage of wind (which was true), of ground (which was only accurate in terms of 'height'), and (most surprisingly because of the appalling weather) of sun.[2] As to the real reason for victory, he had no doubt: St Cuthbert had exacted revenge for James's treatment of the Bishop's castle at Norham.

Ruthall continued: 'All believe it has been wrought by the intercession of St Cuthbert, who never suffered injury to be done to his Church unrequited.'[3] Ruthall's men, carrying St Cuthbert's banner, had even managed to capture the opposing banner of the King of Scots, which 'now stands beside the shrine' of St Cuthbert in Durham Cathedral.[4] St Cuthbert, via his banner, could add to his previous 'victory' at Neville's Cross.[5] Ruthall was still apoplectic about 'the cruel tyranny of the King of Scots' and the razing of Norham. He also took a sideswipe at Andrew Forman, Bishop of Moray, when saying that 'the invasion proceeded of his own [James's] sensual mind, by the instigation of the Bishop of Moray, against the wishes of the nobles'; which is an interesting contradiction of Wolsey's own report to Henry VII five years before, that when it came to renewing the Auld Alliance 'all his [James's] subjects except the Bishop of Moray call on him daily to do so'.[6]

The continuing English reaction was ecstatic. Queen Katherine, as hyperbolic on her own account as she had been for Henry, credited the victory to God himself. When she received the Admiral's dispatch she wrote to the King:

My Lord Howard has sent me a Letter, which I enclose for your Grace within mine. You shall see in detail the great victory our Lord God has given to your subjects in your absence … and to my thinking this battle has been for your Grace and all your realm the greatest honour there could be, and more than if you should win all the crown of France. Thanks be to God for it, and I am sure that your Grace will not forget to do this, which will be the cause of his sending you more such great victories.

If Henry had not known Katherine better, he might have detected a degree of crowing by his Queen. But she also sent him a present: James's blood-soaked surcoat.[7]

Your grace shall see how I can keep my promise, sending you for your banners a King's coat. I thought to send him to you in person, but our Englishmen's hearts would not suffer it. It should have been better for him to have kept the peace than have this reward. All that God sends is for the best.[8]

Brian Tuke, as their secretary, would have seen all the correspondence that came in to Wolsey and Henry. He gave more earthly credit: 'The English halberdiers [billmen] decided the whole affair' and, as previously cited, 'in this battle the bows and ordnance were of little use.'[9]

In Surrey's own epitaph, the credit was spread around: mentioning God's help to honour the King, but also the Earl himself, all other noblemen and 'others the King's subjects that were there with him at the battle'.[10] However, in his role as Lord Treasurer, Surrey applauded himself at the time: he was able to dismiss the army on 14 September, thereby, as he said, 'sparing the wages of 18,689 men by the space of fourteen days'.[11]

What was Henry to make of it all? It was difficult for him to claim this as a personal victory: he wasn't there. Perhaps crediting it to God in honouring the King was the best way of involving him. Maybe Ruthall feared that Henry's absence would cause the leaders of the victory to be undervalued, suggesting to Wolsey that the King should make Surrey a duke and singling out Lords Howard and Dacre, Sir William Bulmer and Sir Edward Stanley for praise.

In the event, Henry had no difficulty in accepting the victory as his. It might not have been a victory by him, but it was most certainly one for him. On Monday, 26 September, bonfires organized by the Earl of Shrewsbury and Lord Herbert were lit and the army besieging Tournai celebrated the triumph. The next day a tent of cloth of gold was set up and a Te Deum sung in celebration by the King's Chapel Choir.[12] No doubt, as always on these occasions, there was a deafening firing of ordnance.[13]

Surrey made forty knights on the battlefield, including his son Edmund.[14] His own recognition was a little slower in coming; it was not until the following February that he was created Duke of Norfolk. Interestingly, this was as the 2nd Duke and not as a new, Tudor, creation – though it had been over twenty-eight years since the death of his father, fighting for Richard III at Bosworth. To maintain the status of a duke, it was necessary to have the income to support the title, and Norfolk was richly rewarded with the gift of thirty manors, but they were spread around the country and none was in his traditional territorial heartland of East Anglia. Henry had no intention of giving Norfolk a consolidated power base akin to a Wars of the Roses magnate.[15] He was, however, now of the same degree in the peerage as the potentially dangerous Duke of Buckingham. And Norfolk's son, the Lord Admiral, became Earl of Surrey.

Flodden had transformed the fortunes of the Howard family. When they had been excluded from the main theatre of war, their prospects had looked bleak indeed. It was clear that they needed a victory in the Scottish campaign to force themselves back into royal favour, and to secure it they were willing to take the risks of dividing their army, of failing to gain the higher ground and of having their retreat cut off by water. Victory gained, favour restored, they were determined that Flodden would be remembered for all posterity and their arms were augmented with an escutcheon that was a variation on the Royal Arms of Scotland. Only the top half of the lion rampant was shown, to ensure the key element could be seen: the arrow piercing the lion's mouth. Considering the nature of James's wounds, this might be considered in extremely poor taste; but it made the point.

Norfolk, if behind Wolsey in power and influence, was back in the inner circle of royal counsels. Together with Wolsey and Fox, he negotiated another Tudor royal marriage, that of Henry VIII's pretty and lively younger sister Mary to the recently widowed Louis XII. Henry and Wolsey were learning: they had anticipated that Maximilian was about to make a separate peace with France and got there first. Louis was now fifty-two and in frail health; within three months, his vigorous eighteen-year-old Queen had 'danced' him to death.[16] Instead of creating a long line of French kings of English descent, she became an interesting footnote in their history: the sole English consort to the French Kings of France in almost eleven hundred years.[17] France's peace with England was made without consulting the Scots.

From this point forward, members of the Howard family were central figures in the increasingly bloody dramas of Henry VIII's reign. When Henry decided on Buckingham's destruction in 1521, it was to the elderly Duke of Norfolk that he turned. Norfolk did not disappoint: he presided over the trial of his fellow duke and, with tears on his cheeks, he announced the death sentence. It was his last great service: he gave up his administrative and ceremonial duties over the next two years and retired to his castle and estates at Framlingham. He died in 1524. As to Norfolk's two sons and fellow commanders at Flodden, the Admiral and Sir Edmund had very different lives. The Admiral was at the heart of political intrigue, becoming the richest peer in the land[18] and surviving – just – until the end of Henry's reign.[19] In contrast, the spendthrift and ineffectual Edmund died in relative obscurity in 1539.[20] Thus he did not live to see his daughter Catherine become Henry's short-lived fifth Queen. She was the second granddaughter of Flodden's victor to become Henry's consort and then victim: the first was Anne Boleyn,[21] his replacement for the discarded Katherine of Aragon.

⊰ ✛ ⊱

The Scots could have no idea of England's real intentions immediately after Flodden. In expectation of a full-scale invasion they began strengthening the defences around Edinburgh; hence the 'Flodden Wall', which in part still survives today. For a country in shock at the size of the defeat, there was the understanding that such a calamitous event must have both great causes and great consequences. That sense of shock was real, vibrant and long-lasting. In the aftermath of the battle and in the decades and centuries that followed, people looked to human agency and above all human weakness for an explanation. Hume, but not Huntly, was blamed for breaking off his attack on the English right. In fact, Robert Lindsay of Pitscottie alleged that Hume said 'he does well that does for himself',[22] as a counter to Huntly's pleas that they aid their King. It was even alleged that, in the very midst of battle, the Borderers on both sides came to an agreement among themselves to stand off. Hume was indeed executed just three years after Flodden, but because he fell foul of the faction-fighting that succeeded it, rather than because of the battle itself. Another target of Pitscottie was Andrew Forman, presented as an evil genius of the King, when he was very much his servant. A further culprit, for both Pitscottie and George Buchanan, was James Hamilton, Earl of Arran. Yet, though Arran was slow to get the fleet into position, modern historians accept it was not through a deliberate disobeying of orders.[23] Even Buchanan's own nineteenth-century editor accuses his author of 'fables too from hatred of the Hamiltons'.[24]

However, the chief target for these post-reformation Protestant storytellers is the pre-reformation Catholic king. They echo Ruthall's 'sensual' critique of James, with James's supposed dalliance with Lady Heron the least of his indiscretions. Their 'James' fits the 'moonstruck romantic' description later given to him,[25] but not the real man and King. Pitscottie's 'History', in particular, is more Hollywood than Holyrood and full of dramatic scenes dedicated to highlighting the historical importance of Pitscottie's own family, the Lindsays. All James's purported acts of doom-laden foolishness are here, such as his supposed 'chivalric' decision to invade by land in return for a ring from Anne of Brittany.[26] James is presented as someone who refused to heed words of warning, either from figures in this world or spectres from the next. Thus Pitscottie tells us of the appearance at the service of Vespers at Linlithgow of an old man in a blue gown, who cautioned James against his English expedition[27] and also, according to the puritanical Buchanan, 'to beware of using any familiarity in associating or advising with women' on pain of disgrace, before promptly disappearing. Following this vision of St John[28] comes an account of a voice at the Market Cross in Edinburgh that incanted what would be later revealed as the roll call of the dead.[29] Buchanan's nineteenth-century editor, James Aikman, added to the mix by declaring these warnings to be contrivances of Margaret, James's anguished Queen, in her attempts to turn her superstitious husband away from war.[30] It was an anguish, according to another nineteenth-century 'historian', that was fuelled by premonitions in Margaret's vivid dreams.[31] More pertinently, James, is also accused by Pitscottie and Buchanan of ignoring her more straightforward counsel, together with that of all his lords who 'would not suffer the king to give battle at that time to a man of inferior degree';[32] and of an important individual (Lord Lindsay, naturally, for Pitscottie,[33] Angus for Buchanan[34]), who begged the King to avoid putting himself in danger. Fantastic or otherwise, these fabrications, with their highlights given lasting resonance by being first versified and then rendered in prose by Sir Walter Scott, are entertaining, but they ought to be treated as entertainments and nothing more.

Pitscottie, who was not born until around twenty years after Flodden, concluded that James was undone 'not by the wisdom or manhood of Englishmen, but by the king's own wilful misgovernance'.[35] His view does not accord with the judgment of recent academic historians nor the documentary evidence of the time. Indeed, James was described as the 'glory of princely governing',[36] by Pitscottie's near namesake, Sir David Lyndsay of the Mount. This, from a man who knew James IV personally, seems nearer the mark.

Flodden was a battlefield defeat of the most comprehensive sort, but it was due to the decisions of days, not of decades. Whatever judgments might be made in matters of 'honour', James fatefully, if not fatally, misread the character of his battlefield opponents, the

Howards. He also took what seemed, from his high vantage point on Branxton Hill, the very small risk of fighting on ground that looked firm from afar. This was not ideal pike country, but if James's part of the battleground had been as firm as that of Hume and Huntly, or if he had been able to accept Surrey's challenge to fight on Milfield Plain, then he would probably have won the day.[37]

Surrey's challenge was, of course, one he could not accept: the very suggestion was an insult. This was a rivalry that James could not acknowledge and the more fatal for it. The Howards sought to treat him not as their superior as an anointed king, but as their equal as a British lord. It was anathema to James because of a far greater rivalry: that with Henry VIII, which was not just to do with their personal, primal competition to father a line of kings. It was something more fundamental even than that: it related to the centuries-old question as to which of them, ultimately, was the overlord of Scotland.

Should James have fought a battle? Most certainly he was right to do so, according to the expectations of his people and of the time. Once forced into war, he would need to negotiate its end, and far better to do this on the back of the famous victory he expected. A historic victory would have fittingly completed a popular and brilliantly successful campaign, but much more than that, it would have adorned a reign of enormous accomplishment with a day of military glory to sit beside Bannockburn. Instead, James's reign and his achievements in raising the crown and country of Scotland to a hitherto unprecedented level of prestige, administrative coherence and geographical unity, are obscured; they are robbed of their lustre by the extent of James's debacle at Flodden, just as Bruce's reign was given increased radiance by the triumph at Bannockburn. The shock of James's military defeat was taken up by the propagandists and storytellers, not the brilliance of what he had done before. This has not been the fate of Joan of Arc, nor indeed of William Wallace.

☙ ✠ ❧

Were the more immediate consequences of Flodden of a scale that echoed the defeat itself? On one level they were, and they stemmed from the very success of James's rule. As Ranald Nicholson puts it at the end of his book, *Scotland – the Later Middle Ages*: 'Sometimes in the past the Scots had suffered a reverse as great as that of 1513 and had quickly recovered; they did not regard Flodden as an irretrievable disaster; but the disaster was not retrieved.'[38] Because, although the machinery for monarchical power was there, it lacked the firm, personal direction that James had given it: one that brought together aristocracy and clergy from all parts of the kingdom. James's kingship had been inclusive and consultative, but when the discussions came to an end it was, as Ayala noted,[39] decisive. In the authoritative opinion of Norman Macdougall, with James's death 'the purpose, drive and unanimity which he had instilled in the political community were shattered, and Scottish self-confidence was lost for the remainder of the century'.[40]

But it is also a measure of James IV's achievements as a ruler that, although the political elite fell into faction during the minority of his young son James V, the country retained a degree of administrative coherence in the succeeding years. As Michael Lynch explains, 'Factions came and went during the minority, but there was a striking continuity of loyal service to the crown throughout the second and third rank levels of the royal administration,'[41] if not among the first.

⊰ ✝ ⊱

Immediately after the battle, even the first rank held firm. Huntly, Hume and Secretary Panter had survived Flodden; Bishop Elphinstone had not been there, nor had Angus nor indeed a number of other lords whose sons had died in their place.[42] Within two weeks the Council had met and James V, aged seventeen months, had been crowned in haste at Stirling.[43]

With the threat of the English invasion having receded, minority government – and this was the fifth successive minority, with two more to follow – could proceed in a calmer manner. However, faction now dominated and events played out as if echoing the unstable periods of the fifteenth century. In his will, James had appointed Margaret 'tutrix' or Regent, to govern with a small council, so long as she did not remarry. But like James II's widow Joan Beaufort, she was an English-born Queen who began to be accused of serial immorality; the difference between them being that, in Margaret's case, there was more than a hint of truth. She certainly lacked wisdom, throwing away her key position by marrying, within a year of her husband's death, Archibald Douglas, a man of her own age (around twenty-five), who was Bell the Cat's grandson and post-Flodden heir. This was a disastrous move, for not only were they both suspected of being pro-English, but Douglas was a large landowner of vaulting ambition, more than ready to make himself a Douglas as powerful as the ones destroyed by James II.

Horrified peers turned to young James V's closest adult relative, the Duke of Albany, son of the brother of James III who had supported the English invasion of 1482. This Albany was rather different: he was French in every aspect but his name. In 1515 he arrived as Governor. Margaret, without young James, fled with Douglas to England, before being invited back in 1517, when Albany had temporarily returned to France.

The lack of a stable and permanent political solution continued right through young James's minority, with matters made even more difficult when Margaret became bitterly estranged from Douglas and sought an annulment to her marriage in order to marry Henry Stewart, a very distant cousin. In the summer of 1528, aged sixteen, James overthrew his stepfather's regime and took power himself. Gradually over the next fourteen years, he restored royal authority. From a much weaker position he sought, with some success, to steer a course between France and England, as Henry VIII spent vast sums of money vainly trying to compete with his younger and richer Renaissance rivals – Francis I of France and Emperor Charles V.[44]

James V augmented his father's palaces with spectacular building projects and tried to build on the work of his father more generally. But in 1542 his army was routed by the English at the Battle of Solway Moss and shortly after he died of plague. His early death, aged thirty, removed 'a very promising Renaissance prince,'[45] but one who was nonetheless a pale imitation of his father. Once again, Scotland was cursed with a minority, that of Mary Queen of Scots. The disasters of Mary's reign and Scotland's Protestant Reformation would break the link with France, though for some the sentimental attachment remained.

Scottish political instability in the decades after Flodden was stoked, both intentionally and unintentionally, by Henry VIII's fluctuating policy. Its one long-term strand was based on Henry's view that his neighbour to the north was of minor interest in comparison to France to the south. Though the Scots might have sometimes feared otherwise, annexation of Scotland was never of interest to him; Henry's consistent strategic concern was containment.[46] More immediately he oscillated between cursory attempts to support a pro-English party and commands for Scottish obedience. In 1542 his demands for recognition of his overlordship culminated in a lengthy recitation of 'his true and right title ... to his sovereignty of Scotland',[47] stretching back into earliest 'history' and authenticated in later times by 'records' listing the homage of Kings of Scotland to their English overlords over half a millennium.

More immediately, after Flodden, while supposedly supporting Margaret, Henry undermined her. His approach was brutal: he gave Dacre free rein. This was not to impose peace, because the desire to bring calm to the Borders had gone with the Perpetual Peace itself. The English aim was to do the opposite: to create a buffer zone of anarchy between the two countries. The English Warden of the Marches was, for a period, the most notorious Border Reiver.

Dacre had not received the same sort of direct rewards as, for instance, Stanley, who in November 1514 was given a stylishly appropriate new title of 1st Baron Monteagle, in recognition of the eagle's claw badge of the Stanleys and his successful hill attack at Flodden. Instead, Dacre was given licence to help himself and over a period of years he kept the Marches in uproar.[48] He was not too choosy about whom he attacked, as shown by the inhabitants of Northumberland making formal accusations against him.[49] Under the new conditions, incidents of reiving multiplied. John Heron the Bastard also took full advantage until, in what might be described as belated justice, he was killed in a foray in 1524. There were periodic crackdowns throughout the remainder of the sixteenth century, such as James V's in 1530, and the Border regularized even within the Debatable Land in 1551,[50] but the settling of the entirety of the Borders had to wait until the unification of the two crowns under James VI and I in 1603. The ensuing solution to the Reiver problem was immediate and crushing: many Reivers were killed, and the Grahams, as one of the most troublesome clans, were forcibly transported en bloc to Ireland in 1606.[51]

But the union of the two crowns under James VI and I did not bring about a union of the countries. The legacy of James IV's rule was that Scotland held together geographically and administratively in the sixteenth century, in spite of its extraordinary political instability and its catalogue of assassination, regime change and foreign intervention. England and Scotland would continue to develop as separate nations, even after James VI became James I of England (having apparently considered changing his name to Arthur, to suit his new doubled role).[52] James sought to combine the emblems of the two nations in a design for a new flag and for a Great Seal (which incorporated the arms of the Celtic Cadwallader and the Saxon Edward the Confessor, as well as those of England and Scotland), but the English Parliament rejected his proposals for a full union in 1607.[53] More disastrously, Charles I was to discover the difference between the two nations when he sought to force a new prayer book on the Scots in 1637 and initiated a dozen years of personal and national calamities.

⊰ ✝ ⊱

As for James IV, after Flodden his body was taken to Berwick, where it was embalmed, sealed in a lead-lined coffin and sent to Richmond. Not to the Palace, but to the Carthusian monastery at Sheen, where it remained unburied. James was excommunicate at his death and could not be laid in consecrated ground until the Pope remitted the sentence. Henry, perhaps out of feeling for his sister – or more likely because he envisaged the funeral as a ceremonial occasion at St Paul's, with himself at its centre, wrote to Leo X. At the same time as asking for remittance for James, he claimed Bainbridge's right as Archbishop of York to oversee the Scottish Church as part of his diocese.[54] This latter request was refused, as was Henry's attempt to nominate the new Archbishop of St Andrews. Bainbridge's influence at Rome was failing, partly due to the counter-plotting of Wolsey's agent, the Italian Silvestro Gigli, Bishop of Worcester, who from 1512 was Henry VIII's special representative in Rome. Gigli, supposedly serving under Bainbridge, was steadily undermining him. On 14 July 1514, in a twist fitting the current popular image of Renaissance Rome, Bainbridge was poisoned by one of his own household who, when tortured, declared that Gigli was his paymaster. Leo formally absolved Gigli of any role in the murder, but the suspicion lingered.[55]

Leo had by this time remitted James's excommunication with the words 'it is to be presumed the King gave some signs of repentance in his extremities'.[56] However, the Scottish King remained unburied. Perhaps he had just been forgotten and no one cared to remind Henry of the fact.

Certainly the absence of James's body proved useful to his widow Margaret. Desperate for an annulment of her marriage to Archibald Douglas, she petitioned the Pope on the basis that James had not died at Flodden.[57] Certainly there had been reported 'sightings' of him after the battle, but then such visions often followed the sudden deaths of kings. Preposterous as Margaret's claim may have been, her petition was presented.

Meanwhile James's coffin stayed above ground at Sheen, where it remained as the decades passed and the cataclysm of the Reformation, including the Carthusian Monastery's own dissolution, unfolded around it. The next known mention is by the antiquarian John Stow, who was personally shown the coffin during the reign of Edward VI, by the owner of the now secularized estate, Lady Jane Grey's father, Henry Duke of Suffolk. It was in a store room, full of old timber, lead and rubble. There it continued until the reign of Elizabeth, when, sadly, the coffin was rediscovered and opened. James's body became a plaything. In the words of John Stow himself: 'Workmen there for their foolish pleasure hewed off his head.' The trunk and limbs then disappeared, their last-known resting place now being covered by the greensward of Royal Mid-Surrey Golf Club. But the head remained and Lancelot Young, Queen Elizabeth's Master Glazier, took it home with him to his house in Wood Street in the City of London. Then, after a time, he asked the Sexton of the local church, St Michael's, to bury it.[58] The church was destroyed in the Great Fire of London and its replacement, built by Wren, was demolished in the nineteenth century.

At the time of writing, the site is occupied by a pub called The Red Herring.

It is a tragedy that there is no fitting last resting place for Scotland's great Renaissance King. Strangely, the same is also true of his English brother-in-law and rival, Henry VIII. Henry planned a magnificent tomb – or rather, Wolsey planned one for himself which Henry requisitioned for his own use after Wolsey's fall. If the father, Henry VII, had not quite gained the full memorial he wanted, then the son, Henry VIII, had no monument at all. The tomb, incomplete at Henry's death, did not suit the zealous Protestantism of the leading councillors of his son Edward VI. Instead, Henry's coffin, which had needed repair after the gases from his bloated corpse had caused it to burst, was placed in the vault at St George's Chapel Windsor on 16 February 1547, with just the slab in the floor above marking the spot. The marble of the tomb was put in store until, like so much else, it was sold off during the Commonwealth period, 1649–60. Only one part remained: the black marble sarcophagus. That survived destruction and can still be seen today in the crypt of St Paul's Cathedral in London. It adorns the granite tomb of a later, very British hero: Horatio Viscount Nelson.[59]

Commemoration

Emperor Maximilian, Henry VIII's 1513 comrade-in-arms, famously said that 'he who fails to create his memorial during his lifetime will have none after his death'. Like other Renaissance rulers whose lineage did not quite measure up, including the Sforza Dukes of Milan and England's Henry VII, Maximilian ensured that his family tree was suitably enhanced and that it included luminaries such as King Arthur and Julius Caesar. Having secured his past, he had an eye to his present (through the ceremonial art of Albrechts Dürer and Altdorfer) and to his future (by commissioning a glorious memorial tomb at Innsbruck). Maximilian choreographed his reign and organised its subsequent celebration. This final element was denied to James IV.

There are three English accounts of the Battle of Flodden from possible eye-witnesses: *Articles of the Battle* (almost certainly written by Admiral Howard); the *Trewe Encountre* narrative of a 'Northumbrian', published by Richard Faques within weeks of Flodden; and, lastly, the report of 'a member of the Earl of Surrey's household' and dedicated to the Earl when it was published by Richard Pynson early in 1514.[1] This last was taken almost verbatim into his *Chronicle* account by Edward Hall.[2] All three are extremely valuable, but even if they are indeed first-hand primary sources, they need to be treated with caution, because all are official versions: the last two because Faques and Pynson were both licensed printers to the crown; the first and third as documents authored or approved by the Howards.

Important secondary sources from soon after the battle include the albeit self-interested writings of Katherine of Aragon and Thomas Ruthall and the aggregation of first- and second-hand material in Brian Tuke's letter to Richard Pace. Tuke was in France and thus

well away from the action in Northumberland, but, as correspondence secretary to Henry and Wolsey, he would have had sight of the
reports sent to the King and his minister. His letter was intended to
be reassuring, but, written by one senior administrator to another, it
also needed to be convincing, thus making Tuke's comments on the
ineffectiveness of the English artillery all the more interesting. All the
same it is a 'political' letter and one has to interpret this, like all the
English material, with care. But at least it exists.

Unfortunately, one cannot compare the English accounts with similar Scottish sources. There are no records from Hume and Huntly
or from other possible credible witnesses. This, combined with the
nature of the defeat, has led over the centuries to less reliable narra-
tives filling the gap and – as a brilliant new essay explains – to the
creation of commemorative traditions that have given a better indication of their own times than of September 1513.[3]

Fortunately the mock-historical varnish of previous centuries is
now being removed. In recent years the Battle of Flodden has been
the focus of important research on both sides of the Border and there
is much more to come, as the following section on 'Related Organiza-
tions' highlights. Though no age can escape leaving a shadow on the
period it interprets, we can be confident that this one will continue to
cast far more light than shade.

SELECT LIST OF FLODDEN-RELATED ORGANIZATIONS AND PLACES TO VISIT

Information at time of going to press.

Immediate to Flodden

Remembering Flodden is a member group of the Battlefields Trust. Working in collaboration with local landowners, it has designed and delivered a battlefield trail with well-positioned and well-judged signboards. Remembering Flodden's Clive Hallam-Baker, who lives in Branxton, has interpreted the battle and battlefield for many years. In preparation for the quincentennial, he has produced campaign maps, a DVD entitled *The Battle of Flodden: Then & Now* and a companion battlefield guide *The Battle of Flodden: Why & How*. These are available through www.flodden.net

The Flodden 500 Project. Commemoration of the Battle is the shared element of the initiatives operating under the umbrella of the Flodden 500 Project. Underpinning the Project is the ecomuseum concept, which brings together places with a common historical connection. Flodden 1513 Ecomuseum sites are nominated for their links to the battle, in terms both of their historical importance and for their resonance in the popular memory. For that reason, though many are close to the Flodden battlefield, some stretch far to the south in England or to the north in Scotland. The Flodden 500 Project's community-based approach is supported by the Heritage Lottery Fund (HLF) with a major grant. The grant is directly funding or indirectly encouraging a full range of initiatives that offer learning, participation and volunteering opportunities for people to get involved in all aspects of Flodden heritage. It includes a range of educational and continuous learning initiatives. For further information on the Flodden 500 Project, which is running an ever-changing calendar of events – not only in 2013 but in the years beyond – see www.flodden1513.com

The Flodden Archaeological 500 project work on sites connected with the Flodden campaign was recognized with the award of a grant by the Heritage Lottery Fund, as part of the Flodden 500 Project. From 2013–2016, they are running a programme of excavations, metal detecting and field walking that will operate in parallel with new documentary research (see below). Site investigations are targeted around Ellemford, Duns, Wark Castle, Ladykirk, Norham, Barmoor and, of course, the immediate battlefield area at Branxton and Flodden. The digs are carried out by volunteers. Potential volunteers can contact The Flodden Archaeological 500 project through its website – www.iflodden.info or by email – Flodden500@gmail.com

Flodden 500 Transcription Project. As part of the Flodden 500 Project, the Berwick-upon-Tweed Record Office and the Heritage Hub at Hawick are leading a volunteer transcription project. The project aims to transcribe primary source material relating to the Battle and its aftermath on both sides of the Border up to c.1603. Documentation relating to this important era of the area's history is kept in various institutions in England and Scotland and the two-year project (from 2013) is consolidating it in digital format. Digital copies of the documents and the transcriptions are being made available in both Record Offices and some information will also be placed on the website – www.flodden1513.com. For further information about the project itself and volunteering opportunities, contact berwickarchives@woodhorn.org.uk

National Organizations and Further Afield

The Battlefields Trust is the UK charity dedicated to the preservation and interpretation of Britain's battlefields. Information on joining and on the 43 registered battlefield sites (including Flodden) is available on the Trust's website, together with the UK Battlefields Resource Centre which has extensive material on 72 British battles, from Maldon (991) to Sedgemoor (1685). www.battlefieldstrust.com

The Royal Armouries is the national museum of arms and armour. It is the UK's oldest museum collection and has sites in Leeds, HM Tower of London, Fort Nelson and Louisville, Kentucky (USA). In addition to personal armour and small arms, the Leeds museum houses the reserve, study and archive collections, and its curators include leading experts on medieval and renaissance warfare; Fort Nelson is the home of the Royal Armouries national collection of artillery. As a starting point for general information, www.royalarmouries.org

The Tower of London and Hampton Court. Henry VIII was the owner of 55 royal palaces. Two of his finest are now managed and run by Historic Royal Palaces, an independent charity which receives no funding from either the Government or the Crown, but which depends on the support of its visitors, members, donors, volunteers and sponsors. For details of opening times and to discover the benefits of annual membership, www.hrp.org.uk

Westminster Abbey, for Henry VII's magnificent tomb and chapel, http://www.westminster-abbey.org/visit-us/highlights/the-lady-chapel

Websites for James IV's Palaces

Holyrood www.royalcollection.org.uk/visit/palaceofholyroodhouse

Edinburgh Castle www.edinburghcastle.gov.uk

Stirling Castle www.stirlingcastle.gov.uk

Linlithgow www.historic-scotland.gov.uk/ under 'Places to Visit'

Falkland www.nts.org.uk/Property/Falkland-Palace-Garden/

Framlingham and the Howards

The Church of St Michael, Framlingham houses the famous Flodden helm of the victorious Earl of Surrey (2nd Duke of Norfolk) and a number of impressive Howard tombs, including that of his son Thomas, Admiral Howard (3rd Duke). For further information, www.stmichaelschurch.onesuffolk.net/home/history-and-tours

Framlingham Castle www.english-heritage.org.uk/daysout/properties/framlingham-castle

NOTES

A number of the primary sources quoted here are also available through British History Online at www.british-history.ac.uk. It has been created by the Institute of Historical Research and the History of Parliament Trust, with the aim of supporting academic and personal users around the world in their learning, teaching and research. It is a tremendous resource – see ◊ in the Select Bibliography for online availability.

PROLOGUE

1. Carey, *Memoirs of Robert Carey, Earl of Monmouth* (1808) p. 7.
2. Just under 43 as the crow flies and just over 52 by modern roads.
3. Sir Robert Carey, later 1st Earl of Monmouth, describes these events in his own words in his memoirs.
4. John Nichols (ed.), *The Progresses, Processions and Magnificent Festivities of King James I*, 4 vols. (1828), Vol. I, p. 60.
5. Borman, *Elizabeth's Women* (2010), p. 391.
6. Smith (ed.), *The Days of James IV* (1890), pp. 75–6 citing Polydore Vergil.

INTRODUCTION

1. Barr, *Flodden 1513* (2001), p. 68.
2. Though there is now some restitution for Richard III.
3. Richardson, *Renaissance Monarchy* (2002), p. 1.
4. Ibid.

1. UNCERTAIN INHERITORS

1. Churchill, *The Second World War*, 6 vols. (1949–54), Vol. II, *Their Finest Hour*, p. 227.
2. The argument that William was invited by members of the English aristocracy does not instantly make his Dutch army of over 20,000 men an English one; besides which, he refused to come without his army. See Vallance, *The Glorious Revolution* (2008), p. 123 for its numbers and its Dutchness; on landing in the south-west, William told the English gentry that what was required was not their 'military assistance' but 'their countenance and presence'. For Prince Louis see King John and Henry III ODNB entries: John Gillingham,

'John (1167–1216)' – doi:10.1093/ref:odnb/14841; and H. W. Ridgeway, 'Henry III (1207–1272)' – doi:10.1093/ref:odnb/12950.

3. This was the fourth time in only twenty-five years that a maritime landing had precipitated a change of monarch, 1460–1, 1470, 1471 being the previous examples.

4. Cunningham, *Henry VII*, p. 42.

5. Indeed there was also a preliminary encounter at Stirling Bridge, which James III won. See Macdougall, *James III* (2009), p. 345; and for the naming of Sauchieburn, which only became established after 1655, see p. 346.

6. Ibid., p. 320.

7. Macdougall, *James IV* (1997), p. 13.

8. Macdougall, *James III*, p. 349.

2. NEW KINGS

1. Proclamation of 23 June 1485 in Gairdner (ed.), *Paston Letters* (Micro Edition) (1909), pp. 81–4.

2. Ibid.

3. Helen Maurer, *Margaret of Anjou* (2003), p. 41 footnote.

4. See Cunningham, *Henry VII*, pp. 16–8 and pp. 25–6.

5. Goodall, *The English Castle*, p. 480.

6. Goodall's 2012 British Library talk on above.

7. Vincent, *A Brief History of Britain* (2011), p. 197.

8. Including Edward III's founding of the Order of the Garter in 1348. See Ormrod, *The Reign of Edward III* (2000), p. 27.

9. Hughes, *Arthurian Myths and Alchemy: The Kingship of Edward IV* (2002), p. 253.

10. With thanks to Thomas Penn for this gem.

11. Hall, *Chronicle* (1809), p. 423 and Polydore Vergil, *Historia Anglica* (1950), (ed. Hay), p. 5.

12. David Starkey, 'Introduction' to Goodwin, *Fatal Colours* (2001), p. xix.

13. Ibid., p. xx.

14. The 'pretender' Lambert Simnel claimed to be Edward Earl of Warwick the heir to George Duke of Clarence; John Earl of Lincoln, eldest son of Richard III's sister Elizabeth had been named his heir by Richard III.

15. Baldwin, *Stoke Field* (2006), p. 22; and Arnold, *The Renaissance at War* (2001), p. 63.

16. Heir to George, Duke of Clarence.

17. Vincent, *Britain 1066–1485*, p. 98.

18. ODNB, Norman Macdougall, 'Douglas, Archibald, fifth earl of Angus (c.1449–1513)' – doi:10.1093/ref:odnb/7864. He explains how the soubriquet

of 'Bell the Cat' was a seventeenth-century invention and the story behind it.

19. Ibid.

20. ODNB, C. A. McGladdery, 'Drummond, Margaret (*d*. 1502)' – doi:10.1093/ref:odnb/8079.

3. 1496 AND 1497 – WAR ON THE BORDER

1. By this time, the province of Burgundy had been annexed by France, leaving the Low Countries, though the name remained.

2. Arthurson, *The Perkin Warbeck Conspiracy* (1994), p. 71.

3. ODNB, S. J. Gunn, 'Henry VII (1457–1509)' – doi:10.1093/ref:odnb/12954.

4. Macdougall, *James IV*, p. 119.

5. G. A. Bergenroth (ed.), *Calendar of State Papers, Spain, Volume 1: 1485–1509* (1862), no. 107, pp. 70–1.

6. Ibid., no. 121, p. 84.

7. Ibid., no. 130, p. 91.

8. Part of a lengthy description by Pedro Ayala. See CSP Spain vol. i, no. 210, pp. 168–79; and Smith, *Days of James IV*, pp. 54–9.

9. Balfour Paul, *Scots Peerage*, 9 vols. (1904–14), Vol. iv, pp. 528–31 James IV's great-aunt had been married to Lady Catherine's father, but Lady Catherine herself was the third daughter by a subsequent marriage.

10. Smith (ed.), *The Days of James IV*, pp. 42–3, citing Polydore Vergil, *Historia Anglica*, xxvi (Basle Edition, 1570).

11. Macdougall, *James IV*, p. 133.

12. Reese, *Flodden* (2003), p. 47.

13. http://www.northofthetyne.co.uk/CastleHeaton.html.

14. Macdougall, *James IV*, p. 133.

15. CSP Spain vol. i, no. 210, pp. 168–79; and Smith (ed.), *Days of James IV*, pp. 54–9.

16. Though her mother was the cousin of Henry's own mother Margaret Beaufort.

17. Cunningham, *Henry VII*, p. 85.

18. Macdougall, *James IV*, p. 134.

19. Starkey, *Henry: Virtuous Prince* (2008), p. 114.

20. Cunningham, *Henry VII*, p. 88.

21. An extremely evocative fictional account of this experience is in H.M. Castor's *VIII* (2011).

22. http://www.edinburghcastle.gov.uk/index/tour/highlights/highlights-mons-meg.htm. Niall Barr in *Flodden 1513*, p. 49 gives us the highly accurate eighteen inches in diameter with a range of 2,867 yards.

23. Ibid. for weight. Distance as the crow flies.

24. Macdougall, *James IV*, p. 138.

25. Ibid., p. 139.

26. Ibid. citing *Accounts of the Lord High Treasurer of Scotland 1473–1513 (T.A.)*, eds. Dickson and Paul, 4 vols., Vol. I, p. 351.

27. Macdougall, *James IV*, p. 139.

28. See National Portrait Gallery Image http://www.npg.org.uk/collections/ search/portraitLarge/mw199830/Thomas-Howard-2nd-Duke-of-Norfolk-Agnes-Howard-ne-Tilney-Duchess-of-Norfolk. David M. Head, 'Howard, Thomas, second duke of Norfolk (1443–1524)' doi:10.1093/ref:odnb/13939.

29. Polydore Vergil, *Historia Anglica* (ed. Hay), pp. 74–5 cited in ODNB, David M. Head, 'Howard, Thomas, second duke of Norfolk (1443–1524)' doi:10.1093/ref:odnb/13939.

30. Cunningham, *Henry VII*, p. 90.

31. Hutchinson, *House of Treason* (2009), p. 15.

4. THE COMMON CONDITION

1. CSP Spain vol. i, no. 204, pp. 159–164.

2. As opposed to John Paul II, for whom there was an authorized biography.

3. Modern English translation from the Latin by Arthur Goodwin. For the best recent *published* translation, see Pius II, *Commentaries*, eds. Margaret Hamilton Meserve and Marcello Simonetta (Harvard University Press, 2 vols., 2003–7).

4. Ibid. Arthur Goodwin.

5. This is a reference to Aeneas's ten-mile barefoot pilgrimage to the shrine of Our Lady of Haddington at Whitekirk. It left him with pains in his feet for the rest of his life. His last-minute decision not to board ship for the homeward voyage almost certainly saved his life; from the safety of the shore, he saw his intended vessel being struck by a storm, just after leaving harbour. It sank and all on board were lost, bar four survivors. Crossing the Channel in winter could be extremely dangerous.

6. We do not know the exact crossing point Aeneas used, but the river in question was the Tweed.

7. Actually it was first built by Robert Curthose, eldest son of William the Conqueror. Even as late as the seventeenth-century ancient English structures from Stonehenge to Norman castles could be described as Roman, see Goodall, *The English Castle* (2011), p. 480.

8. I.e. Italy.

9. Charlotte A. Sneyd (ed.), *A relation, or rather A true account, of the island of England: with sundry particulars of the customs of these people, and of the royal revenues under King Henry the Seventh, about the year 1500*, (1847). Charlotte

A. Sneyd believes that the author was the secretary of Francesco Capello, the Venetian Ambassador.

10. Ibid., p. 12.
11. Ibid., pp. 20–1.
12. Ibid., p. 17.
13. Ibid., pp. 31–2.
14. Williams, *English Historical Documents*, Vol. V (1967), p. 191.
15. Allen. B. Hinds (ed.), *Calendar of State Papers and Manuscripts in the Archives and Collections of Milan: 1385–1618* (1912), no. 553, p. 339.
16. http://www.prestontower.co.uk/thetower.html.
17. Fraser, *The Steel Bonnets* (1989), p. 49 and pp. 56–65.
18. Smith (ed.), *The Days of James IV*, p. 83.
19. Jillings, *Scotland's Black Death* (2007), p. 7.
20. Ibid., p. 39.
21. Hinde, *England's Population: A History Since the Domesday Survey* (2003), p. 64.
22. Fraser, *The Steel Bonnets*, pp. 276–7.
23. Goodman, 'The Impact of Warfare on the Scottish Marches, c. 1481–c. 1513' in *The Fifteenth Century: VII, conflicts, consequences and the crown in the late middle ages*, ed. Linda Clark, p. 207.

5. THE TREATY OF PERPETUAL PEACE

1. Hutchinson, *House of Treason*, p. 15.
2. Hall, *Chronicle*, p. 487.
3. St Ninian is regarded as Scotland's first Saint, see http://www.whithorn.com/saint-ninian.htm. He was regarded as particularly special by James and it was to St Ninian that the King went on pilgrimage to pray for the lives of Margaret and their newborn son. See Chapter 12, below.
4. Hall, *Chronicle*, p. 487.
5. CSP Spain vol. i, no. 210, pp. 168–79.
6. CSP Spain vol. i, no. 210, no. 221, pp. 190–1.
7. Polydore Vergil, *Historia Anglica* (ed. Hay), p. 113.
8. Literally 30,000 gold nobles. A noble was six shillings and eight pence, equivalent to one third of a pre-decimal pound.
9. Smith (ed.), *The Days of James IV*, pp. 81–4 transl. of Rymer's *Foedera*, Vol. XII, p. 804.
10. Perry, *Sisters to the King* (1998), p. 15.
11. John Yonge or Young (Falcon Pursuivant 1486, Somerset Herald 1494 and Norroy King of Arms 1510 until death in 1516 – entry in W. H. Godfrey, *The College of Arms, Queen Victoria Street, being the sixteenth and final monograph*

of the London Survey Committee (1963), pp. 107–8.

12. Yonge's report of the 'Fyancells' and of Margaret's 'Departure from England' can be found in Leland, *Antiquarii De Rebus Britannicis Collectanea*, ed. T. Hearne, 1770. For this comment on the Earl of Surrey, see p. 260.

13. Perry, *Sisters to the King*, p. 45.

14. Tremlett, *Catherine of Aragon* (2010), p. 39 and p. 53.

15. Starkey and Doran, *Henry VIII: Man and Monarch* (2009), p. 16.

16. Starkey, *Henry: Virtuous Prince*, p. 170.

17. Perry, *Sisters to the King*, pp. 21–2 citing Nicholas, *Privy Purse Expenses of Elizabeth of York* (1830), p. 86.

18. Leland, *Antiq.*, p. 266.

19. Ibid., p. 268.

20. Ibid.

21. Ibid., p. 273.

22. His extravagance was such that he died in great debt, ref: Douglas (series ed.), *English Historical Documents*, 10 vols., C. H. Williams (ed.) Vol. V, *1485–1558* (1971), p. 905.

23. Leland, *Antiq.*, p. 274.

24. Ibid., p. 281.

25. Ibid., p. 284.

26. Baildon (ed.), *The Poems of William Dunbar* (1907), pp. 39–45.

27. McAndrew, *Scotland's Historic Heraldry* (2006), p. 275.

28. Macdougall, *James IV*, p. 251 citing Hall, *Chronicle*, p. 498.

29. Hall, *Chronicle*, p. 498.

30. 'Henry VII: January 1504', *Parliament Rolls of Medieval England*. URL: http://www.british-history.ac.uk/report.aspx?compid=116570. Date accessed: 14 December 2012.

31. Ellis (ed.), *Letters Illustrative of English History*, 3 vols. (1824–1846), Vol. I, 2nd edn. (1825), pp. 41–2.

32. Ibid.

33. Hutchinson, *House of Treason*, p. 7.

34. So important to Surrey was this intimacy with the Scottish King that it is mentioned at length on the Earl's epitaph, which also gives us a clue to their conversation with these words, reproduced in his own modern translation by John A. Ferguson in *Battle of Flodden* (2001): 'Notwithstanding any displeasures done by the said Earl in the wars before. And also the said king said then to him, that he loved him the better for such service as he had done before to the king his father(in-law) king of England, though the hurt war had done to him, and his Realm.'

35. Ibid.

6. A NEW MONARCHY

1. Perry, *Sisters to the King*, p. 44.
2. Ibid.
3. Dunbar, *Scottish Royal Palaces* (1999), p. 17.
4. Perry, *Sisters to the King*, p. 45.
5. ODNB, C. A. McGladdery, 'Drummond, Margaret (*d.* 1502)' – doi:10.1093/ref:odnb/8079.
6. See Richardson, *Renaissance Monarchy*.
7. Roger Mason, 'Renaissance Monarchy? Stewart Kingship (1469–1542)', eds. Brown and Tanner, *Scottish Kingship 1306–1542* (2008), p. 256.
8. Ibid.
9. Gillingham, *Wars of the Roses* (2001), p. 20.
10. Cannan, *Scottish Arms & Armour*, p. 59.
11. ODNB, N. F. Blake, 'Caxton, William (1415x24–1492)' – doi:10.1093/ref:odnb/4963.
12. I am grateful to David Starkey for this insight via his 2012 lecture at the British Library.
13. Hardyment, *Malory* (2005), p. 472.

7. RENAISSANCE MONARCHY – POWER

1. Macdougall, *James IV*, pp. 212–13
2. Ibid. In the words of Dr Michael Brown, one of the leading authorities on the subject, in his Introduction to *Scottish Kingship 1306–1542* (ed. Brown and Tanner), p. 1.
3. ODNB, Alan R. Borthwick, 'James II (1430–1460)' – doi:10.1093/ref:odnb/14588.
4. Wormald, *Court, Kirk and Community* (1981), p. 19.
5. Ibid., pp. 19–20.
6. Ibid., p. 22.
7. Ibid., p. 19.
8. A. L. Brown 'The Scottish "Establishment" in the later Fifteenth Century', *Judicial Review*, new ser. 23 (1978), p. 105 as cited by Wormald, *Court, Kirk and Community* p. 19.
9. Lynch, *Scotland: A New History*, (1992), p. 158.
10. Steve Boardman, 'Royal Finance and Regional Rebellion in the reign of James IV' *in Sixteenth-century Scotland*, eds. Goodare and MacDonald (2008), p. 16.
11. With thanks to the Rev. Alan Cartwright.
12. Macdougall, *James IV*, p. 165.

13. Ibid.

14. Boardman, op. cit., p. 16.

15. The islands were originally intended as security for the dowry, but became the dowry itself.

16. Cunningham, *Henry VII*, p. 72.

17. Ibid., p. 140.

18. Ibid.

19. See D. Starkey, 'Intimacy and innovation: the rise of the Privy Chamber, 1485–1547' in Starkey (ed.), *The English Court: from the Wars of the Roses to the Civil War* (1987), pp. 71–118.

20. C. J. Harrison, 'The Petition of Edmund Dudley', *English Historical Review*, 87 (1972), p. 86.

21. Hutton, *A Brief History of Britain 1485–1660*, p. 3.

22. CSP Spain, Vol. I, no. 210, pp. 168–79.

23. ODNB, Sean Cunningham, 'Pole, Edmund de la, eighth earl of Suffolk (1472?–1513)' – doi:10.1093/ref:odnb/22446.

24. Bentley (ed.), 'Extracts from the Privy Purse Expenses of King Henry VII' in *Excerpta Historica* (1831), pp. 132–3.

25. Gairdner (ed.), *Letters & Papers Illustrative of the reigns of Richard III and Henry VII*, 2 vols. (1861–3), Vol. I, pp. 363–4. See also Penn, *The Winter King*, pp. 321–3 and all of Desmond Seward, *The Last White Rose* (2010).

26. It was from Calais that Warwick the Kingmaker launched the initial successful Yorkist invasion in 1460.

27. S. J. Gunn, 'Sir Thomas Lovell (c. 1449–1524): A new man in a New Monarchy?' in Watts (ed.), *The End of the Middle Ages?*, p. 124. Lovell was also the man entrusted with escorting Suffolk from Dover to safekeeping in the Tower and he would be a loyal lieutenant to Katherine of Aragon in 1513.

28. Gairdner (ed.), *LP of R III & H VII*, Vol. I, p. 233.

29. See Bacon, *History of the Reign of Henry VII* (1881).

30. ODNB, S. J. Gunn, 'Henry VII (1457–1509)' – doi:10.1093/ref:odnb/12954.

31. Polydore Vergil, *Historia Anglica* (ed. Hay), pp. 142–7.

32. Ibid.

33. Ibid.

34. Ibid.

8. RENAISSANCE MONARCHY – DISPLAY

1. When Warwick the Kingmaker took Henry VI out of the Tower in 1471 and paraded him in the streets of London as the real King in comparison to Edward IV, the effect was spoilt by Henry's pathetic appearance and shabby blue gown.

2. See McKendrick, Lowden & Doyle (eds.), *Royal Manuscripts: The Genius of Illumination* (2011).

3. 'Extracts from the Privy Purse Expenses of King Henry the Seventh, from December 1491 to March 1505' in *Excerpta Historica*, ed. Bentley, p. 90; and Gunn, 'The Court of Henry VII' in (eds. Gunn and Janse), *The Court as a Stage: England the Low Countries in the later Middle Ages*, p. 143. Of course, jewellery and plate were also a bankable asset, as per Gunn article, p. 138.

4. Cunningham, *Henry VII*, p. 86.

5. Horrox (contrib. ed.), Given-Wilson (gen. ed.), *Parliament Rolls of Medieval England*, 'Henry VII: January 1504', http://www.british-history.ac.uk/report.aspx?compid=116570.

6. Prevenier and Blockmans, *The Burgundian Netherlands* (1986), pp. 223–5.

7. Indeed military defeat was to cost Philip's Successor Charles the Bold the French province of Burgundy – leaving the Duchy its Flemish territories – and his life in 1477.

8. With thanks to Christina Hardyment for this detail.

9. Tabri, *Political Culture in the Early Northern Renaissance: the Court of Charles the Bold* (2004), p. 47. As a testament to Burgundy's influence in England and France, it is fitting that the only surviving copies of Charles the Bold's 'Household Ordinance' of 1469 and the 'Ordinance' of 1478 are in Oxford's Bodleian Library and Paris's Bibliothèque Nationale respectively.

10. Starkey, *Monarchy: from the Middle Ages to Modernity*, p. xxvi.

11. These events are captured in 'The Receyt of the Ladie Kateryne', which can be found in F. Grose and E. Jeffery (eds.), *The Antiquarian Repertory*, Vol. II (1807), pp. 248–331 and with scholarly notes in Kipling, *The Receyt of the Ladie Kateryne* (1990).

12. ODNB, M. M. Condon, 'Bray, Sir Reynold (c.1440–1503)' – doi:10.1093/ref:odnb/3295.

13. A problem came when he tried to get the City of London to pay for it. See Kipling, *The Triumph of Honour* (1977), p. 99, footnote 8; and Kipling, *The Receyt of the Ladie Kateryne*, pp. 146–7.

14. *Antiquarian Rep.*, pp. 289–90; Kipling, *The Receyt of the Ladie Kateryne*, pp. 44–5 and pp. 146–7 citing Fabyan, *The Great Chronicle of London* (1938), eds. Thomas and Thornley, p. 310 as describing the middle king as King Arthur.

15. *Antiquarian Rep.*, p. 314.

16. See Dunbar, *Scottish Royal Palaces*.

17. Steve Boardman, 'Late Medieval Scotland and the Matter of Britain', eds. Cowan and Finlay, *Scottish History: The Power of the Past*, p. 55.

18. Katie Stevenson, 'Royal Propaganda: Snowdon Herald and the Cult of Chivalry in Late Medieval Scotland', in James D. Floyd and Charles J. Burnett (eds.), *Genealogica Et Heraldica Sancta Andreae MMVI: Myth and*

Propaganda in Heraldry and Genealogy, Vol. II (Edinburgh, 2008), p. 797. And see http://www.lyon-court.com/lordlyon/221.185.html.

19. See http://www.stirlingcastle.gov.uk/home/experience/story/forework.htm.
20. Andrea Thomas, 'The Renaissance', eds. Devine and Wormald, *The Oxford Handbook of Modern Scottish History* (2012), pp. 188–97.
21. Dunbar, *Scottish Royal Palaces*, p. 168; and Thomas, 'The Renaissance', p. 192.
22. Dunbar, *Scottish Royal Palaces*, p. 59.
23. Thomas, 'The Renaissance', pp. 189–90.
24. See Katie Stevenson, 'Contesting Chivalry: James II and the control of chivalric culture in the 1450s', *Journal of Medieval History*, Vol. III, no. 2 (2007), pp. 202–3 and 210–11.
25. Measured from the map in Cloake, *The Palaces of Shene and Richmond* (1995), p. 60. For fuller descriptions see *Antiquarian Rep.*, 313–7; Kipling, *The Receyt of the Ladie Kateryne* pp. 70–4 and pp. 159–62. See also Cloake, *The Palaces of Shene and Richmond* (1995), pp. 55–74.

9. HENRY VIII – THE PROTECTED PRINCE

1. Hearn (ed.), *Dynasties* (1996), p. 36.
2. CSP Milan, no. 539, pp. 321–2.
3. ODNB, Rosemary Horrox, 'Arthur, prince of Wales (1486–1502)', – doi:10.1093/ref:odnb/705.
4. Fuensalida, *Correspondencia de Gutierre Gómez de Fuensalida* (1907), p. 449, cited in Starkey, *Henry: Virtuous Prince*, p. 40 and in Mattingly, *Catherine of Aragon* (1941), p. 92.
5. Ibid., cited in Penn, *Winter King*, p. 319.
6. Byrne (ed.), *Letters of Henry VIII* (1968), p. 4.
7. Starkey, *Henry: Virtuous Prince*, pp. 169–70.
8. See Goodwin, *Fatal Colours: Towton 1461*.
9. CSP Spain, Vol. i, no. 210, p. 178.
10. Ibid.
11. For its development see Penn, *Winter King*, in particular pp. 169–70, pp. 232–4 and pp. 324–5.
12. Ibid., p. 339.
13. Mayor (ed.), *The English works of John Fisher* (1876), p. 271.
14. Penn, *Winter King*, p. 334.
15. See Gunn, 'The Accession of Henry VIII', *Historical Research*, Vol. 64, Issue 155 (Oct. 1991), pp. 278–88.
16. Starkey, *Henry: Virtuous Prince*, pp. 260–1.
17. Ibid., pp. 275–7 explains the process.
18. See Goodwin, *Fatal Colours: Towton 1461*.

19. Polydore Vergil, *Historia Anglica* (ed. Hay), pp. 150–1.

10. HENRY VIII – A LIBERATED KING

1. The developments are charted brilliantly in Julia Fox's *Sister Queens* (2011), p. 91, p. 96 and p. 120.
2. By the propagandist Sir Richard Morrison in his *Remedy for Sedition* in 1536, cited in Introduction to Gunn and Monckton (eds.), *Arthur Tudor Prince of Wales* (2009), p. 4.
3. This was not, however, New Year's Day. Until the switch from the Julian to the Gregorian Calendar in 1752, the New Year began on 25 March (known as Lady Day). To avoid madness among historians and confusion among their readers, the former customarily date all years including those before 1752 from 1 January, except in exceptional circumstances.
4. We know about it because he and his Groom of the Stole, William Compton, fought in disguise. When one of them was badly injured some spectators 'in the know' were openly alarmed. The King had to reveal himself as unharmed. Compton recovered to continue his important work for Henry. See Starkey, *Henry: Virtuous Prince*, p. 322, citing Hall, *Chronicle*, p. 513.
5. Fabyan, *The Great Chronicle of London*, p. 374 as cited in Starkey, *Henry: Virtuous Prince*, p. 347.
6. Ibid., p. 369.
7. Ibid., p. 370.
8. *L&P Henry VIII*, no. 734, p. 400; cited by Starkey, *Six Wives*, p. 123.
9. Gwyn, *The King's Cardinal* (1990), pp. 3–4.
10. G. A. Bergenroth (ed.), *Calendar of State Papers, Spain, Volume 2: 1509–1525* (1866), no. 46, pp. 44–5.
11. Ibid., no. 44, pp. 39–43.
12. Starkey, *Henry: Virtuous Prince*, p. 369.
13. Ibid.
14. Brewer, *Letters & Papers, Foreign and Domestic, of Henry VIII*, 21 vols. (1920), Vol. I, 3 parts (1509–14), no. 784/44, p. 424; cited by Starkey, *Henry: Virtuous Prince*, p. 369.
15. Peter Gwyn goes through different interpretations down the ages in *The King's Cardinal*, pp. 4–22.
16. ODNB, C. S. L. Davies, 'Fox, Richard (1447/8–1528) – doi:10.1093/ref:odnb/10051; Margot Johnson, 'Ruthall, Thomas (d. 1523) – doi:10.1093/ref:odnb/24359; Gwyn, *King's Cardinal*, p. 26 for Warham.
17. See Chapter 12 below.
18. Cavendish, *The Life of Cardinal Wolsey* (1920), pp. 4–5.
19. Hannay, *The Letters of James IV* (1953), ed. R. L. Mackie, pp. 107–11.

20. Ibid., p. 108.
21. Ibid., p. 111.

II. JAMES IV AND THE 'REALIZATION' OF SCOTTISH HISTORY

1. Those who offer advice or counsel. These are not necessarily the same people who formed his Council.
2. Smith (ed.), *The Days of James IV*, p. 56.
3. Roger Mason, 'Renaissance Monarchy? Stewart Kingship 1469–1542' in eds. Brown and Tanner, *Scottish Kingship 1306–1542*, p. 259.
4. Ibid.
5. Ibid., p. 258 citing Bower, *Scotichronicon* (1987–98), (ed. Watt).
6. Duncan, *The Kingship of the Scots 842–1292* (2002), p. 1.
7. Roger Mason, 'Renaissance Monarchy? Stewart Kingship 1469–1542' in eds. Brown and Tanner, *Scottish Kingship 1306–1542*, p. 258. See also his footnote 11, p. 275.
8. From a misspelling by Boece as Mons Grampius came the name Grampians for the Mountain Range. See Prebble, *The Lion in the North*, p. 10 footnote. The battle was most likely in Aberdeenshire or Banffshire, see ODNB, Malcolm Todd, 'Julius Agricola, Gnaeus (AD 40–93)' – doi:10.1093/ref:odnb/48290.
9. Breeze, *The Antonine Wall* (2006), pp. 97-102.
10. The Antonine Wall was inscribed as a UNESCO World Heritage site in 2008: http://www.antoninewall.org/.
11. Breeze, *The Antonine* Wall, p. 165.
12. Lynch, *Scotland: A New History*, p. 9.
13. English has been spoken there since the sixth century. See Driscoll, *Alba: The Gaelic Kingdom of Scotland* (2002), p. 23.
14. A. O. Anderson, *Early Sources of Scottish History* A.D. 500–1286, 2 vols., Vol. i (1922), p. 288. See ODNB, Marjorie O. Anderson, 'Kenneth I (d. 858)' – doi:10.1093/ref:odnb/15398 quoting the Scottish Chronicle.
15. ODNB, Dauvit Broun, 'Constantine II (d. 952)' – doi:10.1093/ref:odnb/6115.
16. Oliver, *A History of Scotland* (2009), p. 55.
17. Constantine had recognized Athelstan's father, Edward the Elder at Bakewell in 920 as 'his lord', but Edward had no direct control of England north of the Humber. Athelstan was far more than primus inter pares.
18. Sarah Foot, *Æthelstan: First King of England* (2011), p. 162.
19. Ibid., p. 20.
20. Ibid., p. 23.
21. Chibnall (ed. and trans.), *The Ecclesiastical History of Orderic Vitalis*, 6 vols. (1969–80), Vol. II., p. 233, cited by Borman, *Matilda: Queen of the Conqueror*

(2011), p. 139. It is impossible to give an exact English figure, but two million would seem a reasonably possible one. See Hinde, *England's Population: A History Since the Domesday Survey* (2003), pp. 18–19.

22. Clark (ed.), *The Peterborough Chronicle* (1958), p. 4.

23. Ibid., p. 65.

24. Curthose referring to his short stature, see Borman, *Matilda: Queen of the Conqueror*, pp. 47–8.

25. Watson, *Scotland: A History* (2008), p. 107; J. D. Mackie, *A History of Scotland* (1991), p. 61.

26. Watson, *Scotland: A History*, p. 107. Regarding experience of a minority, Alexander III himself had been a minor. The reason 'the Maid' was a potential Queen designate was because it needed to be discovered whether King Alexander's widowed Queen was pregnant with a son. Ironically, considering that Alexander's death was caused by his ill-judged ride in foul weather to join her for procreation, the King had already achieved his aim to impregnate his Queen. However, the child did not survive.

27. ODNB, A. A. M. Duncan, 'Margaret [the Maid of Norway] (1282/3–1290)' – doi:10.1093/ref:odnb/18048.

28. Ibid.

29. Ibid.

30. G. W. S. Barrow, *Robert Bruce & the community of the realm* (1988), p. 61.

31. Lynch, *Scotland: A New History*, p. 118.

32. Michael Brown, *Bannockburn* (2008), p. 188.

33. Lynch, *Scotland: A New History*, p. 128.

34. ODNB, G. W. S. Barrow, 'Robert I (1274–1329)' – doi:10.1093/ref:odnb/3754.

35. Michael Brown, *The Wars of Scotland* (2004), p. 231.

36. Roger Mason, 'Scotching the Brut', *History Today*, Vol. 35, Issue 1 (1985).

37. Ibid.

38. Ibid.

39. http://www.geo.ed.ac.uk/home/scotland/arbroath_english.html.

40. Ibid.

41. Trevor-Roper, *The Invention of Scotland* (2006), p. 18.

42. Ibid., p. 6.

43. Ibid., p. 19.

44. http://www.geo.ed.ac.uk/home/scotland/arbroath_english.html.

45. Katie Stevenson, 'Royal Propaganda: Snowdon Herald and the Cult of Chivalry in Late Medieval Scotland', in James D. Floyd and Charles J. Burnett (eds.), *Genealogica Et Heraldica Sancta Andreae MMVI: Myth and Propaganda in Heraldry and Genealogy*, Volume II; and Steve Boardman, 'Late Medieval Scotland and the Matter of Britain' in E. J. Cowan and R. J. Finlay (eds.), *Scottish History and the Power of the Past* (2002), p. 50.

12. THEIR RENAISSANCE MAJESTIES

1. Margaret Condon 'The Last Will of Henry VII: Document and Text' in *Westminster Abbey: the Lady Chapel of Henry VII* (2003), eds. Tatton-Brown and Mortimer, p. 137.

2. John Pope-Hennessy, 'The Tombs in Westminster' in *Westminster Abbey*, ed. A. L. Rowse, p. 219, cited by Alan Phipps Darr in *The Anglo-Florentine Renaissance* (2012), eds. Sicca and Waldman, p. 49 and note 2 on p. 74.

3. ODNB, S. J. Gunn, 'Henry VII (1457–1509)' – doi:10.1093/ref:odnb/12954.

4. Darr, op. cit. notes that Henry VIII planned to have his own tomb in the centre of the chapel, relegating the tomb of his parents to its place behind the High Altar.

5. See Hutton, *A Brief History of Britain 1485–1660* for a concise summing up, pp. 14–15.

6. Biddle and Clayre (eds.), *The Castle Winchester: Great Hall & Round Table* (2000), insert.

7. Starkey, 'Intimacy & Innovation: the rise of the Privy Chamber, 1485–1547' in *The English Court*, ed. Starkey, particularly pp. 72–82.

8. Record Commission, *Statutes of the Realm*, ed. Luders et al. (1810–28), III, 8 (St 1 Hen. VIII, c.14, pp. 8–9).

9. Ibid.

10. Rawdon Brown (ed.), *Calendar of State Papers Relating to English Affairs in the Archives of Venice* (38 vols.), *Vol. ii, 1509–1519* (1867), no. 1287, pp. 557–63.

11. Andrea Thomas, 'The Renaissance' in *The Oxford Handbook of Modern Scottish History*, Devine & Wormald (eds.), p. 187.

12. Erasmus, *The Epistles of Erasmus*, 2 vols. (1904), ed. and trans. F. M. Nichols, Vol. II, p. 201.

13. Giustinian, *Four Years at the Court of Henry VIII*, 2 vols. (1854), trans. Rawdon Brown, Vol. I, pp. 85–7.

14. A translation from the Latin in modern English from Smith (ed.), *The Days of James IV*, p. 55.

15. Smith (ed.), *The Days of James IV*, pp. 54–5.

16. From *Encyclopaedia Britannica* online 'monochord, also spelled manichord, musical instrument consisting of a single string stretched over a calibrated sound box and having a movable bridge. The string was held in place over the properly positioned bridge with one hand and plucked with a plectrum held in the other.'

17. Smith (ed.), *The Days of James IV*, pp. 74–5.

18. Macdougall, *James IV*, p. 196.

19. R. L. Mackie, *King James IV of Scotland* (1958), p. 154.

20. One is reminded of the encounter between the King and his peasants in *Monty Python and the Holy Grail*.

21. Macdougall, *James IV*, p. 198.

22. Ibid.

23. Ibid., p. 197 citing Dickson and Paul (eds.), *Accounts of the Lord High Treasurer of Scotland 1473–1513* [*Treasurer's Accounts: T.A.*], 4 vols. (1877–1902).

24. Macdougall, p. 286 *T.A.* iv, p. 108 and p. 358.

25. Macdougall, p. 53 citing *T.A.* iii, p. 250.

26. *T.A.*, iii, p. 172 cited in Barnes, *Janet Kennedy* (2007), p. 30.

27. Read, *Humour and Humanism* (1947), p. 31.

28. Ibid., p. 22.

29. Dunbar, *Scottish Royal Palaces*, pp. 56–7 and p. 59. Also see Thurley, *Royal Palaces of Tudor England* (1993), pp. 27–34.

30. ODNB, Philippe Contamine, 'Stuart, Bérault (1452/3–1508)' – doi:10.1093/ref:odnb/26694.

31. Katie Stevenson, 'Royal Propaganda: Snowdon Herald and the Cult of Chivalry in Late Medieval Scotland', in James D. Floyd and Charles J. Burnett (eds.), *Genealogica Et Heraldica Sancta Andreae MMVI: Myth and Propaganda in Heraldry and Genealogy*, Vol. ii, p. 799.

32. Lynch, *Scotland: A New History*, p. 160; Macdougall, *James IV*, p. 294.

33. See 'Of Ane Blak-Moir' in Baildon (ed.), *The Poems of William Dunbar*, pp. 97–8.

34. Dunbar, *Scottish Royal Palaces*, p. 109.

35. Ibid., citing Pitscottie, *The Historie and Cronicles of Scotland*, (ed.) Mackay (1911), Vol. I, p. 244. Pitscottie credits Andrew Forman with the scheme as one who 'seruit the king at sic tymes for his pastyme and pleasour', but he was the front-of-house man.

13. SEAPOWER

1. Macdougall, *James IV*, p. 196.

2. Rodger, *The Safeguard of the Sea* (1997), p. 168.

3. Macdougall, *James IV*, p. 235.

4. Rodger, *The Safeguard of the Sea*, p. 169. A basilisk was another type of cannon.

5. Eric Graham with Fiona Watson http://www.bbc.co.uk/radio/player/b00zsdss.

6. Fiona Watson, Radio 3, 'The Stewarts: A Love Affair with Firepower', http://www.bbc.co.uk/programmes/b00v3yzj.

7. Ibid.

8. *T.A.*, iii, p. 143.

9. Murdoch, *The Terror of the Seas?* (2010), p. 33.

10. See Chapter 5.

11. Macdougall, *James IV*, p. 243.

12. Indeed, the only Pope to show any real commitment to a crusade after the fall of Constantinople was Pius II, the former Aeneas Silvius Piccolomini who had had such an uncomfortable time of it as a young man in Scotland and Northumberland. But in 1464 Pius had died at Ancona, on the eastern coast of Italy, while waiting for the commitment he needed from putative allies before setting sail.

13. ODNB, David Loades, 'Howard, Sir Edward (1476/7–1513)' – doi:10.1093/ref:odnb/13891.

14. Spont, *Letters and Papers Relating to the War with France, 1512–13* (1897), pp. vii–x.

15. Blackwall is now best known for the Blackwall Tunnel across the Thames.

16. Mackie, *King James IV*, p. 211.

17. Hall, *Chronicle*, p. 525.

18. Lesley, *History of Scotland* (1829), p. 82. Hall, *Chronicle*, p. 525.

19. For a full explanation see Macdougall, *James IV*, pp. 239–42.

20. Spont, *Letters & Papers*, p. xi.

21. Brewer, *Letters & Papers of Henry VIII*, Vol. I, no. 880, pp. 462–3. Also Fox, *Letters 1486–1527* (1929), eds. Allen and Allen, p. 54.

22. ODNB, David M. Head, 'Howard, Thomas, second duke of Norfolk (1443–1524)' – doi:10.1093/ref:odnb/13939.

23. Fox, *Letters 1486–1527*, eds. Allen and Allen, p. 54.

24. Starkey, *Six Wives* (2003), p. 127.

25. ODNB, R. W. Hoyle, 'Darcy, Thomas, Baron Darcy of Darcy (*b.* in or before 1467, *d.* 1537)' – doi:10.1093/ref:odnb/7148.

26. ODNB, Robert C. Braddock, 'Grey, Thomas, second marquess of Dorset (1477–1530)' – doi:10.1093/ref:odnb/11561.

27. Spont, *Letters and Papers*, p. xii.

28. Ibid., xiii Spont.

29. Konstam, *Tudor Warships*, Vol. I (2008), p. 23.

30. Ibid., p. 14 Konstam. In 1536 the ship was uprated to 700 tons.

31. Spont, *Letters and Papers*, p. xvi.

32. Spont, *Letters & Papers*, p. xxiv. For the Trinity *Sovereign* see http://www.maryrose.org/ship/wyndham.htm.

33. Fox, *Letters*, eds. Allen and Allen, p. 57.

34. Spont, *Letters and Papers*, p. xxv.

35. Brewer, *L&P Henry VIII*, Vol. I, no. 1356, p. 628.

14. KING OR VASSAL

1. Statutes of the Realm, 3 Henry VIII, c. 22, p. 43.

2. Mackie, *King James IV*, p. 215.

3. ODNB, C. A. McGladdery, 'Forman, Andrew (c.1465–1521)' – doi:10.1093/ref:odnb/9883.

4. Ibid.

5. Brewer, *L&P*, Vol. I, no. 1604, p. 733.

6. See F. L. Taylor, *The Art of War in Italy* (1921), pp. 180–204 and Arnold, *The Renaissance at War*, pp. 147–50.

7. ODNB, Steven G. Ellis, 'Dacre, Thomas, second Baron Dacre of Gilsland (1467–1525)' – doi:10.1093/ref:odnb/50220. Brougham was then in Westmorland.

8. Brewer, *L&P*, Vol. I, no. 984, p. 495.

9. Spont, *Letters and Papers*, p. 26.

10. Wood (ed.), *Flodden Papers* (1933), pp. xlv–xlvi.

11. Barr, *Flodden 1513*, p. 29. It is difficult to pinpoint the exact date, but it may very well have been earlier: Macdougall, *James IV*, p. 192, says 'two General Councils were summoned – on the last day of 1511 and at the end of February 1512 – whose business must have been the renewal of the Franco-Scottish alliance in March 1512 and its likely consequences'.

12. Actually sent by Dacre to Thomas Ruthall, Bishop of Durham but intended for Henry. It can also be assumed that with such important information Dacre would also have sent to Henry direct.

13. An angel was equivalent to 6 shillings and 8 pence or the equivalent of 1/3 of a pre-decimal £ sterling.

14. Brewer, *L&P*, Vol. I, no. 1342, pp. 623–4.

15. Hall, *Chronicle*, pp. 846–56. See also, Gairdner & Brodie, *L&P*, Vol. 17 (1900), no. 1033, pp. 582–3.

16. Cavendish, *Life of Wolsey*, p. 88.

17. Katie Stevenson, 'Chivalry, British Sovereignty and Dynastic Politics: Undercurrents of Antagonism in Tudor-Stewart Relations, c. 1490–c. 1513' in *Historical Research*, Vol. 86, Issue 234 (Nov. 2013).

18. Wood, *Flodden Papers*, p. xxxvi.

19. Brewer, *L&P*, Vol. I, no. 1297, p. 593.

20. Ibid., no. 974, p. 493.

21. That it was a general rather than individual censure see Wood, *Flodden Papers*, p. lxvi.

22. Bainbridge's power revealed in the letter dated 29 November 1513 from Leo X, Julius's successor, to Henry VIII. See Brewer, *L&P*, Vol. I, no. 2469, pp. 1088-9.

15. 1513 – BREAKDOWN

1. Brewer, *L&P*, Vol. I, no. 1735, pp. 792–4.

2. Ibid.

3. Ibid. He had made the same threat about taking Scotland's best towns to Margaret on the Sunday. See Smith (ed.), *The Days of James IV*, pp. 128–9 and Ellis, *Original Letters*, Vol. I, p. 64.

4. Ibid.

5. Or Paniter.

6. Brewer, *L&P*, Vol. I, no. 1735, pp. 792–4.

7. Ibid.

8. Ibid.

9. Ibid., no. 1775, pp. 809–10. Also Hannay (ed.), *Letters of James IV*, Appendix II, p. 321.

10. Mackie, *King James IV*, p. 235; and Brewer, *L&P*, Vol. I, no. 1775, pp. 809–10.

11. Hannay, *Letters of James IV*, p. 321.

12. Ibid.

13. Ibid., p. 300.

14. Ellis, *Original Letters*, Vol. I, p. 74.

15. In the otherwise brilliant Ellis, *Original letters*, Vol. I, p. 65.

16. See www.dsl.ac.uk under 'Fremmitly' [fremedly].

17. Spont, *Letters and Papers*, p. 85.

18. Ibid., p. xii–xiv.

19. Rodger, *The Safeguard of the Sea*, p. 169.

20. Loades, 'Henry's Army and Navy' in Rimer, Richardson and Cooper, *Henry VIII: Arms and the Man* (2009), p. 51.

21. Spont, *Letters and Papers*, pp. 97–8.

22. Ibid., p. 104.

23. Ibid., pp. 145–9 (letter of Edward Echyngham to Wolsey).

24. Ibid., p. xxxix and p. 136.

25. ODNB, David Loades, 'Howard, Sir Edward (1476/7–1513)' – doi:10.1093/ref:odnb/13891.

26. Spont, *Letters and Papers*, p. 134.

27. Brewer, *L&P*, Vol. I, no. 1852, p. 846.

28. Ibid., No. 1864, pp. 849–50.

29. Hutchinson, *House of Treason*, p. 24.

30. Transl. Arthur Goodwin.

31. Brewer, *L&P*, Vol. I, no. 1912, p. 869. Also Fox, *Letters*, eds. Allen and Allen, p. 70.

32. Hutchinson, *House of Treason*, p. 24.

33. Brewer, *L&P*, Vol. I, no. 1960, p. 890.

34. Wood (ed.), *Flodden Papers*, p. 79.

35. Ibid.

36. Ibid., pp. 79–80.

37. Hannay, *Letters of James IV*, pp. 311–13. It is suggested in *L&P* 2157, 11 August 1513 (note 2) that this might have been Islay Herald. But *Letters of James IV*, p. 313; *Treasurer's Accounts*, iv, p. 417; and Hall, *Chronicle*, p. 545 are sure that it was Lyon King of Arms.

38. Hannay, *Letters of James IV*, pp. 311–13.

39. Ibid.

40. Ibid.

41. Hall, *Chronicle*, p. 545.

42. Ibid.

16. 1513 – KATHERINE, REGENT AND GOVERNESS OF ENGLAND

1. Brewer, *L&P*, Vol. I, no. 2065, p. 942.

2. Ibid., no. 2055/46, p. 933.

3. Only a distant relation to the Bastard.

4. CSP Venice, Vol. ii, no. 211, p. 87.

5. Ellis, *Original Letters*, Vol. I, p. 80.

6. Tremlett, *Catherine of Aragon*, p. 26.

7. Ellis, *Original Letters*, Vol. I, p. 83.

8. CSP Venice, Vol ii, no. 211, p. 87.

9. Brewer, *L&P*, Vol. I, no. 2143 p. 969. Cited by Julia Fox, *Sister Queens*, p. 190.

10. Brewer, *L&P*, Vol. I, no. 2098, pp. 952–3; and no. 2163, pp. 974–5.

11. ODNB, S. J. Gunn, 'Lovell, Sir Thomas (c.1449–1524)' – doi:10.1093/ref:odnb/17065. And see Chapter 7 in this book.

12. Starkey, *Six Wives of Henry VIII*, p. 138.

13. Mattingly, *Catherine of Aragon*, p. 119.

14. Hall, *Chronicle*, p. 555.

15. Ibid.

16. Ibid.

17. Starkey, *Six Wives of Henry VIII*, p. 137.

18. Darcy, as Sir Thomas, had been Margaret's host at Berwick on her journey north. ODNB, Darcy, R. W. Hoyle, 'Darcy, Thomas, Baron Darcy of Darcy (*b.* in or before 1467, *d.* 1537)' – doi:10.1093/ref:odnb/7148 – its author R. W. Hoyle does say that there were signs that Darcy actively lobbied to be taken to France in 1513 and 1514.

19. Hall, *Chronicle*, p. 555.

20. Starkey, *Six Wives of Henry VIII*, p. 145.

21. 'Brewer, *L&P*, Vol. I, no. 2299, p. 1027.

22. Portland of Welbeck Papers, cited by Hutchinson, *House of Treason*, p. 25 and p. 374.

23. http://www.historyofparliamentonline.org/volume/1509-1558/member/bulmer-sir-william-1465-1531.
24. Hutchinson, *Young Henry* (2011), p. 176.
25. Ellis, *Original Letters*, Vol. I, p. 79–80.
26. Brewer, *L&P*, Vol. I, no. 2119, p. 959.
27. Ellis, *Original Letters*, Vol. I, pp. 82–3.
28. Starkey, *Six Wives of Henry VIII*, p. 141.
29. Dudley, *The Tree of Commonwealth* (1859), p. 5.

17. 1513 – WAR

1. Brewer, *L&P*, Vol. I, no. 2026, p. 916.
2. Ibid.
3. D. Caldwell, 'Royal Patronage of Arms and Armour Making in Fifteenth and Sixteenth-Century Scotland' in Caldwell, ed., *Scottish Weapons and Fortifications 1100–1800* (1981), p. 75.
4. Macdougall, *James IV*, p. 264.
5. Brewer, *L&P*, Vol. I, no. 1504, pp. 692–3.
6. Caldwell, op. cit., p. 77.
7. *T.A.* iv, pp. 508–22, cited by Macdougall, *James IV*, p. 264.
8. Robert Lindsay of Pitscottie, *The Cronicles of Scotland* (ed. Dalyell), 2 vols. (1814), Vol. I, p. 264. Mackie, *King James IV*, p. 242.
9. Brewer, *L&P*, Vol. I, no. 2116, p. 958 and no. 2204, p. 990. This is the figure given both times by a Venetian ambassador, correcting the figure he had given previously in *L&P*, no. 2107, pp. 955–6.
10. Wood (ed.), *Flodden Papers*, p. 84.
11. David H. Caldwell PhD Thesis (Univ. of Edinburgh 1982), 'Guns in Scotland', p. 154.
12. Ian Halley Stewart, *The Scottish coinage* (1955), p. 74.
13. Macdougall, *James IV*, pp. 130, 135, 189 and p. 264.
14. Caldwell, 'Guns in Scotland' (PhD 1982), p. 153.
15. Hall, *Chronicle*, p. 556.
16. Barr, *Flodden 1513*, p. 62.
17. Mackie, *King James IV*, p. 246; and Hall, *Chronicle*, p. 556.
18. Starkey, *Six Wives*, p. 143.
19. See Brewer, *L&P*, Vol. I. no. 2170, p. 977 (letter of Henry VIII to Margaret of Savoy); and no. 2200, p. 988 (Katherine of Aragon to Wolsey).
20. Hutchinson, *Young Henry*, p. 179.
21. S. J. Gunn, 'Warfare in Henry's Reign' in Rimer et al. (eds.), *Henry VIII: Arms and the Man*, p. 41.
22. See also Gunn, *Early Tudor Government* (1995), pp. 22–53, pp. 81–9.

23. S. J. Gunn, 'Warfare in Henry's Reign' in Rimer et al. (eds.), *Henry VIII: Arms and the Man*, pp. 42-3.

24. Ibid., p. 43. See also Helen Miller, *Henry VIII and the English Nobility*, p. 137.

25. See Hutchinson, *Young Henry*, p. 179 and Starkey, *Six Wives*, p. 143.

26. Starkey, *Six Wives*, p. 143.

27. Ellis, *Original Letters*, Vol. I, pp. 84–5.

28. Ibid.

29. Brewer, *L&P*, Vol. I, no. 2226, p. 998.

30. Ibid., Vol. I, no. 2261, p. 1014.

31. Ibid., no. 2208, pp. 990–1 and no. 2265, p. 1015; and CSP Milan, no. 660, pp. 404–7.

32. CSP Milan, no. 654, pp. 394-7.

33. ODNB, P. R. N. Carter, 'Tuke, Sir Brian (d. 545), – doi:10.1093/ref:odnb/27803.

34. CSP Milan, no. 660, pp. 404–7.

18. INVASION

1. Caldwell, 'Guns in Scotland' (PhD 1982), pp. 154–5.

2. See Peter Reese, *Flodden*, pp. 3–6.

3. Mackie, *King James IV*, p. 247.

4. Arnold, *Renaissance at War*, p. 32 (and more generally pp. 24–35).

5. Haslewood (ed.), 'The Trewe Encountre or Batayle Lately Don Betwene Englande and Scotlande' manuscript in *Proceedings of the Society of Antiquaries Scotland*, Vol. 7, March 1867 (*Trewe Encountre*), p. 146. Also see MacIvor, 'Artillery and Major Places of Strength in the Lothians' in Caldwell (ed.), *Scottish Weapons and Fortifications 1100–1800*, pp. 98–9; & Phillips, *The Anglo-Scots Wars: 1513–1550* (1999), p. 132.

6. Pitscottie, *Cronicles*, ed. Dalyell, Vol. I, p. 266.

7. Arnold, *Renaissance at War*, p. 31.

8. As Norman Macdougall points out in *James IV*, p. 273, the lack of contemporary or near contemporary Scottish accounts means some estimations have to be made. One instance being the time between when the guns opened fire on Norham and when Scottish troops crossed at Coldstream. Norham surrendered after a six-day siege on 28 August and it is likely that Scottish movements were coordinated – hence the choice of the 22nd as the crossing day. Mackie, *King James IV*, p. 248 also goes for 22 August.

9. Phillips, *Anglo-Scots Wars* (1999), p. 54.

10. Ibid., p. 53.

11. Ibid., p. 114.

12. Sometimes his name is given as Ainslie, but he is given as Anislow on p. 63 of

the *Catalogue of the manuscripts in the Cottonian library deposited in the British Museum*, so he is called that here.

13. See Macdougall, *James IV*, pp. 191–2 for summary of difference between Councils and General Councils.

14. Buchanan, *The History of Scotland*, ed. Aikman, 4 vols., Vol. II (1827), pp. 253–4.

15. Macdougall, *James IV*, p. 307.

16. ODNB, T. G. Chalmers, 'Stewart, Alexander (c.1493–1513)', – doi:10.1093/ref:odnb/26454.

17. Macdougall, *James IV*, p. 272.

18. Hall, *Chronicle*, p. 557.

19. Brewer, *L&P*, Vol. I, no. 2270, pp. 1016–7.

20. Ibid., Vol I., no. 2279, pp. 1019–20.

21. In his letter of 12 August 1513. See Hannay, *Letters of James IV*, pp. 314–5.

22. According to Hall, James had a poor substitute: the Bastard's legitimate half-brother William Heron was in prison within the Humes' Fast Castle near Coldingham in Berwickshire; and, because of that, a prisoner exchange was quickly made for George Hume (a brother of Alexander Lord Hume according to Buchanan, p. 249) and other Scots held locally after their capture in the 'Ill Raid'. See also Hall, *Chronicle*, p. 558; & Smith (ed.), *The Days of James IV*, p. 144.

23. Wood, *Flodden Papers*, p. 79.

24. Vegetius, *De Re Militari Book*, ed. & trans. Milner, on 'General Rules of War', pp. 108–11. See also Helen J. Nicholson, *Medieval Warfare* (2004), p. 14.

25. See Richardson, *Renaissance Monarchy*, especially. pp. 61–3.

26. Mackie, *James IV*, p. 241.

27. See Chapter 13.

28. Grafton, *Chronicle, or History of England*, 2 vols. (1809), Vol. ii, p. 269.

29. Ibid.

30. Brewer, *L&P*, Vol. I, no. 2222/10, p. 995.

31. Ibid., Vol. I, no. 2207, p. 990.

32. Ibid., Vol. I, no. 2313, p. 1037.

33. Hall, *Chronicle*, p. 564; CSP Milan, no. 660, pp. 404–7.

19. PREPARING THE GROUND

1. Hall, *Chronicle*, p. 557.

2. Ibid.

3. Ibid.

4. Ellis, *Original Letters*, Vol. I, no. xxvii, pp. 76–8.

5. Grafton, *Chronicle*, p. 271.

6. CSP Milan, no. 660, pp. 404–7.

7. As the report of the meeting came in a letter from West to Henry, rather than James himself, we cannot be sure whether it was a statement or an oath.

8. Hall, *Chronicle*, pp. 559–60.

9. Ibid.

10. Ibid.

11. Ibid.

12. Phillips, *Anglo-Scots Wars*, p. 119.

13. Ibid.

14. Hall, *Chronicle*, p. 560.

15. Ellis, *Original Letters*, Vol. I, pp. 86–7.

16. See Chapter 3.

17. *Trewe Encountre*, p. 146.

18. Hall, *Chronicle*, p. 560.

19. *Trewe Encountre*, p. 147.

20. Reese, *Flodden*, p. 124. Kightly, *Flodden: The Anglo-Scottish War of 1513* (1975), p. 12.

21. See Goodwin, *Fatal Colours*, p. 170. With thanks to Roger Protz for this information.

22. Peter Brears, 'To Feed the King's Men: Catering for the Henrician Army and Navy', in Rimer et al. eds., *Henry VIII: Arms and the Man*, pp. 314–15.

23. Ibid.

24. The diet of Cromwell's army consisted so predominantly of biscuit and cheese that it became a synonym for provisions – see C. H. Firth, *Cromwell's Army* (1962), p. 223.

25. *Trewe Encountre*, p. 147.

26. John A. Ferguson has reproduced and translated the Epitaph into modern English in his highly valuable collections of contemporary letters and documents (see Bibliography). See specifically, *The Battle of Flodden* (2001), pp. 38–42.

27. With thanks to Bob Woosnam-Savage.

28. Reid, *Battles of the Scottish Lowlands* (2004), p. 10.

29. Ibid. And Cannan, *Scottish Arms & Armour*, p. 35. Cannan says that the spear was typically 8-foot long in the Highlands and 12-foot in the Lowlands.

30. With thanks to Jurg A. Meier, Curator of the Castle Grandson, Basle, Switzerland for information on pike lengths. See also Caldwell, 'Some Notes on Axes and Long Shafted Weapons' in Caldwell (ed.), *Scottish Weapons*, p. 254.

31. See F. L. Taylor, *The Art of War in Italy*, pp. 122–4.

32. See Bert S. Hall, *Weapons and Warfare in Renaissance Europe* (1997), particularly p. 211 and p. 225.

33. These battles, Grandson and Morat, together with Nancy in 1477 led to the permanent loss of the Duchy's territory to France and the death of its Duke Charles the Bold, husband of Margaret of York, at Nancy.
34. Douglas Miller, *Landsknechts* (1997), p. 3.
35. Arnold, *Renaissance at War*, pp. 60–4.
36. For Erasmus statement on War, see Chapter 21.
37. Brewer, *L&P*, Vol. III, no. 2995, p. 1265.
38. Caldwell, 'Some Notes on Scottish Axes and Long Shafted Weapons' in Caldwell, *Scottish Weapons*, pp. 290–3 and p. 297.
39. Barr, *Flodden 1513*, p. 47 citing Hannay (ed.), *Acts of the Lords of Council in Public Affairs 1501–54* (1932), pp. 2–3. The existence of this weaponry was noted by Queen Katherine in her letter to Wolsey of 16 September, mentioning 'a bill in a dead man's purse' found at Flodden – see Ellis, *Original Letters*, Vol. I, pp. 88–9. The details are then given by Tuke in his letter to Pace of 22 September – see CSP Milan, no. 660, pp. 404–7.
40. Black, *European Warfare 1494–1660* (2002), p. 72.
41. Ibid.
42. Ibid.
43. Caldwell, *Scottish Weapons*, p. 308.
44. Ibid.
45. Cooper, *Scottish Renaissance Armies* (2008), p. 28.
46. Phillips, *Anglo-Scots Wars*, p. 62.
47. Cornish, *Henry VIII's Army* (1987), p. 34.

20. FLODDEN – 9 SEPTEMBER 1513

1. With thanks to Chris Burgess for reference to his draft paper 'Strategic Decisions at Flodden'.
2. *Trewe Encountre*, p. 145.
3. According to *Trewe Encountre*, p. 145. Though Hall, *Chronicle*, p. 558, says 1,000 of these were Lancashire men.
4. Hall, *Chronicle*, p. 561.
5. Goodwin, *Fatal Colours*, pp. 107–9.
6. Ibid., pp. 182–5.
7. Phillips, *Anglo-Scots Wars*, p. 118.
8. Hall, *Chronicle*, p. 561.
9. 'Articles of the Battle' in Public Record Office, *State Papers, published under the authority of His Majesty's Commission : King Henry the Eighth.* Vol. 4, Part IV, p. 1.
10. Hall, *Chronicle*, p. 561.
11. Pitscottie, *Cronicles*, ed. Dalyell, Vol. I, p. 277.

12. *Trewe Encountre*, p. 150; and Hall, *Chronicle*, p. 561.

13. ODNB, C. A. McGladdery, 'Graham family (*c*.1250–1513)', – doi:10.1093/ref:odnb/54216.

14. See Paul, *Scots Peerage*, Vols. 1 to 9 (1904–14) for information on Scots commanders at Flodden. *The Trewe Encountre*, p. 148 says that 'the most part of the noblemen of his realm' were with James.

15. The Scots army were reported to have had pavisses at Flodden, but how useful they were with pikes is open to question.

16. With credit to Clive Hallam-Baker for the phrase 'Death from a distance'.

17. That Ambassador being Dr West.

18. Barr, *Flodden 1513*, p. 95.

19. Such as Christine de Pisan. See De Pisan, *The Book of Fayttes of Arms and of Chivalry* (1932), ed. Byles, pp. 18–19.

20. To co-opt David Starkey's description of Henry VIII (see Chapter 12).

21. CSP, Spain Vol. I, no. 210, 168–179 reproduced in Smith (ed.), *The Days of James IV*, p. 56.

22. In the *Articles of the Battle*, p. 1, described as 'an arrow shot apart'. Barr, *Flodden 1513*, p. 39 citing Machiavelli describing it as 'an harquebus shot' according to the Swiss system.

23. CSP Milan, no. 660, pp. 404–7.

24. *Articles of the Battle*, p. 2; Hall, *Chronicle*, p. 562; *Trewe Encountre*, p. 148.

25. *Articles of the Battle*, p. 1. This crucial ridge is worthy of having a name, which Clive Hallam-Baker gives it as 'the Howard Ridge', see his *The Battle of Flodden: Why & How* (2012), pp. 70–1.

26. *Trewe Encountre*, pp. 150-1.

27. The later poem *La Rotta de Scocesi* by 2nd Earl Spencer (cited by Phillips, *Anglo-Scots Wars*, p. 126).

28. *Trewe Encountre*, p. 150.

29. *Grafton Chronicle*, p. 271.

30. *Articles of the Battle*, pp. 1–2.

31. See Cooper, *Scottish Renaissance Armies*, p. 33 and p. 57.

32. Brewer, *L&P*, Vol. I, no. 2283, pp. 1020–1.

33. Ibid.

34. *Trewe Encountre*, p. 150.

35. *Trewe Encountre*, p. 150 re money; Hall, *Chronicle*, p. 564 re 'apparel'.

36. *The Scottish Antiquary*, Vol. 13, no. 52 (April 1899), p. 170: '87 Hays who fell along with the Earl of Erroll [William Hay]'. Other names taken from several sources, most notably Balfour Paul, *Scots Peerage*, 9 vols.

37. Smith (ed.), *The Days of James IV*, pp. 74–5 citing Erasmus, *Adagia* 1634 (ed. 1599).

38. http://www.battlefieldstrust.com/resource-centre/medieval/battleview.asp?BattleFieldId=15.

39. But not, as thought, at Selkirk. See T. Craig-Brown, 'The Flodden Traditions of Selkirk' (1913), extracted from the same author's *The History of Selkirkshire* (1886).

40. UK Battlefields Trust Resource Centre http://www.battlefieldstrust.com/resource-centre/medieval/battleview.asp?BattleFieldId=15.

41. *Articles of the Battle*, p. 2.

42. *Trewe Encountre*, p. 151.

43. Letter of Ruthall to Wolsey of 20 September in Smith (ed.), *The Days of James IV*, p. 171.

44. Barr, *Flodden 1513*, p. 151. Dr Barr cites Henry James (ed.) version of *Articles of the Battle* in James (ed.), *Facsimiles of National Manuscripts from William the Conqueror to Queen Anne* (1865), pp. 2–3. This has the three lines on the activities of the Reivers struck through, but they are readable. They are not in the more official version in *State Papers etc.* (cited elsewhere here). Perhaps thus confirming the English identity of the Reivers concerned.

45. *Articles of the Battle*, pp. 1–2.

46. Ibid., p. 2.

47. Hall, *Chronicle*, p. 564.

48. Younger, 'Crouching enemy, hidden ally: the decisive role of groundwater discharge features in two major British battles, Flodden 1513 and Prestonpans 1745' in Rose and Mather (eds.), *Military Aspects of Hydrogeology* (2012), p. 22.

49. With thanks to Chris Burgess for this information.

50. Barr, *Flodden 1513*, p. 85.

51. *Articles of the Battle*, p. 1.

52. See Goodwin, *Fatal Colours*, p. 178.

53. ODNB, Philippe Contamine, 'Stuart, Bérault (1452/3–1508)' – doi:10.1093/ref:odnb/26694.

54. In Younger, 'Crouching enemy etc.' in *Military Aspects of Hydrogeology* (2012), pp. 19–33.

55. Local historian John Ferguson believes that if James had agreed to fight on Milfield Plain he would most likely have won a victory of sorts. He may well be right.

56. 'Crouching enemy', in *Military Aspects of Hydrogeology*, p. 19.

57. Ignoring the advice of Christine de Pisan in her writings 'not to risk all in battle'. See De Pisan, *The Book of Fayttes of Arms and of Chivalry*, ed. Byles, p. 64.

21. AFTERMATH

1. Phillips, *Anglo-Scots Wars*, p. 2.
2. Letter of Ruthall to Wolsey of 20 September, in Smith (ed.), *The Days of James IV*, p. 172.
3. Letter of Ruthall to Wolsey of 20 September, in Brewer, *L&P*, Vol. I, no. 2283, pp. 1020–1.
4. Ibid.
5. The banner was also carried during The Pilgrimage of Grace, but was burnt in the reign of Elizabeth. http://www.northumbrianassociation.com/cuthban.html. But a replica was created for Durham Cathedral in 2012.
6. Hannay, *The Letters of James IV*, ed. R. L. Mackie, pp. 107–11.
7. CSP Milan, no. 661, pp. 407–8.
8. Ellis, *Original Letters*, Vol. I, pp. 88–9.
9. CSP Milan, no. 660, pp. 404–7.
10. Ferguson, *The Battle of Flodden 1513*, p. 40.
11. Ferguson, *The Battle of Flodden 1513*, p. 16, citing BM Egerton MS 2603, f.30. Also J. D. Mackie (ed.) article, 'The English Army at Flodden', *Miscellany of the Scottish History Society*, Vol. VIII, 1951.
12. Hall, *Chronicle*, p. 564.
13. For ceremonial use of ordnance see Arnold, *Renaissance at War*, p. 32.
14. Brewer, *L&P*, Vol. I, no. 2246, 4ii, p. 1007.
15. ODNB, David M. Head, 'Howard, Thomas, second duke of Norfolk (1443–1524)' – doi:10.1093/ref:odnb/13939.
16. ODNB, David Loades, 'Mary (1496–1533)' - doi:10.1093/ref:odnb/18251.
17. As opposed to Kings of England who claimed the French throne. The only other English-born Queen was Eadgifu, daughter of Edward the Elder, who was consort to Charles III from c. 917 to his death in 929.
18. ODNB, Michael A. R. Graves, 'Howard, Thomas, third duke of Norfolk (1473–1554)' – doi:10.1093/ref:odnb/13940.
19. On 27 January 1547 Henry authorised his execution for Treason, but then died the next day and the sentence was not carried out.
20. Hutchinson, *House of Treason*, p. 302.
21. She was the daughter of the 2nd Duke's daughter Elizabeth.
22. Pitscottie, *Cronicles*, ed. Dalyell, Vol. I, p. 278.
23. ODNB, Elaine Finnie Greig, 'Hamilton, James, first earl of Arran (1475?–1529)' – doi:10.1093/ref:odnb/12079.
24. Buchanan, *History of Scotland*, Vol. II, p. 245.
25. Mackie, *King James IV*, p. 201.
26. Pitscottie, *Cronicles*, ed. Dalyell, Vol. I, pp. 262–3.
27. Ibid, pp. 264–5.

28. Identified as such by Sir Walter Scott. See 'Tales of a Grandfather' in *The Complete Works of Sir Walter Scott*. 7 vols., Vol. VI (1833), p. 62.

29. Pitscottie, *Cronicles*, ed. Dalyell, Vol. I, pp. 266–7.

30. This was James Aikman. See footnote to Buchanan, *History of Scotland*, Vol. II, p. 251.

31. See Robert White's *The Battle of Flodden: Fought 9 Sept. 1513* (1859), p. 6.

32. Pitscottie, *Cronicles*, ed. Dalyell, Vol. I, pp. 267–8 and p. 273. Buchanan, *History of Scotland*, 252–3

33. Pitscottie, *Cronicles*, ed. Dalyell, Vol. I, p. 273–5.

34. Buchanan, *History of Scotland*, Vol. II, pp. 253–4.

35. Pitscottie, *Cronicles*, ed. Dalyell, Vol. I, p. 281.

36. Lyndsay, Sir David, 'Testament and Complaint of the Papingo' in *The Poetical Works of Sir David Lyndsay* (1777), Vol. II, p. 14.

37. Also the judgment of local historian John Ferguson.

38. Ranald Nicholson, *Scotland: the Later Middle Ages* (1974), p. 606.

39. See Chapter 11.

40. Macdougall, *James IV*, p. 309.

41. Lynch, *Scotland: A New History*, p. 163.

42. See Balfour Paul, *Scots Peerage*, 9 vols. and W. K. Emond PhD Thesis (Univ. of St Andrews 1989), 'The Minority of King James V, 1513–1528', pp. 6–7.

43. ODNB, Andrea Thomas, 'James V (1512–1542)' – doi:10.1093/ref:odnb/14591.

44. Starkey, *Henry VIII: A European Court in England* (1991), p. 12.

45. ODNB, Andrea Thomas, 'James V (1512–1542)' – doi:10.1093/ref:odnb/14591.

46. See David M. Head, 'Henry VIII's Scottish Policy: a Reassessment' in *The Scottish Historical Review*, Vol. LXI, I: no. 171: April 1982, pp. 1–24.

47. Hall, *Chronicle*, pp. 846–56. See also, Gairdner & Brodie, *L&P*, Vol. 17, no. 1033, pp. 582–3.

48. ODNB, Steven G. Ellis, 'Dacre, Thomas, second Baron Dacre of Gilsland (1467–1525)' – doi:10.1093/ref:odnb/50220.

49. To the King and Council: see Hodgson, *A History of Northumberland in Three Parts*, Part III, Vol. I, pp. 31–40 – with thanks to Linda Bankier of the Flodden 500 Transcription Project. See also letters from Dacre to Henry VIII and to Wolsey: Ellis, *Letters*, no. 34, pp. 92–9 and no. 50, pp. 131–3.

50. Lynch, *Scotland: A New History*, p. 207.

51. Black, *European Warfare 1494–1660*, pp. 25–6.

52. Lynch, *Scotland: A New History*, p. 238.

53. Ibid., p. 239.

54. Macdougall, *James IV*, p. 300.

55. ODNB, D. S. Chambers, 'Bainbridge, Christopher (1462/3–1514)', – doi:10.1093/ref:odnb/1081; ODNB, Cecil H. Clough, 'Gigli, Silvestro (1463–1521)' – doi:10.1093/ref:odnb/10671.

56. Brewer, *L&P*, Vol. I, no. 2469 pp. 1088–9.

57. With thanks to Helen Castor for this gem. Hannay, *Acts of the Lords of Council in Public Affairs 1501–54*, pp. 241–2, re. granting of annulment.

58. Stow, *A Survey of London*, ed. Kingsford, 2 vols. (1908), Vol. I, p. 298.

59. http://www.stgeorges-windsor.org/archives/archive-features/image-of-the-month/title1/henry-viii-tomb.html and http://www.stpauls.co.uk/Cathedral-History/Explore-the-Cathedral/Discover-the-Crypt. The sarcophagus was placed on top of the tomb a decade after Nelson's funeral.

COMMEMORATION

1. Stevenson and Pentland, 'The Battle of Flodden and its Commemoration, 1513–2013' in eds. King and Simpkin, *England and Scotland at War, c. 1296–c.1513* (2012), p. 359.

2. See Head, *The Ebbs and Flows of Fortune: the Life of Thomas Howard, Third Duke of Norfolk* (1995), p. 301.

3. Stevenson and Pentland, op. cit.

SELECT BIBLIOGRAPHY

◊ Available online through subscription to <u>British History Online</u>

Anderson, Alan Orr. 1922. *Early Sources of Scottish History AD 500 to 1286.* Vol. 1. 2 vols. Edinburgh: Oliver and Boyd.

Armstrong, R. 1911. *The Peel Towers of the Scottish Border.* Galashiels: A. Walker.

Arnold, Thomas F. 2001. *The Renaissance at War.* Cassell's History of Warfare. London: Cassell.

Arthurson, Ian. 1994. *The Perkin Warbeck Conspiracy, 1491–1499.* Stroud: Alan Sutton.

Bacon, Francis. 1881. *History of the Reign of King Henry VII.* Cambridge: Cambridge University Press.

Baildon, H. Bellyse. 1907. *The Poems of William Dunbar.* Cambridge: Cambridge University Press.

Bain, Joseph, ed. 1888. *Calendar of Documents Relating to Scotland.* Vol. IV. 4 vols. Edinburgh: H.M. Register House.

Baldwin, David. 2006. *Stoke Field: the Last Battle of the Wars of the Roses.* Barnsley: Pen & Sword Military.

Barnes, Ishbel. 2007. *Janet Kennedy, Royal Mistress: Marriage and Divorce at the Courts of James IV and V.* Edinburgh: John Donald.

Barr, Niall. 2001. *Flodden 1513: the Scottish Invasion of Henry VIII's England.* Stroud: Tempus.

Barrow, G.W.S. 1988. *Robert the Bruce & the Community of the Realm.* Edinburgh: Edinburgh University Press.

Bentley, Samuel. 1831. 'Extracts from the Privy Purse Expenses of King Henry VII'. In *Excerpta Historica.* London: Samuel Bentley.

◊ Bergenroth, G.A., ed. 1864. *Calendar of State Papers, Spain.* Vols. 1 and 2. 13 vols. London: HMSO.

Biddle, Martin. 2000. *The Castle Winchester: Great Hall & Round Table.* Winchester: Hampshire County Council.

Black, Jeremy. 2002. *European Warfare, 1494–1660.* Warfare and History. London: Routledge.

———. 2011. *War in the World: a Comparative History: 1450–1600.* Basingstoke: Palgrave Macmillan.

Boardman, Steve. 2002. 'Late Medieval Scotland and the Matter of Britain'. In *Scottish History: The Power of the Past,* ed. Edward J. Cowan and Richard J. Finlay. Edinburgh: Edinburgh University Press.

———. 2008. 'Royal Finance and Regional Rebellion in the Reign of James IV'. In *Sixteenth-century Scotland: Essays in Honour of Michael Lynch*, ed. Julian Goodare and Alasdair A. MacDonald. Leiden; Boston: Brill.

Borman, Tracy. 2010. *Elizabeth's Women: the Hidden Story of the Virgin Queen*. London: Vintage.

———. 2011. *Matilda: Queen of the Conqueror*. London: Jonathan Cape.

Bower, Walter. 1987. *Scotichronicon: in Latin and English*. Ed. D.E.R. Watt. New ed. in Latin and English with notes and indexes. Aberdeen: Aberdeen University Press.

Brears, Peter. 2009. 'To Feed the King's Men: Catering for the Henrician Army and Navy'. In *Henry VIII: Arms and the Man, 1509–2009*, ed. Graeme Rimer, Thom Richardson, and J.P.D. Cooper. Leeds: Royal Armouries; Historic Royal Palaces.

Breeze, David John, and Historic Scotland. 2006. *The Antonine Wall*. Edinburgh: John Donald.

◊ Brewer, ed. 1862. *Letters and papers, foreign and domestic, of the reign of Henry VIII*. Vol. 1. 21 vols. London: HMSO.

Brown, Michael. 2004. *The Wars of Scotland, 1214–1371*. The New Edinburgh History of Scotland 4. Edinburgh: Edinburgh University Press.

———. 2008. *Bannockburn: The Scottish War and the British Isles, 1307–1323*. Edinburgh: Edinburgh University Press.

Brown, Michael, and Roland Tanner, ed. 2008. *Renaissance Monarchy? Stewart Kingship (1469–1542)*. Edinburgh: John Donald.

◊ Brown, Rawdon, ed. 1867. *Calendar of State Papers Venice*. Vol. 2. 38 vols. London: HMSO.

Buchanan, George. 1827. *The History of Scotland*. Ed. James Aikman. Vol. 2. 4 vols. Glasgow: Blackie, Fullarton.

Byrne, M. St Clare. 1968. *The Letters of King Henry VIII*. London: Cassell.

Caldwell, David H., ed. 1981. *Scottish Weapons and Fortifications 1100–1800*. Edinburgh: John Donald.

Caldwell, David H. 1979. *The Scottish Armoury*. Scottish Connection. Edinburgh: Blackwood.

———. 1982. 'Guns in Scotland: The Manufacture and Use of Guns and Their Influence on Warfare from the Fourteenth Century to c.1625'. PhD, Edinburgh.

Cannan, Fergus. 2009. *Scottish Arms and Armour*. Oxford: Shire.

Carlton, Charles. 2011. *This Seat of Mars: War and the British Isles, 1485–1746*. London; New Haven: Yale University Press.

Castor, H.M. 2011. *VIII*. Dorking: Templar.

Cavendish, George. 1920. *The Life of Cardinal Wolsey*. London: Macmillan.

Chibnall, Marjorie, ed. 1969. *The Ecclesiastical History of Orderic Vitalis*. Trans. Marjorie Chibnall. Vol. 2. 6 vols. Oxford: Clarendon Press.

Christine De Pisan. 1932. *The Book of Fayttes of Arms and of Chivalry*. Ed. Alfred Thomas Plested Byles. Trans. William Caxton. London: Early English Text Society.

Churchill, Winston. 1949. *Their Finest Hour*. Vol. 2. 6 vols. The Second World War. London: Cassell.

Clark, Cecily, ed. 1970. *The Peterborough Chronicle, 1070–1154*. 2nd ed. Oxford: Clarendon Press.

Cloake, John. 1990. *Richmond's Great Monastery: the Charterhouse of Jesus of Bethlehem of Shene*. Richmond: Richmond Local History Society.

———. 1995. *Palaces and Parks of Richmond and Kew*. Chichester, West Sussex: Phillimore.

———. 2001. *Richmond Palace: its History and its Plan*. Richmond: Richmond Local History Society.

Condon, Margaret. 2003. 'The Last Will of Henry VII: Document and Text'. In *Westminster Abbey: The Lady Chapel of Henry VII*, ed. T.W.T. Tatton-Brown and Richard Mortimer. Woodbridge: Boydell.

Cooper, Jonathan. 2008. *Scottish Renaissance Armies, 1513–1550*. Oxford; Osprey.

Cornish, Paul. 1987. *Henry VIII's Army*. London: Osprey.

Craig-Brown, T. 1886. 'The Flodden Traditions of Selkirk'. In *The History of Selkirkshire*. Edinburgh: D. Douglas.

Cunningham, Sean. 2007. *Henry VII*. 1. London: Routledge.

Driscoll, Stephen T., and Historic Scotland. 2002. *Alba: The Gaelic Kingdom of Scotland, AD 800–1124*. Making of Scotland. Edinburgh: Birlinn with Historic Scotland.

Dudley, Edmund. 1859. *The Tree of Common Wealth: a Treatise*. Manchester: Printed by C. Simms & Co.

Dunbar, John G. 1999. *Scottish Royal Palaces: The Architecture of the Royal Residences During the Late Medieval and Early Renaissance Periods*. Historic Scotland. East Linton: Tuckwell.

Duncan, A.A.M. 2002. *The Kingship of the Scots, 842–1292: Succession and Independence*. Edinburgh: Edinburgh University Press.

Elliot, William. 1911. *The Battle of Flodden and the Raids of 1513*. Edinburgh: A. Elliot.

Ellis, Henry, ed. 1825. *Original Letters, Illustrative of English History: Including Numerous Royal Letters: From Autographs in the British Museum and One or Two Other Collections*. Vol. 1. 3 vols. London: Printed for Harding, Triphook & Lepard.

Emond, William Kevin. 1989. 'The Minority of King James V, 1513–1528'. PhD, UK: St Andrews.

Erasmus, Desiderius. 1901. *The Epistles of Erasmus, from His Earliest Letters to His Fifty-first Year, Arranged in Order of Time: English Translations from the Early*

Correspondence, with a Commentary Confirming the Chronological Arrangement and Supplying Further Biographical Matter. Vol. 2. 3 vols. London: Longmans, Green & co.

Fabyan, Robert. 1938. *The Great Chronicle of London.* Ed. A.H. Thomas and I.D. Thornley. London: Printed by G.W. Jones at the sign of the Dolphin.

Ferguson, John. 2011. *The Encampment of the English Army at Barmoor, 8th September 1513.* Cold Harbour Press.

Ferguson, John A. 2011. *The Battle of Flodden, 1513.* Cold Harbour Press.

Foot, Sarah. 2011. *Æthelstan: First King of England.* London; New Haven: Yale University Press.

Fox, Julia. 2011. *Sister Queens: Katherine of Aragon and Juana Archduchess of Burgundy.* London: Weidenfeld & Nicolson.

Fox, Richard. 1929. *Letters of Richard Fox, 1486–1527.* Ed. P.S. Allen and Helen Mary Allen. Oxford: Clarendon Press.

Fraser, George MacDonald. 1989. *The Steel Bonnets: the Story of the Anglo-Scottish Border Reivers.* London: Collins Harvill.

Gairdner, James. 1861. *Letters and Papers Illustrative of the Reigns of Richard III and Henry VII.* London: Longman, Green, Longman and Roberts.

———. 1904. *The Paston letters, A.D. 1422–1509.* Micro Edition. London: Chatto & Windus.

◊ Gairdner, James, and R.H. Brodie, ed. 1900. *Letters and Papers, Foreign and Domestic of the Reign of Henry VIII,* Vol. 17. 21 vols. London: Longman & Roberts.

Gillingham, John. 1990. *The Wars of the Roses.* London: Weidenfeld & Nicolson.

Giustiniani, Sebastiano. 1854. *Four Years at the Court of Henry VIII.* Ed and Trans. Rawdon Brown. Vol. 1. 2 vols. London: Smith Elder.

Godfrey, Walter Hindes. 1963. *The College of Arms, Queen Victoria Street: Being the Sixteenth and Final Monograph of the London Survey Committee.* Monograph of the London Survey Committee 16. London: London Survey Committee.

Goodall, John. 2011. *The English Castle, 1066–1650.* London; New Haven: Yale University Press.

Goodman, Anthony. 1990. *The Wars of the Roses: Military Activity and English Society, 1452–97.* London; New York: Routledge.

———. 2007. 'The Impact of Warfare on the Scottish Marches, c.1481–c.1513'. In *The Fifteenth Century: VII, Conflicts, Consequences and the Crown in the Late Middle Ages,* ed. Linda Clark. Woodbridge: Boydell.

Goodwin, George. 2011. *Fatal Colours: Towton, 1461: England's Most Brutal Battle.* London: Weidenfeld & Nicolson.

Goring, Rosemary. 2008. *Scotland: The Autobiography.* London: Penguin Books.

Grafton, Richard. 1809. *Grafton's Chronicle, or History of England, to which is added his table of the bailiffs, sheriffs and mayors of the City of London, from the year 1189 to 1558 inclusive.* Vol. 2. 2 vols. London: J. Johnson.

Gravett, Christopher. 2006. *Tudor Knight.* Warrior 104. Oxford: Osprey.

Grose, Francis, and Edward Jeffery, ed. 1807. *The Antiquarian Repertory: a Miscellaneous Assemblage of Topography, History, Biography, Customs and Manners.* New ed. Vol. 2. 4 vols. London.

Gunn, Steven. 1991. 'The Accession of Henry VIII'. *Historical Research* 64 (155) (October): 278–88.

———. 1995. *Early Tudor Government, 1485–1558.* Basingstoke: Macmillan.

———. 1998. 'Sir Thomas Lovell (c.1449–1524): A New Man in a New Monarchy?' In *The End of the Middle Ages?: England in the Fifteenth and Sixteenth Centuries,* ed. John L. Watts. The Fifteenth Century Series no. 6. Stroud: Sutton.

———. 2006. 'The Court of Henry VII'. In *The Court as a Stage: England and the Low Countries in the Later Middle Ages,* ed. Steven Gunn and Antheun Janse. Woodbridge: Boydell.

———. 2009. 'Warfare in Henry's Reign'. In *Henry VIII: Arms and the Man, 1509–2009,* ed. Graeme Rimer, Thom Richardson, and J.P.D. Cooper. Leeds: Royal Armouries; Historic Royal Palaces.

Gunn, Steven, and Linda Monckton, ed. 2009. *Arthur Tudor, Prince of Wales: Life, Death & Commemoration.* Woodbridge: Boydell.

Guy, John. 1990. *Tudor England.* Oxford: Oxford University Press.

Gwyn, Peter. 1990. *The King's Cardinal: The Rise and Fall of Thomas Wolsey.* London: Barrie & Jenkins.

Hall, Bert S. 1997. *Weapons and Warfare in Renaissance Europe: Gunpowder, Technology, and Tactics.* Johns Hopkins Studies in the History of Technology 22. Baltimore; London: Johns Hopkins University Press.

Hall, Edward. 1809. *Hall's Chronicle Containing the History of England, During the Reign of Henry the Fourth, and the Succeeding Monarchs, to the End of the Reign of Henry the Eighth.* London: Printed for J. Johnson.

———. 1904. *The Triumphant Reign of Henry VIII.* Vol. 1. London: T.C. and E.C. Jack.

Hallam-Baker, Clive. 2011. *The Battle of Flodden: Then & Now.* DVD. The Remembering Flodden Project.

———. 2012. *The Battle of Flodden: Why & How.* The Remembering Flodden Project.

Hammer, Paul E.J., ed. 2007. *Warfare in Early Modern Europe 1450–1660.* International Library of Essays on Military History. Aldershot: Ashgate.

Hannay, Robert Kerr, ed. 1932. *Acts of the Lords of Council in Public Affairs, 1501–1554: Selections from the Acta Dominorum Concilii Introductory to the Register of the Privy Council of Scotland.* Edinburgh: H.M. General Register House.

Hannay, Robert Kerr. 1953. *The Letters of James the Fourth, 1505–1513*. Ed. R.L. Mackie. Scottish History Society 3rd series, v. 45. Edinburgh: Scottish History Society.

Hardyment, Christina. 2005. *Malory: The Life and Times of King Arthur's Chronicler*. London: HarperCollins.

Harrison, C.J. 1972. 'The Petition of Edmund Dudley'. *English Historical Review* 87 (No. 342) (January).

Haslewood, Joseph, ed. 1867. 'The Trewe Encountre or Batayle Lately Don Betwene Englande and Scotlande'. *Proceedings of the Society of Antiquaries Scotland*, Vol. 7. 1866-7 (March).

Head, David M. 1982.'Henry VIII's Scottish Policy: A Reassessment'. *The Scottish Historical Review* LXI (No. 171) (April): 1–24.

———. 1995. *The Ebbs and Flows of Fortune: The Life of Thomas Howard, Third Duke of Norfolk*. Athens, Georgia; London: University of Georgia Press.

Hearn, Karen. 1996. *Dynasties: Painting in Tudor and Jacobean England 1530–1630*. London: Tate.

Hinde, Andrew. 2003. *England's Population: a History Since the Domesday Survey*. London: Hodder Arnold.

◊ Hinds, A., ed. 1912. *Calendar of State Papers and Manuscripts, Existing in the Archives and Collections of Milan*. London: HMSO printed by the Hereford Times Ltd. Hereford.

◊ Horrox, Rosemary, contrib. ed. (1455–1504), Chris Given-Wilson, gen. ed. 2005. *The Parliament Rolls of Medieval England, 1275–1504*. Woodbridge: Boydell, National Archives and The History of Parliament Trust.

Houston, R. A., and William Knox, ed. 2001. *The New Penguin History of Scotland: From the Earliest Times to the Present Day*. London: Allen Lane in association with National Museums of Scotland.

Hughes, Jonathan. 2002. *Arthurian Myths and Alchemy: The Kingship of Edward IV*. Stroud: Sutton.

Humphrys, Julian. 2006. *Clash of Arms: 12 English Battles*. Swindon: English Heritage.

Hutchinson, Robert. 2009. *House of Treason*. pbk ed. London: Phoenix.

———. 2011. *Young Henry: The Rise to Power of Henry VIII*. London: Weidenfeld & Nicolson.

Hutton, Ronald. 2010. *A Brief History of Britain: 1485–1660, the Tudor and Stuart Dynasties*. London: Robinson.

Jillings, Karen. 2007. *Scotland's Black Death: The Foul Death of the English*. Stroud: Tempus.

John Hodgson. 1820. *A History of Northumberland in Three Parts*. Vol. I. Part III. Newcastle-upon-Tyne: Thomas & James Pigg.

Kightly, Charles. 1975. *Flodden, the Anglo-Scottish war of 1513*. London: Almark Pub. Co.

Kipling, Gordon. 1977. *The Triumph of Honour: Burgundian Origins of the Elizabethan Renaissance*. The Hague Netherlands: Published for the Sir Thomas Browne Institute by Leiden University Press.

———. 1990. *The Receyt of the Ladie Kateryne*. Oxford; New York: Published for the Early English Text Society by Oxford University Press.

Konstam, Angus, and Tony Bryan. 2008. *Tudor warships. 1, Henry VIII's Navy*. Oxford: Osprey.

Leland, John. 1770. *Antiquarii De Rebus Britannicis Collectanea*. Ed. Thomas Hearne. Vol. iv. London: G. & J. Richardson.

Lesley, John. 1829. *The History of Scotland*. Edinburgh.

Lindsay of Pitscottie, Robert. 1814. *The Cronicles of Scotland, by Robert Lindsay of Pittscottie, published from several old Manuscripts by John Graham Dalyell*. Ed. John Graham Dalyell. Edinburgh.

———. 1899. *The Historie and Cronicles of Scotland*. Ed. Æ J.G. Mackay. Vol. 1. 3 vols. Scottish Text Society. Pitscottie's Chronicles. Edinburgh; London: Printed for the Society by W. Blackwood & Sons.

Loades, D. M. 1996. *Chronicles of the Tudor Kings*. Godalming: Bramley Books.

———.2009.'Henry's Army and Navy'. In *Henry VIII: Arms and the Man, 1509–2009*, ed. Graeme Rimer, Thom Richardson, and J.P.D. Cooper. Leeds: Royal Armouries; Historic Royal Palaces.

———. 2011. *Henry VIII*. Stroud: Amberley.

Luders, A., T. Edlyn Tomlins, J. France, W.E. Taunton and J. Raithby, ed. 1810. *The Statutes of the Realm (1101–1713)*. 3, Henry VIII, c.22. London: Record Commission.

Lynch, Michael. 1992. *Scotland: a New History*. London: Pimlico.

Lyndsay, David. 1777. *The Poetical Works of Sir David Lyndsay of the Mount*. Vol. 2. 2 vols. Edinburgh: Williamson & Elliott.

Macdougall, Norman. 1997. *James IV*. The Stewart Dynasty in Scotland. East Linton: Tuckwell.

———. 2009. *James III*. Edinburgh: John Donald.

Mackie, J. D. 1991. *A History of Scotland*. London: Penguin Books.

Mackie, R. L. 1958. *King James IV of Scotland, a Brief Survey of His Life and Times*. Edinburgh: Oliver and Boyd.

Mason, Roger. 1985. 'Scotching the Brut'. *History Today* 35 (I).

———. 2008. 'Renaissance Monarchy? Stewart Kingship (1469–1542)'. In *Scottish Kingship, 1306–1542: Essays in Honour of Norman Macdougall*, ed. Michael Brown and Roland Tanner. Edinburgh: John Donald.

Mattingly, Garrett. 1941. *Catherine of Aragon*. Boston: Little Brown.

Maurer, Helen. 2003. *Margaret of Anjou*. Woodbridge: Boydell Press.

Mayor, John E.B. 1876. *The English Works of John Fisher*. Early English Text Society. London: N. Trubner & Co.

McKean, Charles. 2001. *The Scottish Chateau: The Country House of Renaissance Scotland*. Stroud: Sutton.

McKendrick, Scott, John Lowden and Kathleen Doyle. 2011. *Royal Manuscripts: The Genius of Illumination*. London: British Library.

Miller, Douglas. 2000. *The Landsknechts*. Men-at-arms Series 58. Oxford: Osprey Military.

Moffat, Alistair. 2008. *The Reivers: the Story of the Border Reivers*. Edinburgh: Birlinn.

Monmouth, Robert Carey. 1972. *The Memoirs of Robert Carey*. Series of Studies in Tudor and Stuart Literature. Oxford: Clarendon Press.

Murdoch, Steve. 2010. *The Terror of the Seas?: Scottish Maritime Warfare 1513–1713*. History of Warfare v. 58. Leiden; Boston: Brill.

Nichols, John. 1828. *The progresses, processions, and magnificent festivities, of King James the First, his royal consort, family, and court*. Vol 1. 4 vols. London: J. B. Nichols.

Nicholson, Ranald. 1974. *Scotland: The Later Middle Ages*. The Edinburgh History of Scotland 2. Edinburgh: Oliver & Boyd.

Nicolas, Nicholas Harris. 1830. *Privy Purse Expenses of Elizabeth of York*. London: W. Pickering.

Oliver, Neil. 2009. *A History of Scotland*. London: Weidenfeld & Nicolson.

Ormrod, W. M. 2000. *The Reign of Edward III*. Stroud: Tempus.

Paul, James Balfour, and Thomas Dickson, eds. 1877–1902. *Accounts of the Lord High Treasurer of Scotland (1473–1513)*. Vols. I to IV. 4 vols. Edinburgh: H.M. General Register House.

Paul, James Balfour. 1904–14 *Scots Peerage*. Vols. I to IX. 9 vols. Edinburgh: David Douglas.

Penn, Thomas. 2011. *Winter King: The Dawn of Tudor England*. London: Allen Lane.

Perry, Maria. 1998. *Sisters to the King: The Tumultuous Lives of Henry VIII's Sisters – Margaret of Scotland and Mary of France*. London: André Deutsch.

Phillips, Gervase. 1999. *The Anglo-Scots Wars, 1513–1550: a Military History*. Woodbridge: Boydell Press.

———. 2012. 'Scotland in the Age of the Military Revolution'. In *A Military History of Scotland*, ed. Edward. M. Spiers, Jeremy A. Crang, and Matthew Strickland. Edinburgh: Edinburgh University Press.

Pius II. 2003. *Commentaries*. Ed. Margaret Hamilton Meserve and Marcello Simonetta. Trans. Florence Alden Gragg. I Tatti Renaissance Library 12. Cambridge, M.A., London: Harvard University Press.

Prebble, John. 1974. *The Lion in the North: a Personal View of Scotland's History*. London: Secker and Warburg.

Prevenier, Walter, and Willem Pieter Blockmans. 1986. *The Burgundian Netherlands*. Cambridge: Cambridge University Press.

Public Record Office. 1830. 'Articles of the Battle'. In *Correspondence Relative to Scotland and the Borders*. Vol. 4. State Papers: King Henry VIII. His Majesty's Commission for State Papers.

Read, John. 1947. *Humour and Humanism in Chemistry*. London: G. Bell.

Reese, Peter. 2003. *Flodden: a Scottish Tragedy*. Edinburgh: Birlinn.

Reid, Stuart. 2004. *Battles of the Scottish Lowlands*. Barnsley: Pen & Sword Military.

Richardson, Glenn. 2002. *Renaissance Monarchy: the Reigns of Henry VIII, Francis I and Charles V*. London: Arnold.

Rodger, N.A.M., and National Maritime Museum (Great Britain). 1997. *The Safeguard of the Sea: A Naval History of Britain, 660–1649*. Naval History of Britain 1. London: HarperCollins in association with the National Maritime Museum.

Rollason, D.W. 2003. *Northumbria, 500-1100: Creation and Destruction of a Kingdom*. Cambridge: Cambridge University Press.

Sadler, John, and Stephen Walsh. 2006. *Flodden, 1513: Scotland's Greatest Defeat*. Oxford: Osprey.

Scott, Walter. 1833. 'Tales of a Grandfather'. In *The Complete Works of Sir Walter Scott*. Vol. vi. 7 vols. New York: Conner & Cooke.

Seward, Desmond. 2010. *The Last White Rose*. London: Constable.

Sicca, Cinzia, and Louis A. Waldman, ed. 2012. *The Anglo-Florentine Renaissance: Art for the Early Tudors*. New Haven: Yale Center for British Art and The Paul Mellon Centre for Studies in British Art; Distributed by Yale University Press.

Smith, G. Gregory. 1890. *The Days of James IV, 1488–1513*. London: Nutt.

Smith, Robert D., and Kelly DeVries. 2005. *The Artillery of the Dukes of Burgundy, 1363–1477*. Woodbridge: Boydell.

Sneyd, Charlotte A. 1847. *A Relation, or Rather a True Account of the Island of England; About the Year 1500*. London: Camden Society.

Spont, Alfred. 1897. *Letters and Papers Relating to the War with France, 1512–1513*. London: Printed for the Navy Records Society.

Starkey, David. 1981. 'The Age of the Household'. In *The Later Middle Ages*, ed. Stephen Medcalf. London: Methuen.

———. 1987. "Intimacy and Innovation: The Rise of the Privy Chamber, 1485–1547." In *The English Court: From the Wars of the Roses to the Civil War*, ed. David Starkey. London: Longman.

———. 2003. *Six Wives: The Queens of Henry VIII*. London: Chatto & Windus.

———. 2006. *Monarchy: from the Middle Ages to Modernity*. London: HarperPress.

———. 2008. *Henry: Virtuous Prince*. London: HarperPress.

Starkey, David, and Susan Doran, ed. 2009. *Henry VIII: Man and Monarch*. London: British Library.

Stevenson, Katie. 2007. 'Contesting Chivalry: James II and the Control of Chivalric Culture in the 1450s'. *Journal of Medieval History* III (no. 2).

———. 2008. 'Royal Propaganda: Snowdon Herald and the Cult of Chivalry in Late Medieval Scotland'. In *Genealogica Et Heraldica Sancta Andreae MMVI: Myth and Propaganda in Heraldry and Genealogy*, ed. James D. Floyd and Charles J. Burnett. Vol. II. Edinburgh: 2008.

———. 2010. 'The Stewarts: James IV'. BBC Radio 3.

———. 2012. 'Chivalry, British Sovereignty and Dynastic Politics: Undercurrents of Antagonism in Tudor-Stewart Relations, c.1490–c.1513'. *Historical Research* 230 (November).

Stevenson, Katie, and Gordon Pentland. 2012. *England and Scotland at war, c. 1296– c. 1513*. Ed. Andy King and David Simpkin. Leiden; Boston: Brill.

Stewart, Ian Halley. 1955. *The Scottish Coinage*. London: Spink.

Stow, John. 1908. *A Survey of London*. Ed. Charles Lethbridge Kingsford. Oxford: Clarendon Press.

Tabri, Edward. 2004. *Political Culture in the Early Northern Renaissance: the Court of Charles the Bold, Duke of Burgundy (1467–1477)*. Lewiston NY: E. Mellen Press.

Tallett, Frank, and D.J.B. Trim, ed. 2010. *European Warfare, 1350–1750*. Cambridge: Cambridge University Press.

Taylor, F. L. 1921. *The Art of War in Italy 1494–1529*. Cambridge: Cambridge University Press.

Thomas, Andrea. 2012. 'The Renaissance'. In *The Oxford Handbook of Modern Scottish History*, ed. T. M. Devine and Jenny Wormald. Oxford: Oxford University Press.

Thurley, Simon. 1993. *The Royal Palaces of Tudor England*. New Haven and London: Yale University Press.

Tremlett, Giles. 2010. *Catherine of Aragon: Henry's Spanish Queen*. London: Faber and Faber.

Trevor-Roper, H. 2008. *The Invention of Scotland: Myth and History*. New Haven; London: Yale University Press.

Urban, William L. 2011. *Matchlocks to Flintlocks: Warfare in Europe and Beyond, 1500-1700*. London: Frontline.

Vallance, Edward. 2007. *The Glorious Revolution 1688: Britain's Fight for Liberty*. London: Abacus.

Vegetius Renatus, Flavius. 1996. *De Rei Militari*. Ed & Trans. N. P. Milner. Liverpool: Liverpool University Press.

Vergil, Polydore. 1950. *The Anglica Historia of Polydore Vergil, A.D. 1485–1537*. Ed. and Trans. Denys Hay. London: Office of the Royal Historical Society.

Vincent, Nicholas. 2011. *A Brief History of Britain: 1066–1485, the Birth of the Nation*. London: Robinson.

Watson, Fiona. 2010. 'The Stewarts: A Love Affair with Firepower'. BBC Radio 3.

————.2008. *Scotland: A History, 8000 B.C.–A.D. 2000*. Stroud: The History Press.

————.2011.'The Great Michael'. *Making History*. BBC Radio 4.

White, John Talbot, ed. 1970. *The Death of a King: Being Extracts from Contemporary Accounts of the Battle of Branxton Moor, September, 1513, Commonly Known as Flodden Field*. Edinburgh: Tragara Press.

White, Robert. 1859. *The Battle of Flodden: fought 9 Sept., 1513*. Newcastle-upon-Tyne: Thomas Pigg.

Williams, C.H., ed. 1971. *English Historical Documents. 5, 1485–1558*. London: Eyre and Spottiswoode.

Wood, Marguerite, ed. 1933. *Flodden Papers: Diplomatic Correspondence Between the Courts of France and Scotland, 1507–1517*. Scottish History Society. Publications ser.3 v.20. Edinburgh: Printed at the University Press by T. and A. Constable for the Scottish History Society.

Woolf, Alex. 2007. *From Pictland to Alba, 789–1070*. New Edinburgh History of Scotland v. 2. Edinburgh: Edinburgh University Press.

Wormald, Jenny. 1981. *Court, Kirk, and Community: Scotland 1470–1625*. The New History of Scotland 4. London: Edward Arnold.

Younger, Paul. 2012. 'Crouching Enemy, Hidden Ally: The Decisive Role of Groundwater Discharge Features in Two Major British Battles, Flodden 1513 and Prestonpans 1745'. In *Military Aspects of Hydrogeology*, ed. Edward P.F. Rose and J.D. Mather. London: Geological Society.

ACKNOWLEDGEMENTS

I am particularly fortunate to be writing at a time when I can consult the work of such academic experts as David Starkey, Norman Macdougall, Steven Gunn, Jeremy Black, Katie Stevenson, Thomas Penn, Sean Cunningham, Gordon Kipling, Gervase Phillips, Glenn Richardson, Michael Brown, John Goodall, Roger Mason, Andy King and David Simpkin, to name just a few to whom I am indebted. I thank those who have given me permission to quote from their work.

I have been able to draw on the work of the fifteenth- and sixteenth-century chroniclers, the great Victorian transcribers and modern historians through online resources as well as books. Foremost among those available electronically are British History Online (open to all through a small subscription) and the Oxford Dictionary of National Biography which brings the lives of almost 60,000 Britons to the desktop and is often accessible through subscription to a local library. I am also grateful for the assistance of librarians at the Institute of Historical Research, the Cambridge University Library, the British Library and my local library in Richmond.

People responsible for protecting our important battlefields and for preserving their memory in the community, whether that be locally, nationally or internationally, are owed a debt by us all. On a personal level, I should first mention Clive Hallam-Baker of the Remembering Flodden Project, who has been generous in giving me his time and the benefit of his years of walking the battlefield and gaining an understanding of its topography; it has been refreshing how enthusiastically he considers new possible interpretations of where and how the troops would have moved at Flodden. Those lucky enough to have enjoyed his personal tour of the battlefield will not quickly forget being called to arms. Flodden is just one of the many British battlefields that are part of the Battlefields Trust and once again I have enjoyed the entertaining insights of Julian Humphrys, including his Spont recommendation, and benefitted from his research on Flodden for his *Twelve Classic Battles*. Though I believe that *Fatal Rivalry* approaches Flodden from a different perspective, I have appreciated the work of others written during the last decade, including Niall Barr, Peter Reese and John Sadler; and I am particularly grateful for the scientific study of Paul Younger, which once again shows the contribution that other academic disciplines can make to the study of history and vice versa.

Others who live close to the battlefield and who have kindly given their time and views are the battlefield archaeologist Chris Burgess, local historians John and Anne Ferguson, and the Reverend Alan Cartwright. The Flodden 1513 Project has played a major part in generating awareness of the 500th anniversary of the battle and in organising its commemoration, and I should particularly like to mention James Joicey, Kendra Turnbull, Becki Cooper and Linda Bankier, as well as Martha Andrews, Bill Purdue and Nick Henderson whom I have met through the project.

This is my opportunity to thank those who have read through the manuscript as a whole or in part, including Julian Humphrys, John Ferguson, Clive Hallam-Baker, Chris Burgess, Gordon Kipling and Stuart Ivinson of the Royal Armouries. They have saved me many a slip and special thanks in that regard must go to Michael Hutchinson. Those who have given me advice on particular aspects are Bob Woosnam-Savage, Timothy Duke, Karen Hearn, Catherine Cullis, David Taylor, Katie Stevenson, Thomas Penn, Helen Castor, James Ross, Sean Cunningham, Jurg Meier, Sam Brown, Giles Proctor, the late Peter Algar, Fiona Paley, Elizabeth Roads, Sam Brown and David Souden on the Imperial Crown.

The book owes its existence to Alan Samson for commissioning it and for giving important tactical advice, and to Lucinda McNeile, my editor, for again being my rock. My thanks go to Holly Harley for picture research, Helen Ewing for design, Anne O'Brien for copy-editing, Douglas Matthews for the index and David Hoxley for the maps. I am also grateful to those at Orion whose work comes after the Acknowledgements are written, including Jess Gulliver in publicity and everyone in sales.

My family has again been extremely supportive: my wife Frances has read through the manuscript and proofs with steely eyes; my son

Arthur has brought his language skills to bear in translating many hundreds of words of Latin, and my daughter Cecily has taken the author photograph for the jacket and assisted by asking some searching questions. This book, like the previous one, is dedicated to them.

INDEX

on English hostility to Scotland,
129; missions to France, 129, 135, 169;
Ruthall criticizes, 214; Pitscottie
condemns as evil genius, 218
Fox, Richard, Bishop of Durham, then
of Winchester: negotiates peace with
Scots, 24, 26, 36–7, 39; and Norham
Castle, 24–6; and Henry VIII's
succession to father, 76–7; serves
on new Privy Council, 78; Henry
VIII's view of as negotiator, 83–4;
relations with Wolsey, 85, 141–2; as
Henry VII's executor, 106; interviews
Scottish seamen, 121; assists Thomas
Howard as Lord Admiral, 141;
conflict with Warham, 148; negotiates
marriage of Louis XII and Princess
Mary, 217
France: as threat to Spain, 38; treaty with
England (1510), 84, 122–3; Henry
VIII's aggression to, 86, 89, 106, 120;
alliance with Scotland, 87–8, 91, 114,
117, 119, 128–9, 132; expansion, 91;
English expelled, 116; conflict with
papacy, 117, 123; England's war with
(1512–13), 123–6, 138, 142–3, 146–8,
150–2; campaign in Italy (1512), 130–1;
naval strength, 139; England invades,
142; Ferdinand's truce with, 147;
Henry's campaign in, 157–61; defeated
at Novara (1513), 185; peace with
England (1513), 217
Francis I, King of France, 108, 222
Froissart, Jean, 71
Fuensalida, Don Gutierre Gómez de,
74
Fuenterrabia, Spain, 124, 159

Gaunt, John of see Lancaster, Duke of
Gaythelos (or Goídel Glas, Greek
Prince), 104
Geoffrey of Monmouth, 103–4
Gigli, Silvestro, Bishop of Worcester,
224–5

Giustinian, Sebastian, 107–10
Gloucester, Richard, Duke of see Richard
III, King
Gloucester. Thomas of Woodstock,
Duke of, 12
Goodall, John, 13
Gordon, Lady Catherine, 20, 24
Gordon, Janet, 197
Grafton's Chronicle, 175
Graham clan, 224
Granada, 147
Great Harry (English ship), 120
Great Michael (Scottish ship), 117–20,
137, 155
Greystoke, Elizabeth, 131
Guinegatte, France, 158
Gunn, Steven, 157–8
Guyane (French gunner), 156
Guyenne, 123–4

Haakon IV, King of Norway, 62
Hadrian's Wall, 93
halberds, 188
Halidon Hill, Battle of (1333), 89, 101,
188
Hall, Edward, 37, 48, 122, 144–5, 165, 167,
174, 179, 195, 227
Hans (Flemish gunner), 156
Hans, King of Denmark, 122
Hardynge, John, 14
Hawley, Thomas, Rouge Croix
Pursuivant, 174–9, 181
Hay family: members killed at Flodden,
208
Heaton Mill, 193
Henry II, King of England, 14
Henry IV, King of England, 12, 55, 102
Henry V, King of England: as model
for Henry VIII, 6, 126, 151–2; near
death at Shrewsbury, 75; takes James
I to France, 89; Scots fight against in
France, 102; campaign in France, 160;
death from dysentery, 180
Henry VI, King of England, 12, 67